THE $25 WRECK
OF THE
ROBERT J. WALKER
PLUS NOAA'S ANTICS AND PRETENSIONS

BY GARY GENTILE

Built: 1847
Previous names: None
Gross tonnage: 358
Type of vessel: *Legare*-class iron-hulled steamer
Power: Two coal-fired steam engines
Builder: Joseph Tomlinson, Pittsburgh, Pennsylvania
Owner at time of loss: U.S. Coast Survey
Port of registry: New York, New York
Cause of sinking: Collision with schooner *Fanny*
Number of fatalities: 20 (or 21)
Location: 11 miles southeast of Atlantic City, New Jersey
GPS: 39-13.230   74-17.269
Sunk: July 21, 1860
Depth: 85 feet
Dimensions: 133' x 24' x 9'

Gary Gentile Productions

Copyright 2016 by Gary Gentile

All rights reserved. Except for the use of brief quotations embodied in critical articles and reviews, this book may not be reproduced in part or in whole, in any manner (including mechanical, electronic, photographic, and photocopy means), transmitted in any form, or recorded by any data storage and/or retrieval device, without express written permission from the author. Address all queries to:

Gary Gentile Productions
3 Lehigh Gorge Drive
Jim Thorpe, PA 18229

Additional copies of this book may be purchased from the same address by sending a check or money order in the amount of $20 U.S. for each copy (plus $4 postage per order, not per book, in the U.S. Inquire for shipping cost to foreign countries). Alternatively, copies may be ordered from the author's website and paid by credit card:

http://www.ggentile.com

Picture Credits

The front cover top image of Robert J. Walker (the man) is on a paper bill in the denomination of 25 cents of fractional currency. The front cover bottom image of the *Robert J. Walker* (the vessel) was painted by W.E. Martin in 1852. The porthole was recovered from the $25 Wreck (see page 80 for details). All uncredited photographs were taken by the author.

International Standard Book Numbers (ISBN)
1-883056-53-5
978-1-883056-53-7

First Edition

Printed in U.S.A.

CONTENTS

GPS NUMBERS   6

PART 1
$25 WRECK

ROBERT J. WALKER – THE MAN   7

ROBERT J. WALKER – THE VESSEL
- CONSTRUCTION AND CAREER   17
- COLLISION AND LOSS   37
- AFTERMATH AND CONJECTURE   53
- DISCOVERY AND IDENTIFICATION   61
- EXPLORATION AND MAPPING   73
- NOMINATION AND FUTURE   83
- NATIONAL REGISTER OF HISTORIC PLACES   98

PART 2
THE HUNTING OF NOAA'S SNARK

MORE TERRITORIAL DEMANDS   165
BATTLE OF THE ATLANTIC   178
     NATIONAL MARINE SANCTUARY ?
THE U-BOAT CONUNDRUM   189
FREEDOM OF INFORMATION – NOT!   193
COPYRIGHT INFRINGEMENT   209
GLOBAL WARMING – ANOTHER NOT!   215

INDEX   217
BOOKS BY THE AUTHOR   222

GPS NUMBERS (OR LORAN) THAT NOAA HAS WITHHELD OR REDACTED

BEDFORDSHIRE	35-54.809 / 75-17.213
BLUEFIELDS	34-45.695 / 75-30.297
DIAMOND SHOALS LIGHTSHIP	35-05.192 / 75-19.626
DIXIE ARROW	34-54.006 / 75-45.031
E. M. CLARK	34-50.604 / 75-32.243
EMPIRE GEM	35-01.824 / 75-28.635
FRANKFURT	37-11.940 / 74-34.562
G-102	26827.3 / 41611.8
LANCING	35-02.016 / 75-26.645
OSTFRIESLAND	37-09.396 / 74-34.562
ROBERT J. WALKER	39-13.230 / 74-17.269
U-85	35-54.811 / 75-17.214
U-117	26877.7 / 41595.3
U-140	37-11.940 / 74-45.410
U-352	34-13.671 / 76-33.892
U-576	34-45.733 / 75-30.449
U-701	35-14.332 / 75-06.691
UB-148	37-09.449 / 74-45.266
V-43	37-16.893 / 74-32.163
YP-389	34-56.445 / 75-23.900

Robert J. Walker – the Man
From Birth to Berth and Casket

Robert J. Walker – the man, not the vessel – was born on either July 19 or July 23, 1801. Sources differ. Sources also disagree on his middle name; some say it was John, others say it was James. In either event, throughout his life his official signature included only his middle initial instead of his full middle name.

Walker grew up in Northumberland, a quaint community in the Commonwealth of Pennsylvania, located in the V that was formed by the confluence of the Susquehanna River and the West Branch of the Susquehanna River.

After local schooling, he attended the University of Pennsylvania. During the course of his studies he made the acquaintance of Mary Bache, a granddaughter of Benjamin Franklin. Their courtship commenced immediately. They got married shortly after Walker received his diploma.

Walker graduated in July of 1819. He was eighteen years old. His first occupation was working as a surveyor for the Holland Land Company "in the northwest corner of the state, but in this raw region his principal interest was the study of law, for in three years he was ready to begin the practice of that profession; and he located in Pittsburgh in 1822."

Thus he followed in the footsteps of his father, who was at that time a judge on the Pennsylvania Supreme Court. Coincidentally, Walker's brother-in-law, George M. Dallas, was assistant United States district attorney for eastern Pennsylvania. Thus the newly formed family was largely engaged in the legal profession.

Once, when asked if he was born in Pennsylvania, Walker replied with pride, "I was born there, sir, and spent the early years of my life in that State, and I still look upon the old Keystone as the brightest in the federal arch." (Pennsylvania was and still is known as the Keystone State.)

Walker then went on to say that when he left the services of the Holland Land Company, his employer, Harm Jan Huidekoper, "presented me with a purse [of three thousand dollars], with which I purchased my law library – locating in Pittsburg [sic]." (Pittsburgh, with an "h," was the capital of Pennsylvania.)

One source intimated that Walker once owned slaves. At first blush this seems unlikely, as Pennsylvania was a free state. However, Walker did put on record the fact that he believed in slavery – or at least he accepted the concept as expedient because slave labor enabled Southern plantation owners to sell cotton cheaply.

For example, on May 30, 1857 – after he was appointed as Governor of Kansas – he declared, "Four weeks ago to-day I was in New York. I thought I would like to hear that eccentric preacher, Henry Ward Beecher. So I paid a visit to his church. He gave us a genuine anti-slavery speech. If he had known I was in the audience I should have believed it was designed expressly for my ears; but it was impossible for him to have known I was there. The following Sunday I spent in Buffalo [New York]. There I had the pleasure of listening to another anti-slavery sermon. I came up the Missouri on a steamer with Senator Wilson. The passengers teased him to make a speech, and of course it was anti-slavery. To-day I am going to the Unitarian church to hear Rev. Mr. Nute. I expect I shall be entertained with another sermon of the same sort. Possibly they will convert me to their views yet."

Understand that those who believed in slavery were in a position never to become slaves. If their roles had been reversed, believers would probably have become dissenters.

In 1823, Walker lobbied for Andrew Jackson, who was running for President of the United States. Jackson did not win . . . that time. The voters elected John Quincy Adams.

The year 1826 found Walker following his brother Duncan to Natchez, Mississippi, which hugged the east bank of the Mighty Mississippi River. They started a law firm called Walker and Walker. Duncan died in 1839, leaving Robert the sole proprietor of the practice.

The Mississippi Land-Grab

Mississippi was a slave state with a population of 136,000 people, half of whom were slaves. This may be the time and place at which Walker owned slaves, and came to believe that slavery was a necessary evil.

Mississippi was also a state of unrest. There were literally millions of acres of land that pioneers ached to own and develop, mostly into cotton fields. "Fortunes were won in a few years and great plantations speedily took the places of canebrakes and stagnant swamps. . . . Money-making was a mania and everybody had a hand in speculations, large or small."

There was one large problem with exploiting all this so-called vacant land. It was not unoccupied. It was populated by Indians . . . Indians who had inhabited this land for thousands of years.

In many ways, and particularly with respect to land, Indians had cultural values that differed greatly from those of Caucasian pioneers. A pioneer believed that land existed in the form of discrete parcels or tracts that a person or small family could own and control to the exclusion of all others. They thought of land as private plats, or plots, or lots, or segmented properties with specific boundaries that outsiders were not permitted to cross.

Indians – especially the nomadic tribes – believed that land could not be owned by an individual or a group of individuals; that land was unowned and unownable and existed for the use of all. In other words, they believed that land was present in abundance for everyone to utilize as needed. To them, land had no boundaries, or property lines, or political borders.

These two cultural philosophies were diametrically opposed. Opposition leads to conflict. Conflict leads to strife. Strive leads to confrontation and eventually to bloodshed. And so it was that the great land-grab wars erupted in Mississippi. Indians had to be displaced before U.S. land acquisition could proceed.

Walker was an active participant in these land-grab wars.

The U.S. government then passed what was called the Indian Removal Act. This Act of Congress paved the way for displacing Indians by moving them from fertile territories to desert territories, in order to make the fertile territories available to farmers and ranchers.

THE MAN

In the mid-twentieth century, Walker's likeness adorned several types of revenue stamps, like the $10 Silver Tax stamp shown above, plus the $10 Documentary stamp and the $10 Stock Transfer stamp. Considering the appellation that was given to the shipwreck that bore his name, it is unfortunate that he was not shown on a $25 stamp.

The Treaty of Dancing Rabbit Creek was proclaimed on February 24, 1831. This so-called "treaty" was forced upon the Choctaw, who involuntarily ceded eleven million acres of their ancestral homeland in Mississippi in exchange for fifteen million acres of property in what eventually became the State of Oklahoma. For accepting this trade-off they were granted "perpetual peace."

Tens of thousands of Choctaws walked more than five hundred miles along the "Trail of Tears" to their newly designated reservation. Later, other Indian tribes were squeezed in with them. In the 1880's, the U.S. government redefined the words "perpetual" and "peace" by repossessing half the Indian's acknowledged landholding in piecemeal fashion.

Squatters rapidly moved into the newly vacated Mississippi landfall.

When public land sales were announced in 1833, Walker "organized some two hundred of the prospective purchasers into an association of which he became the principal spokesman and beneficiary. These gentlemen, men of the first consequence in Mississippi and the neighboring states, Government officials, directors of banks, and judges of the courts, entered into an agreement whereby they were not to bid against each other at any of the sales of public lands. Walker and his appointees were to manage the bidding and afterwards apportion the proceeds. They made arrangements with squatters and small farmers to procure for them their little tracts on condition that they would not bid against the association. The charge for this service was a dollar an acre above the Government minimum. Eventually this scheme of defrauding the country was so popular that Walker was given a public dinner by the farmers and squatters at the conclusion of the sales.

"The plan of the association was carried out everywhere, the Federal land officers lending their aid and receiving their reward [they were bribed]; and Walker and his friends thus came into possession of great tracts of land which were easily sold at prices ranging from two to twenty dollars per acre. Many of the fortunes of the lower South were the result of this campaign against the treasury of the United States; but it might be regarded as ungracious, even at this late day, to publish a list of the names of the men who at that time made no denial of their part in the transaction.

"The scandal of the land sales of October, 1833, was so great that Senator Poindexter, one of the foremost public men of the time, succeeded in getting an investigation of the subject, and a report was made to the senate in the summer of 1834, which showed something of the character of Walker's word in this his first important undertaking. Senators from Tennessee, Alabama, and Louisiana resisted Poindexter's efforts to give the widest publicity to the report, and especially his proposition to punish the guilty parties. Nothing was done except to print the report, which appeared in many newspapers of the time without any severe criticism of the transaction. Henry Clay and Daniel Webster supported the investigation, while others said that the practice of defrauding the Government had gone so far and involved so many eminent characters that it was well-nigh impossible to punish anyone."

Corruption was a fundamental element in United States politics. And still is!

Senatorship

After making himself rich, Walker used some of the money to purchase a plantation in Madison county. As long as he was on a financial roll, he responded to Poindexter's anti-criminal crusade by running against him for Mississippi's senatorial seat. Speculators and small farmers supported Walker's campaign as a way to repay him for his efforts in their behalf.

"The outcome was a decided victory for Walker, though the election in the legislature became at once the subject of an investigation, which, however, only led to a 'whitewash'."

The thirty-six-year-old Democrat senator was called "the Wizard of Mississippi." He immediately started to make a name for himself as the people's representative, first by proposing the free homestead policy, then by demanding the "re-annexation" of the Republic of Texas, no doubt with the rallying cry, "Remember the Alamo."

But wait, there's more! He also wanted to annex Mexico. All of it. Later he decided to settle for Yucatan, but that did not happen either. There was too much heated opposition from the Mexicans. (Judging by how hard Mexicans strive to cross the border today, they must wish that they *had* been annexed.)

Walker used his new position of authority to expand his money manipulations. "Under Walker's leadership Mississippi borrowed more than ten million dollars from Nicholas Biddle and his clients on state credit and then loaned the money to planters and others in need of funds on the uncertain security of lands and slaves. Walker, himself, is said to have borrowed huge sums and even to have taken, without security, a portion of the sinking fund of the state banks, whose directors were the medium of all these transactions. Nobody seems to have thought that a debt of ten millions was any burden to a population of less than four hundred thousand, including slaves.

"When the day of reckoning came Walker and his party escaped the natural result by inducing the legislature to repudiate practically the whole debt and on the pretext that Nicholas Biddle had negotiated with the agents of the state a loan which was contrary to the mandates of the Mississippi constitution! Before 1844 the slate was clean and Walker gave himself no concern about the transaction, while it was quite generally regarded as a fine stroke to have outwitted the President. Of the 'monster bank' whom most followers of Jackson felt to be legitimate prey for honest Democrats. Walker suffered, however, in his personal fortunes, and he was brought to the humiliating necessity

THE MAN

of promising his creditor, Martin Van Buren, a lien on his meagre salary as a senator."

Nonetheless, Walker's machinations continued. He served ten years in the Senate. Then . . .

Secretary of the Treasury

. . . in one of the greatest ironies of American politics, when James Polk took office as the President of the United States, in 1844, Walker turned down his appointment as attorney-general of the country, and asked instead for a cabinet position as Secretary of the Treasury!

"The man who had completely bankrupted himself and his state and had brought dishonor upon all who had been allied with him in financial matters became head of the national treasury."

Talk about putting a fox in the henhouse!

Any indiscretions that Walker made in his new office were effectively covered up. His term as Secretary is remembered mostly for the Walker Tariff. An international trade tariff was a tax on imports and exports. Walker proposed to boost the country's flagging economy by reducing tariff rates from 32% to 25%, and by standardizing tariffs across the board (instead of having different rates for different products). The adoption of this new policy stimulated trade between the U.S. and the rest of the world, especially Great Britain.

Much of the country's increased income was used to fight the Mexican-American War, from 1846 to 1848. Like Walker, Polk was an ardent expansionist who believed that the United States had a manifest destiny to subsume the entire North American continent. This was what Walker had wanted all along. When the war ended, the U.S. gained New Mexico, Arizona, Utah, Nevada, and California: about one third of Mexico's land mass. (Polk had already convinced the Republic of Texas to join the Union, in 1844.)

Because the U.S. Revenue Marine Service operated under the Department of the Treasury, Walker managed to have one of the new revenue cutters named after him. The name stayed with the vessel when she was transferred to the U.S. Coast Survey.

Walker was relieved of his position as Secretary of the Treasury after Polk's single term ended, and Zachary Taylor became President of the United States. Walker remained in Washington and worked largely out of the limelight as a lawyer for the next eight years.

Kansas Statehood

Walker's last political bow transpired when President James Buchanan asked him to assume the office of Governor of the Territory of Kansas, in 1857. Walker consented.

He quickly learned that Kansas was a hotbed of hostility. Walker described its inhabitants as "a band of disorganisers [sic] and revolutionists." The reason for the animosity was the proposed adoption of statehood: should it enter the Union as a slave state or a free state? Opinions differed. Bloodshed ensued.

Outsiders from both factions descended upon the territory. Settlers from Missouri and Arkansas wanted their neighbor to be a slave state. Abolitionists from New England wanted a free state. They clashed not only with guns but with political persuasion. (Walker had previously gone so far as to insist that Texas be admitted as a slave state.

He was overruled.)

The worst fanatic to enter the fracas was abolitionist John Brown. He and his sons and a ragtag group of followers started hostilities by murdering a handful of suspected slave staters by dragging them out of bed in the middle of the night and shooting them in the head. He also openly engaged in some full-scale battles in which hundreds of men participated, some with cannons that were filled with grapeshot. These quasi-military actions are what made Bleeding Kansas a battle cry. This is the same John Brown who later raided the federal arsenal at Harper's Ferry (Virginia at the time, now West Virginia), was captured, and was hung for treason.

Other slave staters took a different tack. They stuffed the ballot boxes with fraudulent votes from fictitious settlers. For example, the town of Oxford was populated by only half a dozen legal voters, yet it returned 1,626 votes – all for slavery. The names seemed to have been copied from a city directory.

McGee county returned some 1,200 votes for slavery, yet "there was not a legal voter in the county, it being Indian territory, and not open to settlement."

This was the situation that Walker faced when he assumed the office of Governor. His position with regard to slavery had softened somewhat over the years. Despite the fact that he still believed in slavery as an economic expedient, he did not let his personal persuasion interfere with the situation at hand. He openly avowed that his job was not to sway the vote in either direction, but to let the legitimate residents choose for themselves the way they wanted to enter statehood.

His first priority was to call the army for protection against abolitionist raids and confrontations with armed free-staters. The President grudgingly dispatched troops to the territory, but they turned out to be a wretched bunch of malingerers who were largely ineffective in quelling the insurrection. They engaged half-heartedly in some of the skirmishes between armed opponents, but for the most part they chose to remain on the sidelines and let the opponents duke it out without military interference.

The army's most effective role was in dealing with Walker's second priority: protecting the voters from violence at the ballot boxes. In this regard the army was largely successful in quelling agitation.

Walker conducted a full investigation into the fraudulent votes, and discounted those that had obviously been faked. Yet local newspapers made accusations against him, in particular that he had allowed soldiers to vote. Thus he found himself being investigated. In his defense, when witnesses were called to testify, Lieutenant Carr denied the allegation that troops under his command had been allowed to vote. He stated that the governor was standing by the polls when a soldier asked if he was permitted to vote.

"Gov. W. inquired of Mr. H. if he had voted. The latter replied that he had not; that he was a resident of Missouri. 'Then,' said the Governor, 'you have no right to vote.'"

According to the Territorial enactment of February 20, 1857, "All citizens of the United States, who have resided in the Territory six months before the election, shall be permitted to vote." Walker stood by the law, and disqualified all non-residents from voting in the election.

Although the majority of voters wanted free-state status, when politicians in the legislature convened the constitutional convention, they tried to include provisions for slavery by substituting a fake constitution (called the Lecompton Constitution) for the

THE MAN

This portrait of Robert J. Walker was painted by William Garl Brown in 1879.

real one. Walker protested this chicanery by tendering his resignation. He went to Washington, DC to discuss the matter with President Buchanan. Buchanan was sympathetic to the Southern cause for slavery. The very reason that he appointed Walker to the governorship was because of Walker's pro-slavery background and his long residence in the slave state of Mississippi. Buchanan had expected Walker to settle the dispute on the side of slavery. When Walker remained adamant in his stance, Buchanan accepted his resignation.

Walker then lobbied Congress to repudiate the substituted constitution and to accept the original one that Kansas residents had voted to accept, or a new version that coincided with the wishes of the majority of voters. Buchanan backed the fake constitution. Another election was held in Kansas amid bouts of violence. Nonetheless, the fake constitution received 1,788 votes for slavery, and 11,300 against. This landslide election ensured that Kansas would enter the Union as a free state.

Civil War Service

The Kansas squabbles and free-state proclamation contributed substantially to fomenting civil war among the fractionizing United States. In the next Presidential election, Buchanan – the puppet of Jefferson Davis – was ousted, and Abraham Lincoln secured his position as Commander-in-Chief in the White House.

When the War of the Rebellion became a reality, Walker "was sent to Europe as special financial agent of the Federal Government, bearing a letter of credence from President Lincoln." This action once again put a larcenous fox in a financial henhouse, but if any improprieties occurred during his tenure, they went unrecorded. Walker seems to have mended his earlier thieving ways.

As a measure of economy, the Union issued fractional currency to replace gold and silver coinage during the War between the States. Three Union administrators used the privilege of their positions to have their faces engraved on the obverse of this newly printed paper money: Francis E. Spinner (Treasurer of the United States), William P. Fessenden (U.S. Senator and Secretary of the Treasury), and Spencer M. Clark (Superintendent of the National Currency Bureau).

This selfish favoritism created somewhat of a furor. Congressional critics claimed that the busts of living persons constituted an abuse of administrative privilege. As a result, Congress enacted legislation that banned this preferential practice, to wit, "that no portrait or likeness of any living person hereafter engraved, shall be placed upon any of the bonds, securities, notes, fractional or postal currency of the United States."

As far as I know, this Act of Congress has never been repealed. That is why you will never see your picture on a United States stamp. Robert J. Walker's likeness was not printed on the 25-cent bill until 1874, five years after his decease in 1869.

Walker established his headquarters in London, England. "The Confederacy was then borrowing money both in England and France without difficulty, while the finances of the United States showed a weakness and derangement which augured the success of their enemy. England and France treated the representatives of the Lincoln administration with ill-concealed hostility."

There was a very good reason for this anti-Union attitude. By placing blockades around Confederate ports, the Union prevented free trade between the South and European merchants. England and France needed Southern cotton for clothing, and they had goods to sell to the Confederates in exchange. Thus France and England recognized the Confederacy as a sovereign nation.

"The purpose of Walker's appointment was to break down the credit of the South and at the same time to sell the bonds of the United States."

Walker started his campaign by shifting the blame of the Mississippi bond disaster, which he had orchestrated, to Jefferson Davis, who was now President of the Confederate States of America. Many Europeans had lost money on the deal and were still riled about it – and rightfully so. Walker, ever the conniver, made his twisted story sound plausible. He wrote newspaper articles and issued thousands of pamphlets in which he "published the most glowing account of the soundness of the Federal finances and of the resources of the North on which her securities were based."

All rubbish, but he made it look good on paper – a confidence game at which he was quite experienced. In 1862 and 1863, he sold some twenty-five million dollars' worth of bonds that were guaranteed to pay 6% interest when they matured in twenty years.

At the same time, he denounced the South in order to bolster his scheme in the bond market. Walker remarked, "No form of Confederate bonds, or notes, or stock, will ever be recognised [sic] by the Government of the United States, and the cotton pledged by slaveholding traitors for the payment of the Confederate bonds is all forfeited for treason, and confiscated to the Federal Government by Act of Congress."

Shades of Mississippi!

British pundits in the know referred to Walker as Slyboots: a person who was charming on the outside but stealthy and manipulative on the inside. They also called him an artful dodger for his Mississippi machinations.

If these testimonials sound reminiscent of descriptions of today's political leaders and congressional representatives, so be it. Today's politicians recapitulate yesteryear's.

The Alaska Purchase

After Walker's return to the United States, in 1864, he found himself at loose ends and without a job. "The South regarded him as a traitor; and now the North, whom he served with a zeal which allowed of no defeat, seemed to be ashamed of him. He took up his work of lobbyist again and more than once he had the pleasure of seeing some-

THE MAN

thing of the 'seamy' inside of things at the capital."

In 1868, Walker used his vast repertoire of Machiavellian skills in support of the Alaska Purchase, better known as Seward's Folly. Russia desired to sell Alaska to the United States as a way to add money to its empty coffers, to weaken England's grip in North America, and to cement relations with the expanding United States. The American Civil War had interrupted negotiations.

As the United States reorganized after the war, Senator Charles Sumner proposed a bill to purchase the Arctic wasteland. Secretary of State William H. Seward wholeheartedly agreed with the senator from Massachusetts, that the property could prove to be a valuable asset, not only because of the vast natural resources that the land contained, but because its proximity to Asia could create new markets for American products.

Although most Congressional representatives were against the purchase, Secretary Seward and Russian Minister Eduard Andreevich Stoeckl negotiated a treaty. They then ran into a stumbling block: the House of Representatives refused to approve funding for the purchase.

Great persuasion was needed to gain allies to endorse the unpopular legislation. Seward and Stoeckl "engaged John W. Forney, editor of the Washington *Chronicle*, the leading paper at the capital, to advocate the immediate payment of the money called for in the treaty, already ratified by the senate. The minister paid Forney $30,000 for his services. He then employed Walker, for a consideration of $26,000 in gold, to 'engineer' the desired measure through the recalcitrant house."

Then as now, the way to change the mind of a politician was by bribery. Walker "plied the arts known to be effective with many statesmen and with the aid of the resources at his command he persuaded the congress . . . to vote the appropriation."

Secretary Seward went on record as saying "that the price of votes ran as high as $10,000."

Politics!

This was how Alaska was sold to the highest bidder. Russia has been crying in its beard ever since.

Lonely Demise

The Alaska Purchase was Walker's final political fracas. He sided with ardent expansionist Sumner in demanding the cession of Canada to the United States as reparation for the damage done to Union shipping by blockade runners that had been built surreptitiously in British shipyards, but that appeal went nowhere.

Robert J. Walker passed away on November 11, 1869, at the age of 68. He was buried in the Oak Hill Cemetery in Washington, DC.

Perhaps it is best that today most of Walker's nefarious indiscretions have been largely forgotten, and that he is remembered mostly for the survey vessel that was named in his honor – or dishonor, as the case may be.

It is woefully ironic that Robert J. Walker was such an industrious imperialist as a man, and that NOAA, which claims association with the vessel that was named after him, is the most treacherously imperialistic governmental administration in the world today.

Another *Robert J. Walker*

It is interesting to note that two vessels carried the name *Robert J. Walker*: the one that is the subject of the present volume, and a merchant vessel that was built during World War Two.

The latter was a Liberty ship that was constructed in 1943 by the Oregon Ship Building Corporation for the War Shipping Administration: one of more than 2,700 "ugly ducklings" that transported cargoes for the Allies' prosecution of the war. Unfortunately, her career was cut short by a Nazi torpedo when she was only one year old, on December 25, 1944.

The miscreant was the *U-862*, Korvettenkapitan Heinrich Timm. According to John Gorley Bunker, author of *Liberty Ships*, "On Christmas Day of 1944, the *Robert J. Walker* was off the coast of Australia when a torpedo took off her propeller and destroyed the steering engine. The submarine, evidently chary of expending any more torpedoes than necessary, waited around for the ship to sink. When a second torpedo was seen about two hours later, gunners blew it up only a hundred yards from the ship. The submarine then tried a third shot that hit, despite a rain of 20-millimeter shells directed at it. The crew escaped without casualties and was picked up by HMAS *Quickmatch*. Despite two torpedoes, the *Robert J. Walker* did not sink and had to be sent to the bottom by the destroyer's guns."

German records confirm the date of the attack, but *Lloyd's War Losses* states that the attack occurred on December 24 (Christmas Eve). Then, the ship was "subsequently sunk by gunfire on December 25."

On her final voyage, the *Robert J. Walker* was bound in ballast from Calcutta, India via Fremantle, Australia for Sydney, Australia. Of her 79 crew members, two were lost either in the attack or while abandoning ship.

German records give the attack position as 36° 45" south latitude, 150° 43" east longitude. British records give the position as 36° 35" south latitude, 150° 43" east longitude. The disparity could be the difference between the attack position and the sinking position.

As noted previously, Walker's likeness adorned several types of revenue stamps in the twentieth century: the $10 Stock Transfer stamp that is shown below, plus the $10 Documentary stamp and the $10 Silver Tax stamp.

Robert J. Walker – the Vessel
Construction and Career

The *Robert J. Walker* was built during a number of transitional phases in vessel construction.

One phase was converting from wooden hulls to iron hulls. According to Captain Alexander Fraser, Commandant of the United States Revenue Marine Service, "The principle advantages arising from the use of iron are: economy in the original construction; durability, lightness of material, and consequently, increased buoyancy; increased strength, particularly in the ability to withstand shocks sustained by taking the ground when passing shoal water bars; and the value when worn out, of the old materials."

Iron hulls possessed other advantages over wood. The two greatest banes concerning wooden hulls were rot and marine boring animals such as teredos. Teredos are often called worms but in fact they are mollusks. They burrow into wood under water the way termites eat into wood on land.

Another blight on hulls in saltwater is the barnacle (which cannot survive in freshwater). Barnacle larvae are free swimming organisms that search for a suitable substrate to which to attach themselves. After they glue themselves onto a vessel's hull, they grow a calcareous shell whose size and angles defeat the hydrodynamic design of the carefully laid lines of the underside. Increased friction causes a reduction in speed and efficiency of movement.

Unfortunately for mariners, barnacles are attracted to iron hulls the same as they are attracted to wooden hulls, and they are every bit as difficult to remove. That is why wooden-hulled vessels that are intended to ply equatorial waters, where barnacles are more prolific than in colder northern waters, have their hulls coppered. That is, copper sheets are nailed to that portion of the hull that extends below the waterline. In this respect, it is easier to fasten copper sheets to wood than it is to iron. I have never heard of iron hulls that were coppered.

Another phase was switching from sail to steam. A great deal of experimentation resulted in both engine and boiler designs. In some cases, both hull and propulsion changes were incorporated at the same time: from wooden-hulled sailing vessels to iron-hulled steamships. The *Robert J. Walker* fell into the latter category.

A third phase was involved in the evolution of transportation over water: this one in the manner of steam propulsion, from paddle wheel to propeller. In this regard, the *Robert J. Walker* fell into the former category. Note that there were two kinds of paddlewheel designs: a single paddlewheel in the stern of the vessel, and a pair of paddlewheels with one placed on either side of the hull near midship.

Stern paddlewheel steamers worked well on protected inland waterways such as the Mississippi River. The narrow hull and shallow draft enabled such steamers to slip between shoals and obstructions (such as islands and stranded tree trunks), and to dock close to unimproved shores. In the open ocean, these steamers rolled from side to side in storms, and were difficult to maneuver.

Sidewheel steamers worked better in the ocean where the deep draft was not an impediment, and where the wide beam – with paddlewheels projecting to the sides – added stability.

Thus each configuration had advantages and disadvantages with regard to its intended employment.

Propeller-driven vessels were in their infancy at the time the *Robert J. Walker* was constructed. The initial problem with their design was in keeping the hull from flooding through the packing glands. Engineers were experimenting with suitable materials to pack around the propeller shaft where it passed through the hull. Materials that worked on the drawing board often broke apart or worked themselves free as the shaft turned or was jostled by rough water. The shafts of a paddlewheel were located high above the water.

Yet a fourth phase comprised this rapidly moving progression: a gradual change from wood to coal as fuel to burn beneath the boilers that heated water into steam to power the engine. River boats utilized wood because they could dock along the banks and cut down trees for fuel. The lumber was free, requiring only labor to collect it. Ocean-going steamers had to operate independent of forests of fuel, so they filled their bunkers with bituminous or anthracite. Travel distance was limited by the size of the bunkers. The *Robert J. Walker* was a coal burner.

During the course of a single generation in the early part of the 1800's, vessel design leaped from millennia-old wooden-hulled sailing vessels to modern-day propeller-driven steamships. Thus it could be said that the *Robert J. Walker* represented an intermediate design that escaped the past and presaged the future.

It should be noted that global governments had nothing to do with this riverine and ocean-going progress. It was all accomplished through private enterprise. The only part that the U.S. government played was in acknowledging the development of marine propulsion, and conceding that it could be useful for federal vessels.

In 1843, the U.S. government authorized the construction of a fleet of six iron-hulled steamships of various designs, both paddlewheel and propeller. Two more vessels were authorized in the succeeding two years. The last of these eight vessels was the sidewheel steamer *Robert J. Walker*, whose construction was authorized by Congress in January 1845. These vessels were constructed primarily for the "enforcement of customs."

In other words, these so-called revenue cutters were tax collectors, or revenuers.

Despite the authorization date of the *Robert J. Walker*, the contract for her construction was not awarded until 1846, when Congress opened its purse strings. By this you can see that Congress was not any more efficient in olden days than it is now. Actual construction was not commenced until March 1847 (two years after authorization) at the yard of Joseph Tomlinson, in Pittsburgh, Pennsylvania. The cost of construction was $104,825.53 – right down to the penny, as penny-pinching Congress authorized.

The hull was launched in November 1847. The completed vessel grossed 358 tons. She measured 133 feet in length, had a beam of 24 feet (not counting paddle wheels), and had a depth of hold of 9 feet.

The Lighthall Engine

According to NOAA, the engines to turn the paddlewheels were two Lighthall patent lever half-beam engines. Included in NOAA's report on the *Robert J. Walker*

THE VESSEL ~ CONSTRUCTION AND CAREER   19

was an illustration and meager description of Lighthall's engine in patent number 6811, dated October 23, 1849. This information is somewhat irrelevant to the *Robert J. Walker* as the application postdates by two years construction of the vessel and installation of her engines.

By the time of the patent date of that particular engine, the *Robert J. Walker* had already been built, launched, and been doing survey work for more than a year and a half.

Ordinarily I would go no farther in describing the engine and Lighthall's subsequent improvements, but as the subject of this entire book is only a single vessel, and as the engine on the site was crucial to establishing the wreck's identity, I will quote the appropriate patent application:

> William A. Lighthall, of Albany, New York.
> Steam-Engine
> Specification of Letters Patent No. 696, dated April 14, 1838.
> To all whom it may concern:
> Be it known that I, William A. Lighthall have invented or discovered certain new and useful improvements in steam engines intended for propelling vessels, which combined improvements I designate as "Lighthall's improved horizontal and beam engine," and that I am desirous of obtaining a patent for the said improvements.
> The following explanations refer to the drawings 1 and 2 accompanying this, specification A at the working beam, B Z, the connecting-rod, C, the crank, and end of the shaft, C E the crank, E E the piston rod and l link to the lower end of the beam, F, the yoke, G G the brace to support the yoke, H the connecting rod from the beam to the bell crank of the air pump, I the bell crank for working the air pump, J the connecting rod from the bell crank to the piston of the air pump, K K the air pump and reservoir, L L L the condenser, foot valve, and connection to the air pump, M the steam pipe.
> N the exhaust pipe to the condenser, O O the valve rods, P the eccentric wheel and rod, 0 the rock shaft for working the valves, R R the cut off valve, T T the keelson or keelson's, E Q the piston rod, UV the center of crank motion, X the center or fulcrum of the beam, Y the pinon journal of the connecting rod, l, 2, the yoke, 3 the point of coupling with the connecting rod, 4 L the cylinder.
> The following being a description of the aforesaid improvements will be more clearly understood by referring to their drafts or drawings herewith submitted. To obviate many serious inconveniences and existing defects in the present form and disposition of the steam engines now in use, I have combined the leading characteristics of the beam engine, with those of the horizontal engine, in order to embrace the advantages of both and avoid the defects of either, and I accomplish this object in the following manner. I lay the cylinder (or cylinders if a double power be required) horizontally on or upon the keelson T T, and place the working beam A A at the proper distance in a vertical position, with its lower end A at such a height as to range with the piston rod E E in the same manner as when the working beam is horizontal and the cylin-

der erect. If the length of the working beam when thus vertically placed corresponds with the height of the shaft C and the center of crank motion U then the arrangement is completed, and the desired effect produced. But if the size of the wheel and other circumstances require the shaft to be placed lower than on a horizontal level with the upper end of the working beam, I then bend or incline the upper half arm of the working beam to such an inclination or angle that a line drawn from the center or fulcrum X of the working beam, to that point where the central line of the connecting rod would intersect it shall be at right angles to a line drawn from the center of the shaft U to the said point of intersection and consequently to the center of crank motion; or in other words if a line be drawn from center U of the shaft, to the center of the pinon journal Y of the connecting-rod in the working beam, then a line drawn from the center or fulcrum X of the beam, intersecting at right angles the former line will give the requisite bend of the beam or the necessary deviation V from its vertical and rectilinear direction, with sufficient accuracy for all practical purposes.

The proper bend or inclination of the working beam and the requisite length of yoke hereafter specified (Z. E., the proper positional relation between the center of beam vibration and the center of crank motion) can be obtained by other methods or rules equally well known as that which I have adopted.

But as in this case considerable accuracy in the radius, and of such length as to remove the point 3 of its coupling with the connecting rod B B so many degrees forward as it would otherwise be necessary to bend the working beam. This yoke may be attached to any working beam in a vertical position and will be the same in effect as though the working beam itself were bent to the angle required.

To secure the yoke in its place a strong brace G G is attached from the upper arm of the working beam, say about the center of its length to the forward end of the yoke near the point 3 of its coupling with the connecting rod which brace will give in all cases the necessary firmness. Thus it will be seen that the yoke is a substitute for the weight instead of being as it now is a necessary and unavoidable encumbrance will act in a great measure as judiciously stowed ballast Y.

That in vessels of war or armed steamers all the essential and vital parts of the machinery will be completely protected from an enemy's fire, and that the acting engineer can perform his duty not only with safety but with that self possession which personal security could alone insure.

Should additional power be required, two cylinders similarly placed on opposite sides of the beam in line with each other might be worked upon the same beam, or one could be doing the work while the other was undergoing repairs, almost essential for vessels navigating the ocean.

In vessels calculated for shallow waters by the application of the yoke or the bent working beam, any length of stroke may be obtained with the cylinder lying horizontally on the keelson without any loss of power, and with the cylinder thus firmly attached to the keelsons there will be less jar and of course less strain and injury to the vessels than when the cylinder is raised or sup-

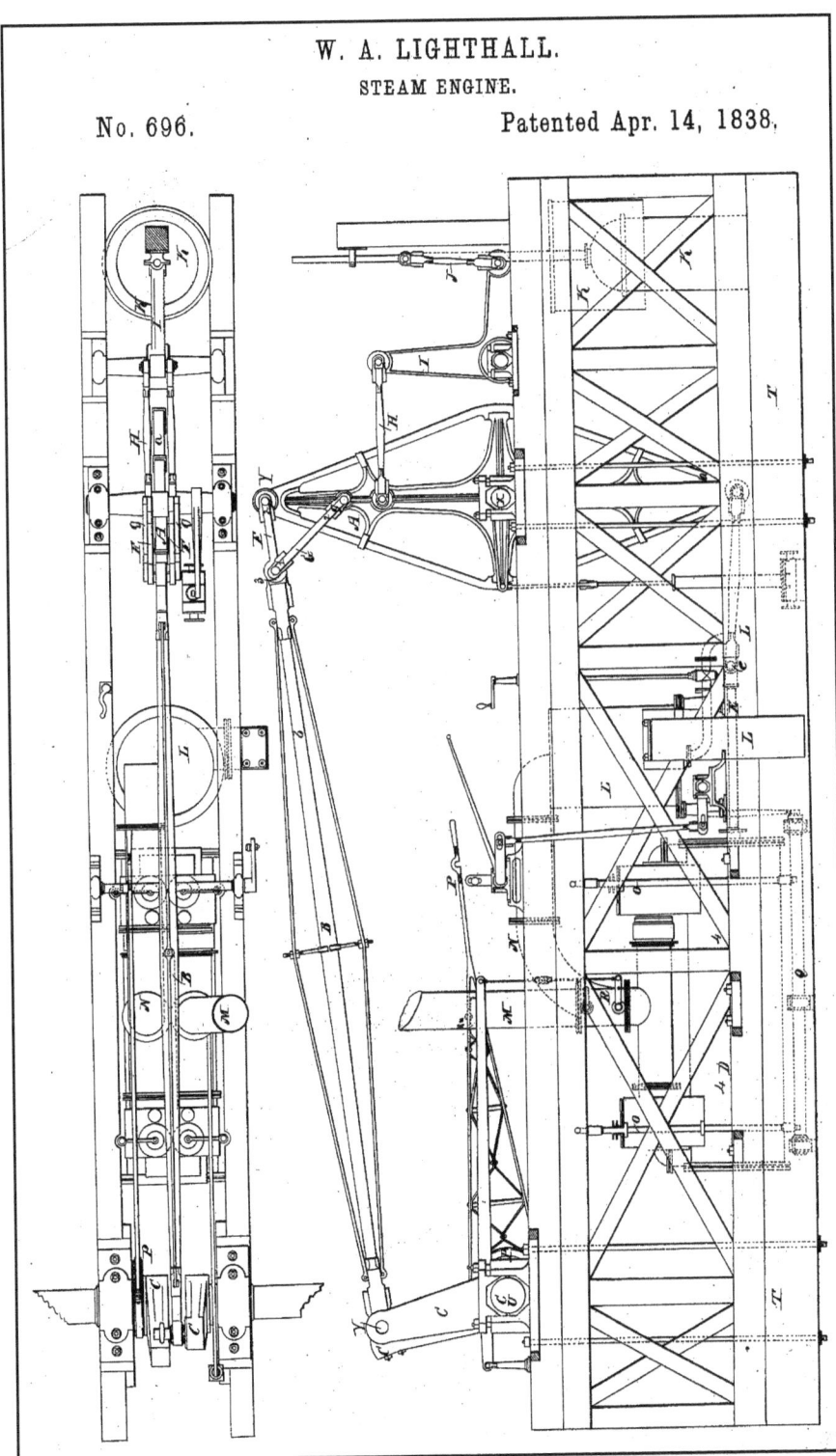

ported on the deck beams or on a frame at a distance from the keelson.

The arrangements of the essential improvements having been described it is thought unnecessary to specify in detail the slight variations which might be required or deemed expedient to be made in the relative situation of its minor parts. Such changes may be made in a variety of ways and would naturally suggest themselves to the relative and combined disposition of the cylinder, the beam working vertically, with it and the crank, to wit, the cylinder lying horizontally on or upon the keelson or keelsons at right angles to the lower end of the working beam, while the upper end of said beam is in connection with and gives motion to the crank upon the shaft. V Y Y 3. The curved or bent working beam, working vertically in combination with the horizontal cylinder in their relative and combined disposition as herein before intended to be described, and as shown in the drafts or drawings accompanying this specification.

1. To avoid bending the working beam in cases in which it is desired to place the shaft lower than on a horizontal level with the upper end of the working beam, I claim the yoke herein before specified in combination and connection with the vertical working beam, working vertically and also in combination with those combined disposition of parts, as set forth and described in the first and second foregoing claims.

If you read any of the foregoing engine description, do not feel bad if you did not understand all of it – or any of it – because neither did I. Engineering language is for specialists. (Note that a two-engine propulsion system has one engine as a back-up.)

Despite Lighthall's claims for a better marine engine than then existed, the Navy turned him down. On May 4, 1839, three members of the Board of Navy Commissioners – Captain M. C. Perry, William Kemble, esquire, and engineer Charles Haswell – met with Lighthall and his associates in New York City. Armed with drawings and models, Lighthall explained the efficacy of his latest steam engine.

After the demonstration, the three Board members wrote in concurrence, "The undersigned do not consider the alleged superiority of Mr. Lighthall's arrangement of the engines sufficiently established to induce them to change the opinions already officially expressed of the expediency, under existing circumstances, of placing on board the two steamers contemplated to be built – in one, a pair of American inclined engines; and in the other, vertical beam engines, of the same nominal [horse] power and arranged after the European manner."

On the other hand, three dissident Board members – Humphreys, Hartt, and Lenthall, naval constructors – voted to accept the Lighthall engine. Nonetheless, on May 24, 1839, the Navy settled the issue as if the Board members were on a jury at a murder trial:

"In the opinion of the department, it is not expedient to adopt any alterations or alleged improvements in the contemplated engines for the steam-frigates, the superiority of which is not established, by time and experience, beyond all reasonable doubt.

"It appears to the department that untried experiments, involving great expense, and perhaps the risk of serious delay and ultimate disappointment in the expectations of all parties concerned, is a policy which ought to be avoided in the construction of

THE VESSEL ~ CONSTRUCTION AND CAREER 23

our public vessels of any kind."

No doubt this was sound judgment on the part of a recalcitrant Navy. The Navy department wanted to sit back and watch others take the financial risk, and to prove over time that the Lighthall engine could do everything that Lighthall claimed it could do. Those "others" who were willing to take such risks were stockholders in public companies that were engaged in the business of aquatic transport.

In the meantime, Lighthall submitted another patent application in which he stated that he had "discovered certain improvements in Half-Stroke or Cut-Off Valves for Steam-Engines, which I call the Double-Plunge Half-Stroke Valve." This application was dated November 26, 1840. Here is another engineering description which you may either skim through or skip altogether:

> A A A A, the steam chest; B B, the valve stems; C C, the plunge valves of equal diameter, with their rims or collars E E being from three to six inches deep in accordance with the required throw and recoil of the valve, thus allowing the valves sufficient play or motion while they are in the openings and still continuing to close them; D D, four lugs or guides upon each valve having their outer edges gradually tapering inward toward the stem or rod which together with said stem or rod secures the entrance of the valves into F F, the valve seats or openings, which being turned or bored square instead of beveling or conical allow the cylindrical formed valves to enter in and partially through said opening and work as plungers with little or no friction. Thus it will be seen that this valve differs in structure and mode of working from any valves now or heretofore used. The collar part of the valve being cylindrical instead of conical, the lugs or guides being sufficiently tapered inward, and the seat or valve openings being also turned square or cylindrical on their edges instead of conical or beveling the valves, work by plunging into and

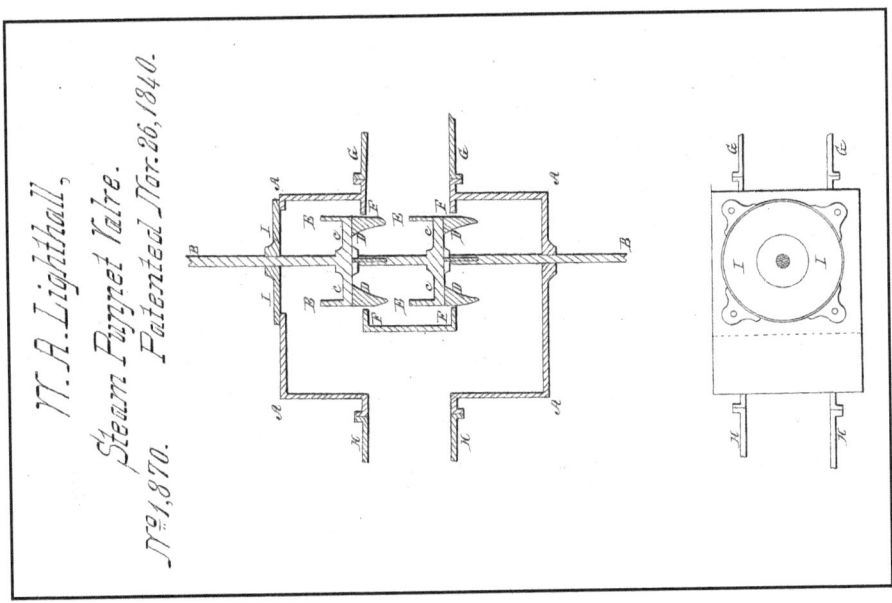

partially through the seat or opening, the lugs or guides are never entirely withdrawn from the openings when lifted but on the return stroke or motion may pass completely through the openings, the collars or rims still continuing to close the apertures. G G the opening to the side pipes. H H the opening to the steam pipe. I I the top view showing the top and bonnet of the steam chest.

The whole apparatus will thus be seen to consist of a cast iron steam chest or box A A A A partially divided by an interior apartment division or chest with apertures F F for admitting the steam from the exterior into the interior chest. The valves the steam pipe H H from the boiler opens into the exterior box or chest, and the steam pipe G G to the cylinder communicates with the interior box chest or apartment, when therefore the valves are lifted out of the openings the steam is admitted from the exterior chest or apartment into the interior and thence to the side pipes upon the cylinder.

The advantages obtained by my improvements in the cut off valve as set forth in the specification and drawings herewith submitted may be thus briefly enumerated: First. It shuts off the steam more perfectly than the cut off valves now in use, and sufficiently perfect for all the practical purposes of a half stroke valve. Second. It requires less power from the engine to work it, because having two valve plates on one stem of equal superficies it is, when in situ in equilibrium, floating as it were, in the steam that surrounds it, the least possible force destroys that equilibrium, and admits the steam. In this respect it is an improvement on the ordinary double balance valve for that requires the diameter or superficies of one valve plate, larger than the other to keep it in its seat, consequently greater force to displace it to admit the steam is necessary. Third. It works without noise and consequently obviates the wear and tear from the collision which in the ordinary valves occasion that noise. The conical or beveled rims or edges of the ordinary double valves strike on thin seats and bring up with a jar and recoil that soon renders readjustment and repair necessary and the recoil impairs their effect. If force be applied to counteract the recoil, then they bring up the harder. Fourth. By passing through instead of on the seat these difficulties are obviated – the valve will wear longer without getting out of order and the collars or rims allow it to vibrate (or work up and down) in the openings still keeping them closed, which is not accomplished in the ordinary half stroke valve.

In the foregoing specification I claim as my invention or improvement – The combination of two valves working on one stem constructed as herein before described, to wit – with rims or collars of sufficient depth to allow the requisite degree of motion while in their seats, and yet continuing to keep the openings closed, and with lugs or guides which prevent the Valves first from being displaced and allow the steam to pass freely through the space between them.

Whew! Again, I do not profess to comprehend much if any of Lighthall's secondary description. His patent applications are included here merely for the purpose of completeness. Lighthall really knew his stuff.

The proof of the pudding came from two commercial steamships that navigated

THE VESSEL ~ CONSTRUCTION AND CAREER

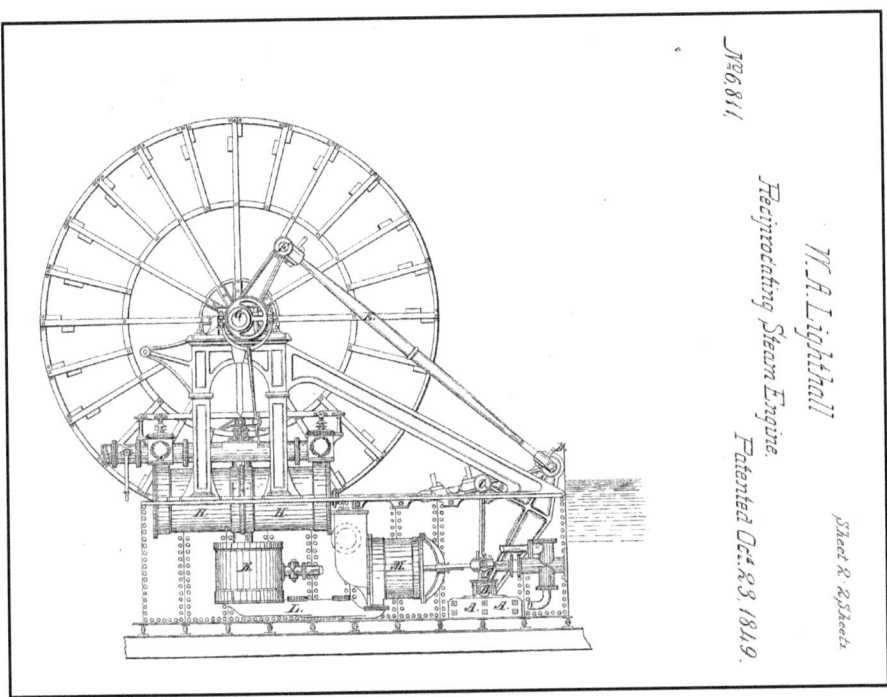

Pictured above and below are the engine that NOAA included in its report, and which it relied upon to identify the $25 Wreck as the *Robert J. Walker*. Note that the patent date is 1849, whereas the vessel was built two years earlier, in 1847.

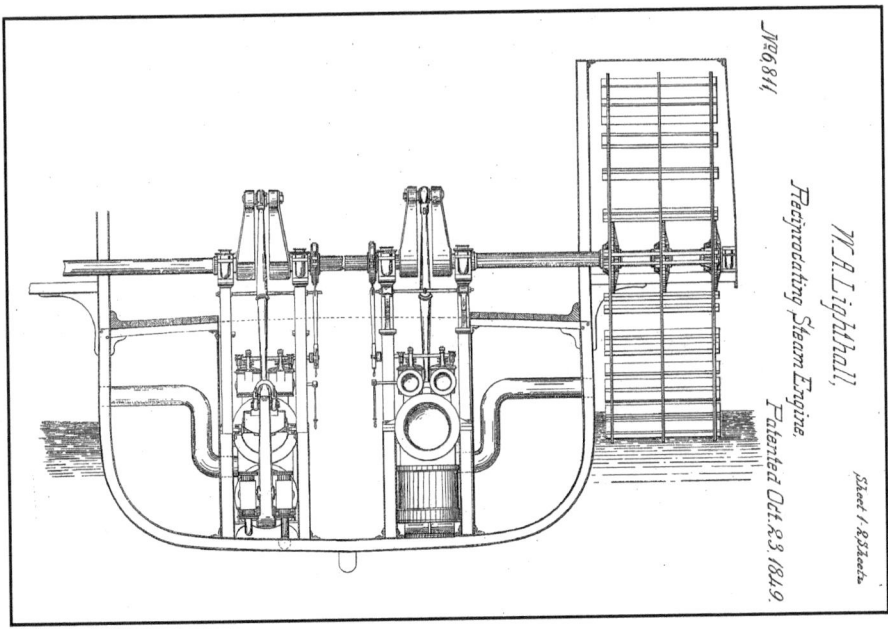

the Hudson River in New York State. The 294-foot-long *Troy* was built in 1840. "She has two of William A. Lighthall's patent horizontal steam engines, low pressure, and is fitted up exclusively for a day boat."

The 330-foot-long *Empire* was completed in 1843. "She is fitted up as a day or night boat, and has fifty state-rooms, a saloon two hundred feet long and seventeen feet wide on her promenade deck, with two of Lighthall's patent horizontal half beam low-pressure engines."

It took all of this and more before the Navy approved Lighthall's engine for the *Robert J. Walker*.

By the way, William Lighthall stayed in the marine engineering business for the rest of his life. He bequeathed the company to his son, who continued the business. The company was still in operation well into the twentieth century.

The Coast Survey

Early steam engines were subject to frustrating breakdowns. For that reason, the *Robert J. Walker* was fitted with two masts that were rigged with canvas, so she could proceed under sail in the event of mechanical malfunction. The sails on the foremast were square-rigged (side-to-side), while those on the mainmast were schooner rigged (fore-and-aft). This configuration was called a brigantine rig.

After sliding down the ways, the *Robert J. Walker* was equipped with armament in the form of three 32-pounders: that is, guns that could fire a shell that weighed 32 pounds. She then steamed down the Ohio River, thence down the Mississippi River, toward her base of operations at Mobile, Alabama.

Before reaching her intended destination, the revenue cutter received new orders. Along with four of the other eight newfangled steamships, she was transferred from the Revenue Marine Service to the United States Coast Survey, and was ordered to proceed to New Orleans, Louisiana, where she arrived on February 11, 1848. It is possible that, because of her reassignment from revenuer to survey vessel, her guns were removed. They have not been found on the wreck site.

According to Benjamin Isherwood, Chief Engineer of the U.S. Navy, "The experiment tried by the Treasury, of substituting steam for sailing cutters, having signally failed from the too large size of the steamers, the expense of maintaining them, and the abortive character of their machinery and propelling instruments, they were either turned over to the Coast Survey, or otherwise disposed of. Of the eight, only three now remain in the Government service, viz: the *Legare*, the *Bibb*, and the *Walker*, and they are employed as Surveying steamers."

In other words, the Navy was not sold on the concept of steamships for use as revenue cutters.

The U.S. Coast Survey was created in 1807 at the behest of President Thomas Jefferson. Jefferson was the same President who negotiated the Louisiana Purchase with Napoleon Bonaparte, in 1803, and who then dispatched Meriwether Lewis and William Clark on their historic expedition of discovery across the continent to the west coast. Jefferson was a staunch advocate of expansion of the United States, and of exploration of the country's land resources and waterways.

Although the Navy excoriated steamships and favored sailing vessels, the advantages of steam over sail in the conduct of coastal surveys were clearly promoted by

THE VESSEL - CONSTRUCTION AND CAREER

Lieutenant Commandant Charles Davis, captain of the *Bibb*, in his 1848 report to Alexander Bache, Superintendent of the United States Coast Survey:

> The following statement of the comparative advantages of steam and sailing vessels, in the service of the coast survey, is derived from my own experience and observation during the present season of active employment.
>
> It must be premised that steam vessels are required only in large fields of work, where long lines can be run, and where the depth is sufficient for ordinary navigation.
>
> In such cases, the superior advantages possessed by the vessel propelled by steam over the sailing vessel, may be classed under two heads, direct and indirect.
>
> Of the direct advantages, the first in importance, is the independence of steam upon wind and tide. Having the means of going in any direction, the surveyor is able to make a comprehensive and careful project of his work, and to carry it out with certainty; while, with sails only, he is obliged to accommodate his traverse to the direction of the wind and the course of the tide, and generally much time is lost in retracing his steps to windward to obtain a suitable position for continuing and connecting his work. As the wind and tide are constantly changing, the plans which depend upon them must change also; those which have been adopted must be left unfinished and new ones be taken up, and thus blanks remain upon the sheets, to fill which is attended with difficulty and loss of time. The greatest evil here, however, is the loss of accuracy, the consequence of a want of system and previous arrangement.
>
> The most favorable days for sounding are those on which the sea is calm, and then the steamer will accomplish the best work, both in amount and quality; but the sailing vessel lies idle for want, of motive power.
>
> When sounding in deep water it is often necessary to lessen the speed in order to get the depth accurately, and to ascertain the character of the bottom. The steam-vessel does this easily, without diverging from her track; the sail vessel must change her course to lie to. By this, time is lost, labor is increased, and the continuity of the lines is broken.
>
> So again, if places unexpectedly occur which demand careful examination, the steam-vessel, moving equally well in all directions, can resume her position when the examination is completed. The other must frequently begin anew.
>
> The speed at which the steamer moves can be regulated with ease and precision; and equality of speed contributes to correctness. The sailing-vessel is almost always unequal in her rate of going for any considerable length of time.
>
> The strict test of the relative value of these two methods of working is the cost of each, compared with the results produced. This test shows very largely in favor of the steam-vessel. The hydrographical party under my command was employed on the Nantucket shoals, during the month of August, 1846, with sailing vessels only, and in 1847 the same party was employed there with the addition of a steam-vessel to its former force.

On both occasions the hire of tenders and the pay of pilots was nearly the same. It will only be necessary, therefore, to compare together the expenses of the two principal vessels—the schooner *Gallatin*, in 1846, and the steamer *Bibb*, in 1847.

The current expenses of the *Gallatin* are estimated at $100; those of the *Bibb* at $450, or four and a half times as much. But the work executed by the latter exceeded that of the former in the proportion of at least fifteen to one; and it is here that the ability of the steam-vessel, to move without regard to wind and tide, is particularly valuable. The numerous shoals and ridges over which the sea readily breaks, can only be approached with safety in calm weather; and near them the current runs with such rapidity that a sail vessel requires a good breeze to stem its force. It is impossible, therefore, for the latter to pursue the work systematically. The loss, too, of the best days, those in which the wind is light or calm, is unavoidable.

By the mention of this field of survey, I am led to speak of the indirect advantages of the steam-vessel, the chief of which is her power to tow other vessels where they are wanted.

On the Nantucket shoals, two or three vessels are anchored as stations. Their positions are to be frequently changed. This is done by the steamer without the delay occasioned by the lack of wind, &c.

It is to be counted among the incidental advantages of a steam vessel, that she works on an even keel; and the inclination of sailing vessels, on the contrary, frequently increases the ordinary fatigue and labor; that she can move into narrow places or stop at a particular spot, less room for manoeuvreing [sic] being required; that she can begin work at pleasure, and continue it until the latest hour; not being compelled to allow for a failing or contrary wind, or an ebbing tide, to get a secure anchorage before night; that she has no sails to interfere with signals while engaged in company with other vessels; that her greater height makes her more conspicuous when observed on from fixed stations, and in the same way is convenient to observers on board when the signal points are distant; the limits of work are thus extended; finally, that she is moved without fatigue to her crew, which, in sailing vessels, is an obstacle to progress.

The year 1848 found the *Robert J. Walker* working in earnest in the Gulf of Mexico. According to the NOAA report, "In the first year, *Walker* finished surveying the offshore approaches to Mobile Bay [Alabama] and the approaches to Cat and Ship Islands [Mississippi]. The work accomplished by the vessel also helped to determine the somewhat unique nature of tides in the Gulf of Mexico. Because of the small range of tides in the Gulf of Mexico, coupled with the great influence of winds on the tidal levels, it was a triumph of perseverance and analysis to discern that the tides in this area were composed of only one high and one low per day as opposed to the twice daily tides of both the Atlantic and Pacific coasts. Studies of shifting channels, accreting and eroding barrier islands, and appearing and disappearing islands – all issues in the Gulf of Mexico today – were first noted in the 1848 report. In addition, the commercial significance of the survey of Mobile Bay and entrance was not lost on the mayor of Mo-

THE VESSEL – CONSTRUCTION AND CAREER 29

bile: '...We trust sir, that the labors you are about to bestow upon Mobile Bay will fully confirm our present anticipations, and establish beyond controversy, the fact that our bay and harbor are capable of affording at least equal facilities with any other southern port to shipping of any description.' . . . Plans were in the making for a Mobile and Ohio Railroad and, if the railroad was to be successful, it was necessary to ensure that Mobile Bay would be able to handle deep draft vessels."

Politics!

In effect, the mayor told the surveyors to fudge the results (depths) of the survey in order to promote Mobile Bay as a suitable port for ocean-going vessels. (For additional fudging practices, see "Global Warming – Another Not!" for NOAA's gross misrepresentation of the facts in regard to the chapter title.)

Upon completion of the survey, the *Robert J. Walker* steamed to her official home port in New York City, where she arrived on July 29, 1848.

She departed for her next cruise on January 16, 1849. Her destination was again Mobile Bay, to complete the work that she had started the previous year. During five months of survey work, she "obtained 71,745 soundings, and ran 1,160 linear miles."

Get the Lead Out!

In case the number of soundings does not sound like a daunting challenge, my readers should know that in those days most soundings were made by casting the lead – by hand! To give you an idea of the amount of work this involved, understand that a lead line or sounding line consisted of a wire that was weighted by the element for which the mechanism was named, in order to measure the depth of water under the survey vessel.

The lead sinker was usually cylindrical in shape, and varied in weight in accordance with the depth of water in which it was to be dropped. The "hand lead" was cast and retrieved manually in waters less than 150 feet. So that the depth could be quickly read, the line was marked at increasing depths with strips of leather, white duck, or red bunting. These different materials enabled the depth to be read quickly. In darkness, an experienced hand could determine the depth by the feel of the material.

Sometimes, the lower part of the sounding lead was deeply indented or hollowed out so that when it struck the bottom, sediment would be compacted into the cavity and brought to the surface for examination.

Generally, the lead was cast while the vessel was in motion. In order to obtain an accurate reading, the lead had to be cast ahead, then reach the bottom before the vessel's forward motion placed the caster directly overhead. The caster retrieved the slack in the line as the vessel proceeded forward. The actual depth was obtained when the line was taut and perfectly vertical. This job was not as easy as it "sounds," and could be accomplished only by sailors with strong bowling arms.

The lead line was also used by vessels in making their approach to an unfamiliar shore or shoal water, especially at night or in fog. Thus, when Samuel Clemens worked as the "leadsman" on a Mississippi riverboat, and called out "By the mark, twain," he was not just creating his future penname; he was informing the skipper that the water was twain (two) fathoms deep. (A fathom is six feet of depth.)

For surveying deeper water there was the "coasting lead." In this device, the lead cylinder weighed fifteen to thirty pounds, and was used for depths up to 350 feet. For truly deep water, there was also a "deep sea lead" that weighed in at more than fifty pounds. These leads could not be cast ahead, but had to be lowered and retrieved by means of a sounding machine.

In its simplest form, a sounding machine consisted of a spool of wire much like a large fishing reel or deep-sea rig. It was mounted on a stand that resembled the pedestal

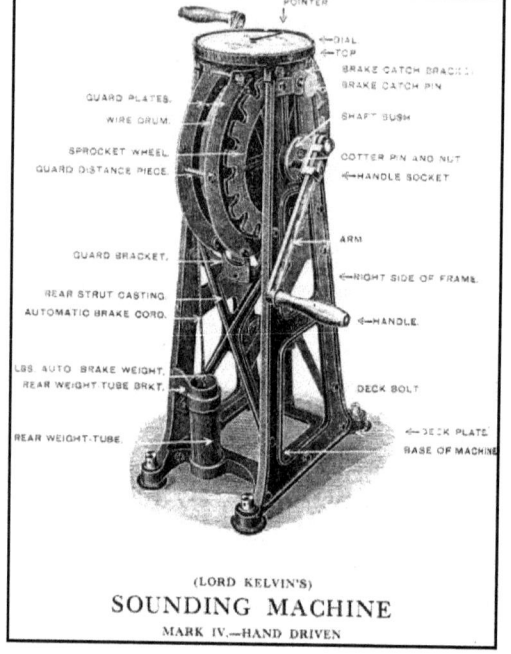

Archival illustrations of sounding leads. On the right (below) are a pair of hand leads with rope secured to the top of each; note the indentations for bottom sampling; the indentation would be partially packed with tallow, which acted as an adhesive to which sediment would stick. Below is a hand-cranked sounding machine, alias a deep-sea sounding apparatus. This device used wire in place of rope. A brake prevented the wire from unspooling too fast. At the bottom is a deep-water lead that was designed for use with a sounding machine; the hemispherical bowls opened upon striking the bottom, then scooped up sediment as the lead was dragged.

(LORD KELVIN'S)
SOUNDING MACHINE
MARK IV.—HAND DRIVEN

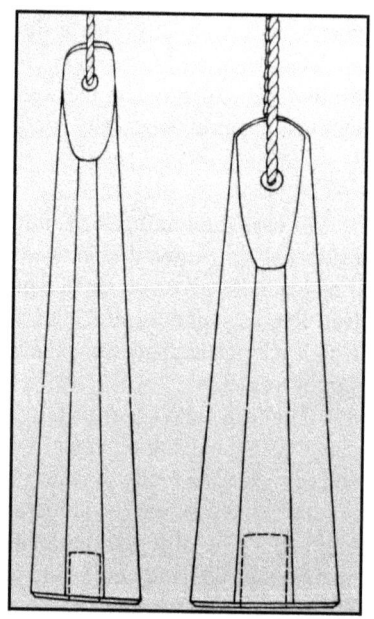

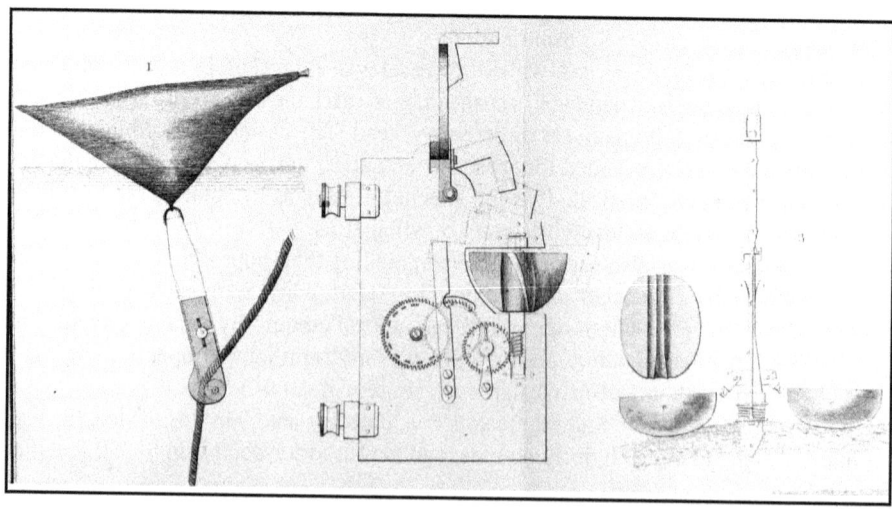

THE VESSEL ~ CONSTRUCTION AND CAREER

for a pelorus or engine order telegraph. Attached to the end of a wire was a heavy lead weight which was dropped overboard. The weight unspooled the line until the lead struck the bottom, at which point the wire went slack. The length of the dispensed wire was measured, and the vessel's speed was factored into calculating the actual depth, as the line paid out at an angle aft. The lead was then retrieved by cranking the reel by hand. Twentieth-century sounding machines were cranked by an electric motor.

All this puts into perspective how much physical effort was required to take soundings and do survey work in antebellum days.

Mobile in Mobile

There was a downside to this season's numerous accomplishments. NOAA report: "Notable on this cruise was the death of Passed Assistant Surgeon Silas Holmes and five men who were with him in a small boat that capsized in a squall off Mobile on May 21. Only one man in the boat's complement lived, 'sustaining himself on an oar.' "

The 1850 season was not as fruitful. The *Robert J. Walker* wintered in the Gulf of Mexico, then was loaned out to an "unnamed agency." By the time the vessel was reclaimed, refitted, and crewed, there was only enough time left to "do a reconnaissance of Cedar Keys, Florida," during which she discovered "the existence of a shoal extending out eight or ten miles from Sea Horse Key." For navigational safety, it was recommended that a flashing light mark the end of the shoal.

Additionally, the Mobile Delta survey was completed. Later, she did some survey work "offshore of the Virginia Capes and Maryland. This was one of the few occasions when *Walker* conducted work anywhere but in Section VIII."

In 1851, the *Robert J. Walker* "was occupied with offshore work south of Dauphin Island and Petit Bois Island, in shore [sic] work north of the same islands, and in special examinations of Pass Christian Harbor and the mouths of the Mississippi [River]. A steam launch, specially constructed for inshore and harbor work, was lost in a storm off the Chandeleur Islands in May."

New boilers were installed in Philadelphia, Pennsylvania in 1852. The *Robert J. Walker* then "continued surveying in Mississippi Sound from Dauphin Island to the longitude of round Island including Horn Island Passage, made outside soundings (ten miles to sea) from the middle of Petit Bois Island to the middle of Horn Island, conducted reconnaissance to the South and Southwest Passes of the Mississippi Delta, and made a survey of Naso Roads at the north end of Chandeleur Island."

Lest this work sound repetitive or unnecessary, understand that at that time virtually nothing was known about the coastal regions that surrounded the country. This work was important for commerce so that transport vessels did not run aground on uncharted shoals.

Nor was the *Robert J. Walker* the only survey vessel in operation. Survey work was a three-pronged operation. Other vessels were assigned to survey the eastern seaboard and the west coast shoreline.

Nor was survey work limited to taking soundings. Magnetic studies were also undertaken. Vessels steered strictly by compass when they were out of sight of land. It was crucial to map magnetic deviations and anomalies so that ship masters knew how to adjust their compasses as they passed through various regions.

Tidal variations were also noted.

THE VESSEL ~ CONSTRUCTION AND CAREER

The Great Mobile Hurricane struck the *Robert J. Walker's* working area in 1852. As a result, 1853 found her redoing some of her earlier work in the search for changes of the sea floor. "The ship then began work in Mississippi Sound. The crew made 69,079 soundings over 1,430 sounding miles."

Instead of making the long passage to New York, the *Robert J. Walker* spent the following off-season in Pensacola, Florida. Seven crewmembers died when a yellow fever epidemic struck the area.

The 1854 season was hampered by a lack of personnel. After a late start, the *Robert J. Walker* surveyed the east pass of the Mississippi River, and took deep sea soundings and temperature measurements far to the south – all in two and a half months. She then proceeded for Philadelphia for repairs.

The 1855 season commenced with "a succession of gales" that postponed survey work for two months. Despite the late start, the *Robert J. Walker* still managed to take 105,591 soundings. She also "ran soundings in the Gulf Stream while running north at the end of the season and then in October ran the section south from Nantucket, one of the more difficult sections run in the past because of its length."

To give an idea of how much work was accomplished, the original records occu-

The 1853 chart below shows the kind of work in which the *Robert J. Walker* was engaged. The numerous depth soundings were vital to finding the best ways to enter St. George's Sound, Florida, without running aground.

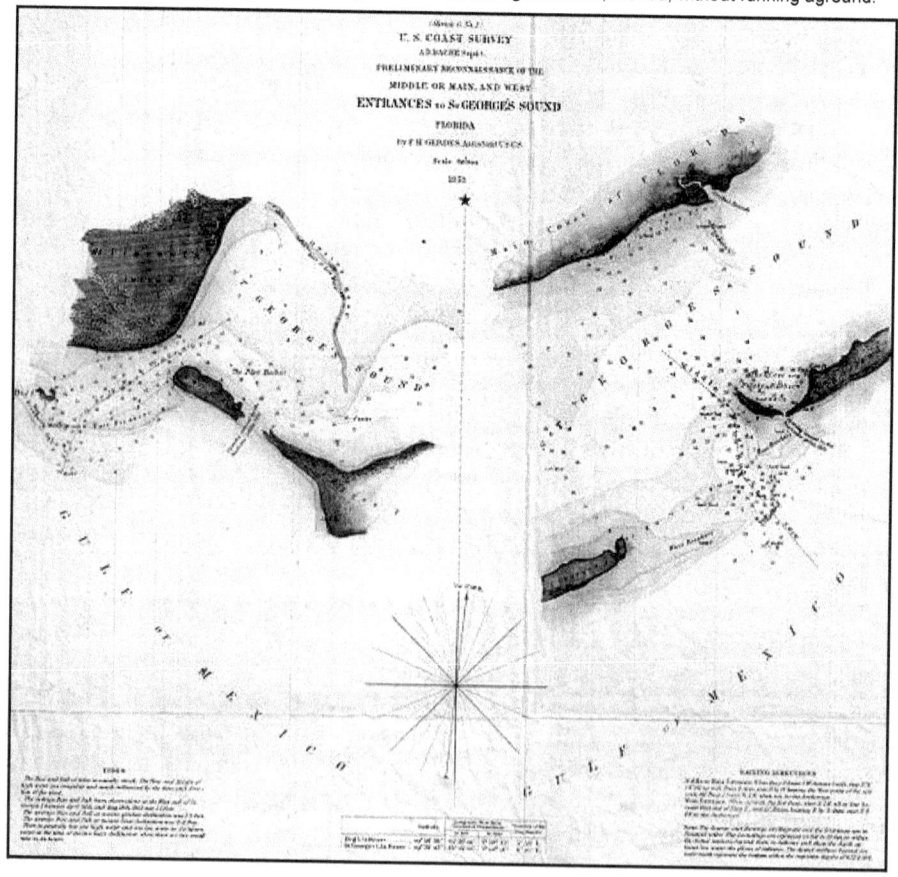

THE VESSEL – CONSTRUCTION AND CAREER

Historical photographs of the first two skippers of the *Robert J. Walker*. On the left is plank owner Carlile Patterson, who commanded the survey vessel in 1847 and 1848. On the right is James Alden, who was in command between 1849 and winter of 1851.

pied twenty volumes of observations, "another volume of observations in determining angles, another of tides observed, and thirteen diagrams." All in one season!

Ice clogged the Delaware River in the winter of 1855-1856. This prevented an early departure. Not until the middle of March did the *Robert J. Walker* attempt to escape the big freeze, "but the ice damaged its paddlewheels necessitating further delay at New Castle [Delaware] for repairs. A stormy passage south allowed for no deep sea soundings until reaching the latitude of Cape Fear [Wilmington, North Carolina]. From there, *Walker* ran soundings to Cape Canaveral [Florida]. From Key West, it ran deep sea soundings north to the Mississippi Delta."

The 1857 season resulted in 75,529 soundings. According to the hydrography report for that year, "The deepest sounding made on the passage to Key West was at 1,511 fathoms, registered by the indicator with 2,070 fathoms of line out, and an ample specimen of light blue mud was brought up."

Also recorded at extreme depth was a temperature of 38° Fahrenheit, or 6° above the freezing point of water.

A separate topographical party was dispatched to Matagorda Bay, Texas. Appended to the report:

> The general character of the country is prairie; along the shores of the bays the land is subject to overflow at very high tides; but, at a distance of ten or fifteen miles from the Gulf, the shores of the bays are fronted by bluffs rising from fifteen to thirty feet high, with frequent patches of timber, especially near the streams.

THE VESSEL ~ CONSTRUCTION AND CAREER

Above left is an historical photograph of Benjamin Franklin Sands, who started his service as commander of the *Robert J. Walker* in March of 1851. The woodcut of Thomas B. Huger shows his likeness after he commanded the survey vessel in 1858 and 1859.

Matagorda island is mostly low, butt ridges, or 'rolls,' rising from eight to ten feet above the Gulf, extend throughout its entire length. Immediately along the Gulf shore some sand hills occur, varying in height between five and thirty feet.

The soil of the island is fertile; but high winds prevail constantly during spring and summer. All kinds of garden vegetables grow in great perfection and abundance. Fruit trees generally, and the peach and fig, thrive very well in sheltered localities, but the chief attention is given to the raising of cattle, mules, and sheep.

In 1858, "While detained at Pensacola, assistance was rendered by Commander Sands, with the men and boats of the steamer *Walker*, on the occasion of a fire which happened at Fort Pickens on the night of the 20th of January."

Also lending assistance was the hydrographic party of the Coast Survey schooner *Varina*. The *Varina* was an auxiliary which assisted the *Robert J. Walker* by fetching supplies so that the survey vessel could remain on station.

The season ended with an additional 75,951 soundings.

In 1859, 69,447 soundings were added to the score card of the *Robert J. Walker*. Her area of operations was Atchafalaya Bay, Louisiana. According to NOAA, "During the survey work, *Walker* was primarily used as a hotel ship because of shallow waters in the working area. The ship conducted deep sea soundings on the trip south to Key West and then ran a section of Gulf Stream from the Tortugas to Havana while on the way north."

New and Final Skipper

The last skipper of the *Robert J. Walker* was John Julius Guthrie. He took command on October 10, 1859. His time aboard lasted a mere eight months.

THE VESSEL - CONSTRUCTION AND CAREER

Guthrie was born in Washington, North Carolina only two months after the final flickering flames of the War of 1812. The year of his birth was 1815. The date of his birth was either April 15 or April 27 (sources differ). Aside from the fact that he was educated by Reverend Doctor William McPheeters in Raleigh, North Carolina, almost nothing was recorded of his childhood. Standard biographical sources skip to 1833, when he enrolled as a cadet in the U.S. Military Academy at West Point. A year later he joined the ranks of the U.S. Navy as a midshipman. As most sailors did, over the next quarter century he served aboard a number of Navy vessels and, as today's posters promise, he saw the world.

His first recorded service was on the USS *John Adams*: an old wooden-hulled 44-gun frigate which, construction having been completed in 1799, was older than Guthrie. (Despite her age, the *John Adams* survived in fighting trim until after the Civil War.) This was long after the Second Barbary War, but piracy was still alive and well in the Mediterranean Sea. The *John Adams* patrolled the north coast of Africa, and convoyed American vessels to ensure their safety in hostile waters.

After four years of his first service afloat, Guthrie returned to the United States and was transferred to the USS *Columbia* in time to embark on a cruise around the world. This 44-gun frigate was younger than Guthrie. The *Columbia* spent two years circumnavigating the globe. After passing the Cape of Good Hope, at the southern tip of Africa, the *Columbia* sailed to the East Indies. Along the way she met the *John Adams*. The Columbia returned via Cape Horn, at the southern tip of South America, then proceeded north through the Atlantic Ocean. The next two years were spent in home waters.

Guthrie achieved the rank of lieutenant in 1842, when he was transferred to the USS *Warren*: a 32-gun sloop-of-war with a compliment of 190. She sailed around the Horn, proceeded North on the Pacific Ocean, and spent the rest of her career on the West Coast of the United States.

An historical photograph of John Julius Guthrie in his younger days.

Guthrie's next assignment was on the USS *Union*. This was a brand new paddlewheel steamer: an experimental design in which the paddlewheel shaft was placed below the waterline and extended outboard through a cofferdam on either side of the hull.

This introduction to steam machinery lasted only a short while. Guthrie spent the years 1845 to 1846 aboard the USS *On-Ka-Hy-e* (also spelled *Onkahye*), a 2-gun schooner that patrolled in the Caribbean Sea and as far south as Brazil.

His service aboard the 6-gun schooner USS *Flirt* occurred during the Mexican war (1846-1847). The *Flirt* did not engage in hostilities, but primarily carried mail and supplies between New Orleans, Louisiana and Galveston, Texas. She also did some blockade duty.

Guthrie's next station was the USS *Brandywine*. For three years, the 44-gun frigate patrolled off the coast of Brazil "protecting United States interests in the region." Sharing a 175-foot-long vessel with 430 men was a typical situation for Navy personnel.

He then found himself aboard the USS *Saranac*. This sidewheel steamer was armed with nine 8-inch guns; she was classified as a sloop-of-war. Two uneventful years on the *Saranac*'s home service were punctuated by one noteworthy event: that of returning Brazilian Minister Chevalier de Sodre to his homeland.

Between 1855 and 1858, Guthrie served aboard the USS *Levant*. This second-class sloop-of-war saw action in China during hostilities between that country and England. The United States was neutral in the Second Opium War. Nonetheless, the U.S. warships *Levant*, *Portsmouth*, and *San Jacinto* were dispatched to the Celestial nation.

What should have been nothing more than guard duty escalated to armed conflict when, according to Navy records, "At the outbreak of hostilities between the British and the Chinese, *Levant* arrived Whampoa 28 October. Comdr. A. H. Foote then sent a landing party from *Levant* and his own ship, *Portsmouth*, to Canton to protect American lives and property there. On 15 November, while in the process of withdrawing this force, Commander Foote was fired on while passing in a small boat by the 'Barrier Forts' on the Pearl River below Canton. On the 16th *Levant* was towed upriver to join *Portsmouth* and *San Jacinto* in keeping the Pearl open to American shipping. As the forts were being strengthened in disregard of American neutrality, Foote was ordered by Commodore James Armstrong, commanding the squadron, 'to take such measures as his judgment would dictate...even the capture of the forts.'

"Commander Foote complied with all the dash and courage for which he became famous during the Civil War. On 20 November he took the first fort by leading an amphibious assault with 300 men, then silenced the second with cannon captured from the first. Next day he took the third, and by the 24th all four were in American hands and the Pearl once again safe for American shipping.

"*Levant*, close in through most of the action, received the major part of the Chinese bombardment, with 22 shot holes in her hull and rigging, one man dead, and six injured. Destruction of the earthworks was completed by 5 December, and *Levant* cruised between Hong Kong and Shanghai until she departed Hong Kong 7 December 1857 for home, arriving at the Boston Navy Yard 6 April 1858."

Guthrie took an active part in the attack on the forts. He personally hauled down the Chinese flag from the first fort. For more in this regard, and events involving Guthrie after the loss of the *Robert J. Walker*, see "Aftermath and Conjecture."

A contemporary likeness of Guthrie in his later years.

Robert J. Walker – the Vessel
Collision and Loss

New York Times
The following article is copied verbatim from the *New York Times*:

LOSS OF THE U. S. STEAMER *WALKER*.
TWENTY PERSONS MISSING.
Particulars of the Disaster – Arrival of the Survivors at this port –
List of the Saved and of the Lost.

"A telegraphic dispatch, received late on Thursday, from Cape Island, New Jersey, announced the loss of the United States Coast Survey Steamer *Walker* by collision with an unknown schooner off Absecom, early on Monday morning of that day, and stated that twenty of her crew were supposed to be lost, while the survivors, some forty in number, had been saved in the boats. By the arrival, yesterday, of the steamer *Kennebec*, Capt. Johnson, from Cape May, with forty of the crew of the unfortunate steamer, we have been enabled to gather full particulars of the disaster, and a complete list of the saved and lost. The *Walker*, Lieut. J. J. Guthrie commanding, which has been absent for several months, engaged in the work of the coast survey, at the South, was returning to New-York for repairs. She left Norfolk on Tuesday, the 19th inst. And, at the time of the collision, had passed Cape May, and was within about ten hours sail of New-York. The wind had been blowing fresh from Northeast, and there was a heavy head-sea, which considerably retarded the progress of the steamer. She was, however, making about seven knots an hour under steam. At about 2 1/4 o'clock A. M., the man on the look-out saw a schooner approaching under full sail, and steering head on. He notified the man at the wheel, and gave the usual order to port the helm. The order was obeyed, the helm being put hard a-port; but at the same time the schooner was observed to put her helm a-starboard thus rendering a collision inevitable. As both vessels were under full headway, there was no time for either to alter his course, and the shock was instantaneous and terrible. The schooner struck the steamer on the port-bow, near the forward chains, her head-rail taking under the steamer's plankshear, staving in the iron plates, and opening her down to the water-line. The vessels then swung clear of each other, and the schooner was observed to round to and remain with her sails shaking for four or five minutes. She then filled away and kept on her course. An effort was made to hail her from the steamer, but it failed. The shock of the collision immediately brought all that were below on deck and word was passed that the steamer was sinking. Captain Guthrie ordered the vessel headed in shore, and sent men below to stop the leak if possible. Hammocks and mattresses were stuffed into the opening, but the hole was so large and the force of the water so great that it was found impossible to stop it. In fifteen minutes the water had risen to the furnaces and extinguished the fires, causing the engines to stop. Orders were now given to clear away the two boats, (one having been destroyed by the collision,) and to drop them astern, that they might be ready for use. There was no time to be lost, however, as she was fast sinking. The mainmast was ordered to be cut away, and the booms and spare spars cut loose to afford the crew the means of sustaining themselves in the water. The boats were now hauled up, and one of the crew who was sick, and the only lady passenger on board, first put into one of them. Implicitly obeying the commands of Capt. Guthrie and his officers the boats were then filled with as many as they could safely sustain, and, at the word of command, pulled away from the sinking ship. The next moment she went down, carrying with her all who were on her decks. The crew were now seen clutching at the floating spars and loose materials of the wreck, or clambering up the rigging to save themselves by clinging to the topmast head. The boats were very deeply loaded, there was a heavy sea running, and their crowded condition left little or no room to pull at the oars. They were some ten miles from the land, and, even if they were able to reach it, the heavy surf which broke upon the beach would render it impossible to land without swamping the boats, and probably losing many lives. In the extremity a vessel was seen bearing down for them. She was hailed, and immediately answered by rounding to and giving them a line. All the crew were put on board, excepting men enough to man each boat, both of which then returned to search for those who were still clinging to the wreck or floating spars. All who could be found were picked up. At this time another schooner was seen, apparently engaged in the same work, but she soon kept away, and how many she may have picked up, if any at all, is not known. It is hoped that, of the twenty persons missing, some at least are on board of this unknown vessel, which has probably carried them to some Southern port.

"The schooner which picked up the boats, and rendered such timely and important service, proved to be the *R. G. Johnson* [sic], Capt. Hudson. He remained in the vicinity of the sunken steamer, searching for the missing men until 2 o'clock P. M., Thursday, when, the weather being thick and it blowing fresh, the vessel was headed for Cape May. Here they were all landed, and the same afternoon the steamer *Kennebec*, Capt. Johnson, brought them to this City [New York]. They have lost everything they possessed.

LIST OF THE SAVED

The following is a list of those who reported themselves on board of the receiving ship *North Carolina* yesterday:

Mr. Guthrie, son of Lieut. Guthrie, in charge of the crew. John McMullen, Captain main-top. John Burton, master-at-arms. Charles Clifford, John Brown, J. R. Hall, Essex D. Corcoran, (sick and unable to report himself,) Quartermasters. Robert Bell, Joseph Meary, George Penn, Joseph Peterson, John Desmond, John Rowe, Joseph Clark, John Brien, Andrew Young, William Logan, William J. Jones, John Smith, James A. Golden, seamen. James Clark, James Delorse, Alonzo Hood, John A. Minor, John W. Walsh, Burnett Canah, ordinary seamen. John C. Johnson, boatman's mate. James Young, gunner's mate. Edward Lynch, arms mate. Joseph Wilson, sailmaker. John Taylor, fire-

THE VESSEL - COLLISION AND LOSS

man. Michael Lyons, Daniel Evans, Frederick Dougherty, Henry Hunter, Michael Boyle, coal passers. Peter Decker, (boy.) John Harrison, C. T. Thomas Rixley, Lds. William H. Mapes, 1st C. F. Henry Dick, S.S.

There were three others known to have arrived in the steamer, making forty-four in all who are saved.

LIST OF THE MISSING

The following list of the missing crew has been supplied by Mr. Charles Gifford, Quartermaster on board of the *Walker*, to whom we are also indebted for the particulars of the collision:

Marcus (or Marquis) Buoneventa, ward-room steward.
Michael M Lee, ship's cook, (colored.)
James Patterson, ward-room cook, (colored.)
Henry Reed, second mate.
Timothy O'Connor, second gunner.
John Driscol, seaman.
Michael Olman, seaman.
George W. Johnson, son of Mr. Johnson, the actor.
Charles Miller, ordinary seaman.
Robert Wilson, seaman.
John M. Brown, captain of after guard.
Jeremiah Coffice, cooper.
Cornelius Crow, landsman.
John Farren, fireman.
James Farren, fireman.
Samuel Sizer, fireman.
George Price, fireman.
Joseph Bache, fireman.
Daniel Smith, fireman.
Peter Conway, fireman.
    Total 20

RECAPITULATION
Names of those saved   44
Names of those missing   20
    Total of the crew   64

The foregoing list corresponds with the names of the lost as telegraphed from May's Landing, N.J., and signed by N. G. Porter, but afterwards the following names are added:

        S.J. HUDSON.
        JOHN ENGLISH.
        E. SMITH.
        WM. TAYLOR.

New York Herald

The *New York Herald* published a somewhat different account; that is, one that accentuated different aspects of the event by adding some particulars, and by dismissing details that another correspondent emphasized. The combination of both articles presents a more rounded view of the catastrophe. According to Quartermaster Charles Clifford:

> At the time of the collision Lieutenant J. A. Sewall, the executive officer, was on watch. It was about quarter past two in the morning. We saw the schooner ahead, coming before the wind, and put the helm hard aport to clear her. The schooner was close aboard of us. The lights of both vessels were burning clear. The atmosphere was cloudy, and the wind blowing fresh from the northeast.
>
> The schooner thereupon put her helm hard astarboard, which made a collision inevitable. She struck the steamer forward of the port guard and wheelhouse, cutting her down to the water's edge, and carried away her own head booms. The schooner hung for a moment, then swung alongside, and carried away the forward and quarter boats of the steamer. Getting clear of the schooner, we worked ahead, but found the *Walker* was sinking; cut away her mainmast booms, and got everything movable on deck, to make a raft for the men. Everybody cool, and the officers behaving with great presence of mind, lowered both starboard boats and dropped them astern for use when the vessel went down.
>
> By this time every soul was on deck except those who may have been killed or injured by collision, and a sick man on board, nearly seventy years of age, almost helpless, had been carefully lifted out and put in one of the boats. All was orderly. The men stayed by the steamer until she was sinking, and then, without confusion, such of them as could took to the boats. Many of the crew went down with the steamer, however, clinging to the spars and portions of the wreck, and expected to be saved in that way. The captain stayed on board until the steamer went down, and just before she disappeared from sight jumped into the water, and was picked up by one of the boats.
>
> Lieutenant Sewall was drawn down in the vortex, and, after remaining for a considerable time floating on a portion of the wreck, was also rescued by one of the boats. A heavy sea was running, and many of the men were doubtless washed off the spars and drowned from the mere exhaustion of holding on, while others were killed or stunned on rising to the surface by concussion with spars and other parts of the wreck.
>
> The steamer had entirely sunk from sight in thirty minutes after the collision. Many of the crew were rescued by the boats, in which were about forty-four persons, and they were in turn picked up by the schooner *R. G. Porter*, Captain S. S. Hudson. He did nobly, keeping his vessel about the spot where the wreck went down until two o'clock in the day, and using every endeavor to render us comfortable and afford the desired assistance. Finding that it was useless to remain longer in searching for the missing, Captain Hudson stood in to Cape May [New Jersey], where he arrived about four o'clock on Thursday afternoon.

Clifford's account was appended with:

THE VESSEL - COLLISION AND LOSS

The above account is corroborated in all particulars by that of Lieutenant Commanding J. J. Guthrie, United States Navy, with whom another of our reporters likewise had an interview at a later hour in the evening. He states, in addition to the above, that on arriving at Cape May a schooner was there with a rent in her foresail, her head spars carried away and her cutwater injured.

The name of this vessel was the *Fanny*, and the time of her arrival was such as to make it almost certain that she was the author of the accident. While in Cape May the officers and crew were provided with much needed refreshments and clothing by the citizens. Prominent among those who rendered assistance were Mr. West, the proprietor of Congress Hall, J. C. Little, of Our House; Captain Johnson, of the steamer *Kennebec*, and Captain Cannon, of the *Delaware*, and Messrs T. M. Quicksall and J. W. Burton, of Philadelphia. Lieutenant Guthrie speaks in the highest terms of the conduct of the crew under the trying circumstances, and states that when the steamer went down every man was at his post, there being in the boats only three individuals and a dog.

A heavy gale was blowing at the time and a rough sea running, which caused the steamer to careen and settle much more rapidly than she otherwise would have done, as well as prevented those engaged in the work of rescue from saving all those who were enabled for a time to keep themselves above water. It is hoped that as a number of schooners were in the vicinity others may have been picked up, and, indeed, from the maneuvers of one of them, the captain states that it is almost certain that such is the case. The survivors who came on to this city [New York] have reported themselves to the Commandant of the Navy Yard, and been paid off. All are in a destitute condition, however, officers and crew having lost everything except the clothes on their backs. In view of these circumstances, and the bravery and discipline manifested on the trying occasion, it behooves the government to take some steps to recompense them for their loss.

NAMES OF THE SAVED.

John J. Guthrie, Lieut. Com.
J. A. Sewell (and lady), 2d officer.
B. W. Guthrie, 4th officer.
Jas. Bellum, Surgeon.
R. B. Swift, Engineer.
Henry Dick.
John C. Thompson.
John Burton.
John Walsh.
John McCaffrey.
Chales [sic] Clifford.
John R. Hall.
John Brown.
John Taylor.
William H. Mapes.
William F. Jones.
Robert Dell.
Jos. Clark.
John Dryan.
George Henn.
Jos. Morg.
John Smith.
Jos. A. Golding.
William Logan.
John Rowe.
Jos. Peter.
James De Courcey.
William Doyes.
Bernard Carrah.
Thomas Riley.
John A. Minor.

James Harrison.
John McMillan.
Edward Lynch.
Daniel Evans.
James Wilson.
Jefferson Cravens.
Andrew Young.

Alonzo Hood.
James Clark.
Peter Decker.
Michael Boyle.
Patrick Doherty.
Michael Lyons.
Henry Hotten.

NAMES OF THE MISSING.

Henry Reed.
Timothy Connor.
Jeremiah Coffey.
John M. Brown.
Michael M. Lee.
Marquis Bonevents.
Jas. Patterson.
Michael Allman.
John Driscoll.

Robert Wilson.
Cornelius Crow.
Chas. Miller.
Geo. W. Johnston.
Saml [sic] Sizer.
Daniel Smith.
John Farren.
Joseph Bate.
James Farren.

George Price.

Explanatory Remarks

The astute reader will have noticed that Clifford's account in the *New York Herald* noted that the executive officer was Lieutenant J. A. Sewall; yet neither name nor position of such an individual was mentioned in the *New York Times* article, either as a survivor or as a victim.

The astute reader will also have noticed that no female names were given in either list. The *New York Herald* listed only a "lady" next to Sewell's name. Note the difference in the spelling of Sewall and Sewell.

Also, the *New York Herald* provided a list of the saved and lost that differs slightly from the list that was provided by the *New York Times*: not only in the way some of the names were spelled, but in the number of names on each list. The *New York Herald* gave 45 saved and 19 missing, instead of 44 and 20.

To add to the confusion, NOAA claimed that the name of the executive officer was spelled Joseph A. Seawell. NOAA also claimed that the total number of individuals onboard at the time of the collision was seventy-two instead of sixty-four. NOAA then claimed that one of those saved later died of his injuries, which raised the total of deceased to 21.

Where NOAA obtained these data is unknown to me. Considering the difficulty that I had in obtaining documentation from NOAA in this regard, it is unlikely that the Administration will divulge its sources to me. In Part 2 I will relate how NOAA reacted the last time I asked for a single item of information, by not providing it unless I paid $294.00 in advance, with other charges to follow. At other times, NOAA refused even to reply to my request for information. The information that NOAA posted on its website is only the tip of the iceberg: thousands of images have not been released.

The reader should also understand that historical documentation is seldom precise. Minor variations among sources are common. The best that a researcher can do is to draw attention to disparities in the historical record, so that readers are kept informed.

THE VESSEL - COLLISION AND LOSS

Steering Convention

Most of my readers know that "port" on a vessel means "the left side" if you are looking forward (toward the bow). Consequently "starboard" means "the right side" if you are looking forward. Thus when a vessel turns to port it turns left, and when it turns to starboard it turns right.

But in the eighteen hundreds, when a vessel "ported the helm" it meant that the vessel turned to the right, not to the left. Likewise, when the helm was "put aport" it meant that the vessel turned right, not left. Antebellum mariners understood this distinction but most modern landlubbers do not.

Thus you might have been confused when reading the passages about the collision between the *Robert J. Walker* and the *Fanny*. When both vessels ported their helms, you might have thought that they both turned to the left, thus exposing their starboard sides to the oncoming vessel. Yet the way the collision occurred, the bow of the *Fanny* struck the port side of the *Robert J. Walker*. In reality, both vessels turned to the right.

This counterintuitive steering convention was a holdover from the ancient days of sail when vessels were steered not by a helm but by a tiller that was connected directly to the rudder. When the tiller was pushed to the left, the rudder was turned to the right, and the vessel's direction of travel was consequently turned to the right. When helms replaced tillers, time-honored traditions were maintained, so if the top spoke of the helm (or steering wheel) was moved to the left (so that the wheel rotated counterclockwise), the vessel turned to the right. Thus the command "port your helm" meant "turn the vessel to starboard," or right.

This steering convention was changed gradually in the middle of the twentieth century. Steamships were the first to adopt the new steering convention that broke away from old-time rudder commands, so that turning the helm clockwise (pushing the top spoke to the right) turned the vessel to the right, the way it does today in vehicles; and vice versa. But for many years sailing vessels clung to the old standard. Furthermore, some countries were slow to adopt the new convention. For a number of years "port your helm" could have meant "steer" right or left, depending upon whether you were on a steamship or a sailing vessel, and in which country the vessel was constructed and the crew was trained.

Eventually, when international rules of the sea were standardized, the new convention became global. Now if we could only get the Brits to drive on the "right" side of the road . . .

Official Report

Guthrie's report to Superintendent Alexander Bache was shorn of drama and more succinct than either of the newspaper articles:

> It becomes my painful duty to report to you the loss of the U.S. Coast Survey Steamer "Walker" which was sunk at sea in five fathoms [30 feet] of water about six miles SE of "Absecum Light" on the coast of New Jersey, in consequence of being run into by a schooner – supposed to be the "Fanny" on the morning of the 21st of this month about 2:20 A.M. Two of the boats were stove in and rendered useless by the collision, the two remaining ones were lowered, and many of the crew saved by this means, and the timely as-

sistance of the "R. G. Porter" of Mays Landing, N. J., Captain Hudson, who came to our assistance in this hour of need. I cannot withhold profound regret for the melancholy fate of that portion of the crew who are still missing and who it is to be feared have found a watery grave. During this sad catastrophe the sea was running high and the wind very fresh. I need not add that the loss of my own professional reputation, necessarily incident to such an accident occasioned very slight regrets compared to the depths of sorrow I endure for the missing – and heartfelt sympathy entertained for the anxious and bereaved families and friends – I am sure you understand the workings of the heart sufficiently to render it unnecessary for me to essay to unfold mine in written terms.

Bache asked for more detail, to which Guthrie responded:

> On the night of the 21st about 2:20 A.M., I was awakened by an unusual noise on deck, and my first thought was that the 1st officer was getting a case of the lead, but soon after heard the Executive Officer tell someone to call the Captain – an officer came down and reported to me that the vessel was sinking – I went on deck and directed her [the vessel] to be headed inshore, and to give her all the steam speed possible, seeing Abseceum Light distinctly – being about West-Nor.West – distant about nine miles. A schooner was near us, which I hailed and requested to keep by as we were sinking – soon after this the engineer reported the fires extinguished – and the water gaining very rapidly on us. – I had previously sent men down in the coal bunkers to see if the leak could be stopped in any possible way – it was found to be impracticable – finding she must inevitably go down soon – I directed the mainmast to be cut away – the boats to be lowered and some of the ladders to be towed astern for buoys – and also directed the quartermaster to get a case of the lead – he reported five fathoms water – Soon after she sunk. It was found two of the boats had been crushed. The two remaining ones picked up what portion of the crew they thought they could carry in safety; Nothing was saved, except what was on and about the persons of those who were rescued – all the Note Books, Instruments, charts of the vessel etc. went down with her and as all the records are gone – I have to depend upon memory for the facts – all of which it is impossible to remember distinctly.

All these accounts differ slightly in detail, some giving facts that the others omitted, and some giving facts that seem to contradict those of the others. Keep in mind that each of the witnesses who provided an account saw events from a different perspective, with himself at the center of activity. Minor discrepancies are bound to infiltrate the stories of survivors in a state of distress.

What is remarkable about the rescue of the survivors is that the crewmembers of the *R.G. Porter* were able to hear the shouts of floating men above the gale that was filling their canvas, and they were able to see the men in the water in the ebony of night. Also remarkable is the fortuitous appearance of the rescue vessel: a savior that smacks of divine intervention.

THE VESSEL – COLLISION AND LOSS   45

Yet Another Account

The most complete account of the disaster was published shortly after the event, but far enough removed in time to allow additional facts to come to light. The article duplicates many of the facts that were published in the dailies only a day or so after the loss of the *Robert J. Walker*, but its twice-yearly publication of happenings of the previous six months enabled the periodical to add many details that had accumulated in the interval. *Vincent's Semi-Annual United States Register* told the story in full:

> Loss of the U.S. Steamer *Walker* and Twenty of Her Crew. – This day [June 21, 1860], the U.S. steamer *Walker*, under the command of Lieut. John Guthrie, which had been on the Coast Survey, and was on her way back to New York, having got as far as the Absecom light-house, the look-out sighted a vessel right ahead, coming toward the steamer. The vessel seen proved to be a fore-and-aft schooner of about three hundred tons burden; her name was not discovered. Scarcely ten minutes elapsed from the time the schooner was first sighted until she struck the steamer. Mr. Sewell, the deck-officer, seeing the approach of the schooner, and believing a collision inevitable, unless both vessels altered their course, at once ordered the man at the wheel to port his helm. This order was immediately obeyed, and some three or four minutes before the collision the steamer had sheared off from the course of the schooner.
>
> He ordered the schooner to port her helm also. Instead, however, of porting her helm, she appeared to have put it hard astarboard. It was too late to shift round. The schooner being before the wind, with a northeast half gale blowing, and the sea running very high, she struck the *Walker* on the port side, about two feet forward of the paddle-box, and cutting the second cutter in two. She hung on to the steamer for several minutes, then her bow rolled right up on top of her; she then slid off, and the two vessels dragged side by side for about three minutes more. During this time no voice answered from the schooner, nor was any one seen on board. While the vessels were dragging together, the fourth cutter was smashed so completely as to be rendered utterly useless. The schooner then dropped astern, and in ten minutes afterward was out of sight.
>
> The gale continued to blow with unabated vigor, and the sea ran high, making it exceedingly perilous to put out either of the two remaining cutters which were on board the steamer. Vessels last seen had left close-reefed. No time was lost, however. It was ascertained that the vessel was taking water very fast. Some of the men were sent down into the coal-bunker, where they found the water rushing in. They tried to stop the leak with beds and blankets, but found it impossible, as the hole was so large that they no sooner put a bed into it than it was carried through. In this way, one bed after another was lost in the effort.
>
> Finding their endeavors all in vain in that direction, and the vessel fast sinking, they were ordered to clear the boats and to have them ready for lowering. At the same moment an order was given to run the vessel for shoal water. This order was promptly obeyed, and she was heading finely for the

shore, when, owing to the influx of water into the boiler-room, the fires were drowned and the engine stopped. To prevent explosion, the engineer at once ordered the steam to be blown off, which was done forthwith. The order was also given to cut away the mainmast, for the purpose of making a raft, but before it could be disentangled from the rigging, it went down with the vessel.

The order to lower away the first and third cutters was next given and obeyed. Mr. Sewell's wife was then placed in the first boat, which was dropped astern in tow, while the crew was endeavoring to sail the vessel. Finding this impossible, the boats were ordered to be manned. In four minutes after this order was given, the steamer went down by the head, the captain standing aft on the poop-deck until she was two-thirds hid in the water. He then jumped overboard, and was picked up by the third cutter. When the steamer went down, Mr. Sewell was standing on the poop-deck and went down with her. He was subsequently picked up by one of the boats. Owing to the continued roughness of the sea, it was impossible to crowd the boats. So long as there was any hope of saving the vessel, every man on board the steamer worked with a will. Every order was obeyed with alacrity and promptitude. The men were cool and self-possessed. As the steamer went down, the screams and shrieks of the perishing echoed terribly through the boisterous elements.

After the steamer went down, the boats pulled to the leeward of the wreck, among the drift, and picked up as many as they could of those who were yet floating about. Finding it too dangerous to go close to the wreck, and seeing a sail in the distance, it was thought best to pull out athwart the bow of the approaching vessel. As soon as she came within hailing-distance, she hove to. She proved to be the schooner *R. G. Porter*, Captain Hudson, bound to Philadelphia. All who were in the boats, with the exception of a sufficient number of men to work them, were taken on board the schooner. The boats then proceeded on a search for the remainder of the crew. Both boats pulled away for the wreck, and succeeded in saving about a dozen more, who were drifting about, some clinging to chairs, some to chicken-coops, some to planks, and some to ladders. Finding it impossible to pull the boats to the windward of the wreck, they pulled back to the schooner and got the captain to beat to the windward, and at about ten o'clock they fell in with Mr. Sewell, in a greatly-exhausted state, and four others of the crew, clinging to the poop-deck, which had been separated from the steamer by the force of the sea.

Mr. Sewell had got his leg entangled in the ridge-rope, which was fastened to the stanchions. This kept him in water nearly up to the neck, the sea at times breaking over him and smothering him. At length, however, by the continuous efforts of the men who were on the poop-deck with him, the stanchion which yet remained was unshipped, and he was released at once and taken on board the schooner, as were also the others. One of the four just mentioned – a young man named William Logan, – in diving to get at the rope and cut it, got away from the place, but was picked up and put on board the schooner also, - not, however, until he was almost drowned. The schooner then stood to the windward again, in search of more men, but saw no one until about half-past eleven o'clock, when they fell in with a man, who appeared

THE VESSEL - COLLISION AND LOSS

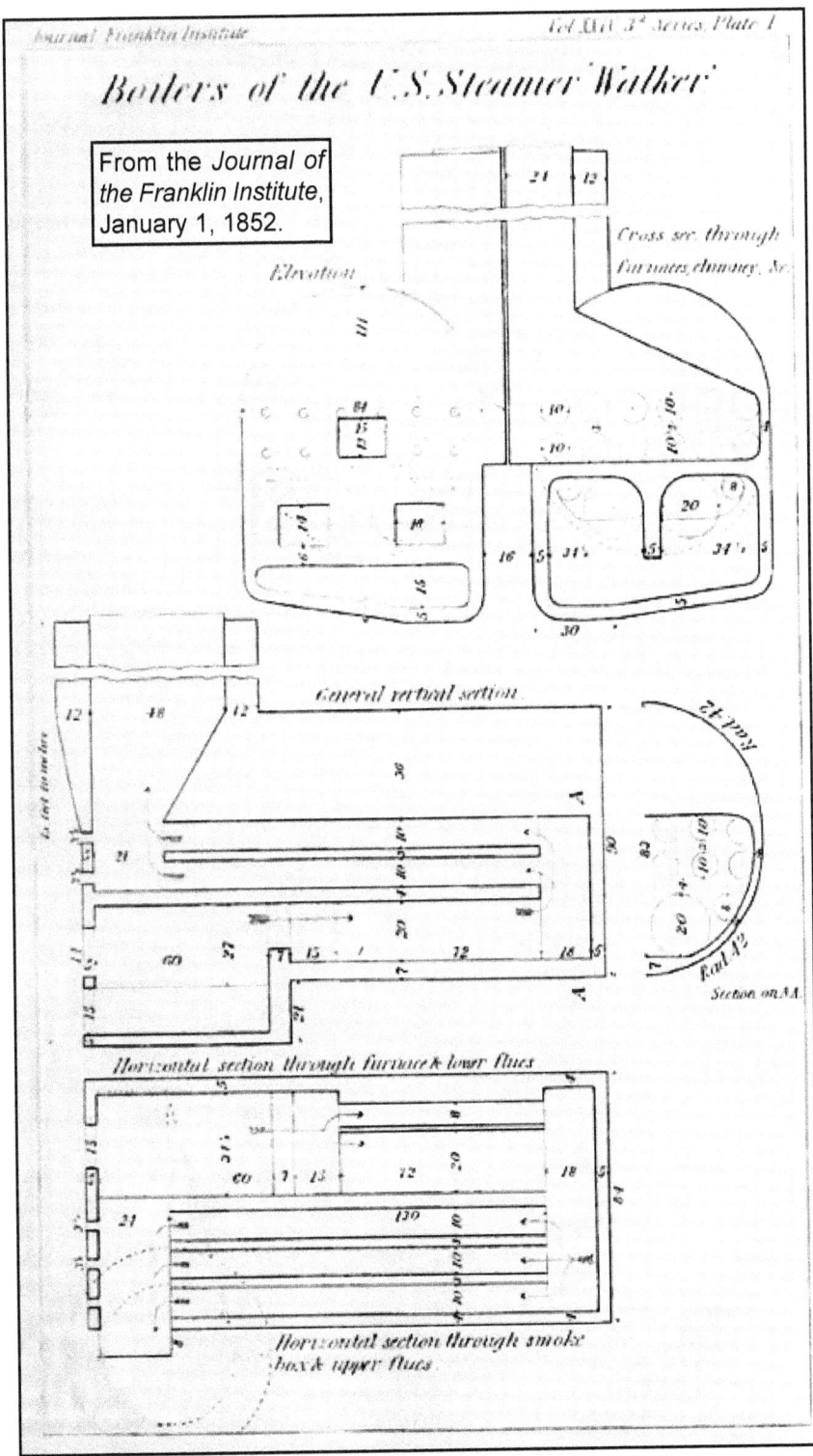

From the *Journal of the Franklin Institute*, January 1, 1852.

to be naked, swimming toward them.

They hove to and manned a boat, the sea at this time running very high, but before they could get to him they lost sight of him. They pulled backward and forward for three-quarters of an hour in the trough of the sea, expecting to be swamped every moment, but they could see nothing of the man. They went on board again and beat up to the windward of the wreck, so that they could examine the topgallant foremast, the top of which was still above water. Five men, who had taken to the mast, had been seen clinging to it when the stanchion was unshipped and the poop-deck floated away.

The reason of their taking to the mast was an impression which they had that they were in shallow water, and that the rigging would be a safe resort. But the masthead was examined in vain: no one was there. They bore away for Cape May, where they arrived on Thursday afternoon. The people, seeing their destitute condition, treated them very kindly, giving them such food as could be found.

Most of those saved took passage on board the steamer *Kennebeck*, for New York. Some, however, took passage in the steamer *Delaware*, for Philadelphia.

The men spoke in praiseworthy terms of the officers. Not one of them got into either of the boats, the doctor, or course, excepted.

At the time of the collision, an old man, named Essex Cochrane, one of the crew, who had been very sick for some time, was brought on deck, passed into one of the cutters, and put on board the schooner *R. G. Porter*.

Lieut. Guthrie, the officer in command, speaks very highly of the good order maintained by the men.

The utmost order prevailed during the whole time of the catastrophe, until the vessel sank and they were left to the mercy of the waves. The sea was very rough. When the vessel went under, part of the deck got loose and floated on the water, fortunately for the men, as it afforded a means of support without which a great number of those rescued must have been swallowed by the waves.

After the fate of the vessel had become certain, Lieut. Guthrie ordered the cannon to be fired; but the powder was wet, and the next moment each man was forced to struggle for dear life. The schooner that ran into the *Walker* disappeared, notwithstanding their urgent need of assistance. There were other vessels about, however. The *R. G. Porter*, a Jersey schooner, Capt. S. S. Hudson, came timely to their aid. The energetic efforts and good offices of Capt. Hudson were beyond all praise. He and his mate, Mr. E. Smith, made almost superhuman efforts for the rescue of Lieut. Guthrie's men, and are remembered by them with the warmest gratitude.

At Cape May, Capt. Cannon, of the *Delaware*, and the captain of the steamer *Kennebeck*, whose name is not ascertained, betook themselves earnestly to supplying the wants of the wrecked.

Mr. John C. Little, of "Our House," took in some of them, and furnished carriages to convey the others to Congress Hall, at the request of Capt. West, of that place, and to other houses in that vicinity. Messrs. T. M. Quicksall and

THE VESSEL – COLLISION AND LOSS 49

G. M. Burton, of Philadelphia, freely furnished them all the money they needed, and, besides, went around among the people to collect stray boots and jackets, (for the seamen had cast theirs off,) and food, which they, by this time, felt the want of, laboring most generously until all had been made comfortable.

The saved unite in returning thanks to the whole community, in short; for everybody seem to busy himself or herself in their behalf.

At this point the article reprinted verbatim the narrative of Quartermaster Charles Clifford, the only difference being a change in the spelling of name of the executive officer from Sewall to Sewell. It then provided the names of the survivors and the missing, which I will furnish because the lists contain slight dissimilarities from those that were published in the dailies.

Names of the Saved. – John J. Guthrie, Lieut. Com., J. A. Sewell (and lady), second officer, B. W. Guthrie, fourth officer, James Hellum, surgeon, Charles Marriott, assistant surgeon, R. B. Swift, engineer, Henry Dick, John C. Thompson, John Burton, John Walsh, John McCaffrey, Charles Clifford, John R. Hall, John Brown, John Taylor, William H. Mapes, James Harrison, John McMillan, Edward Lynch, Daniel Evans, James Wilson, Jefferson Cravens, Andrea Young, William F. Jones, Robert Bell, Jos. Clark, John Bryan, George Henn, John Cazmer, Jos. Morg, John Smith, Jos. A. Golding, William Logan, John Rowe, Jos. Petter, James De Courcey, William Boyes, Bernard Carrah, Thomas Riley, John A. Minor, Alonzo Hood, James Clark, Peter Decker, Michael Boyle, Patrick Doherty, Michael Lyons, Henry Hotten.

Names of the Missing. – Henry Reed, Timothy Connor, Jeremiah Coffey, John M. Brown, Michael M. Lee, Marquis Bonevents, Jas. Patterson, Michael Allman, John Driscoll, Robert Wilson, Cornelius Crow, Charles Miller, Geo. W. Johnston, Samuel Sizer, Daniel Smith, John Farren, Joseph Bate, James Farren, George Price.

The crew of the *R. G. Porter* all behaved gallantly, and it was owning to their noble exertions that many lives were saved. Their names were S. J. Hudson, E. Smith, John Englison, and William Taylor.

Note that the names of the saved now number 49, and the names of those missing now number 19, giving a total of 68. There are also spelling differences from the lists that were published in the dailies. There was no mention of anyone dying the day after the event.

Also, the four names that were now given as crewmembers of the *R. G. Porter*, had been appended to the lists in the dailies as men who were missing from the *Robert J. Walker*. Again there are some differences in spelling.

To continue:

The vessel which came into collision with the *Walker*, and caused so much loss of life, proved to be the schooner *Fanny*, Capt. Mahew, bound from Philadelphia for Boston. She was a vessel of about two hundred and fifty tons, long and narrow, built upon the model of a canal-boat, and loaded with two hundred and forty tons of coal, her bow being exceedingly strong, as was evidenced by the effects of the collision by which the steamer was sunk, her bow being but slightly injured, and no damage done to the vessel except the carrying away of her bowsprit and a portion of her railing. She did not leak a bit after the accident. The captain of the *Fanny* says that his vessel was headed for Cape May, and running before the wind, her course having been changed in consequence of the high wind and heavy sea. The lights of the steamer were seen for some distance, but her hull was not discovered until the vessels were within two hundred yards of each other. The captain of the *Fanny* then eased his vessel off a little, he says, to avoid a collision, and at the same time the steamer, it is alleged, changed her course, bringing her directly toward the *Fanny*, and in a moment the two came together. The first contact was near the bow of the steamer; and, as the bowsprit of the *Fanny* did not break at this time, it is thought the anchor over the bow knocked a hole in the iron side of the *Walker*. The schooner got clear for a moment, but again struck the steamer, aft the wheel-house, breaking her bowsprit, railing, &c. The captain of the *Fanny* then examined his vessel and tried the pumps, and, no leak being found, he continued on his course, not thinking, he says, 'that there was any probability of the steamer sinking, his fears being altogether for his own vessel.' He also states that his vessel, after the loss of her jib, was entirely unmanageable, and that he could not have gone about to render any assistance."

And Yet Another Account

As part of a biography of the skipper of the *R. G. Porter*, a concise version of the catastrophe was published in the *Daily Union History of Atlantic County*. This item stressed his providential appearance after the sinking of the *Robert J. Walker*, and his gallant efforts to render aid to the survivors and to search for the missing. It provided a slice of life as it was in the mid-1800's. It also provided his full and correct name instead of the mistaken initials that were ascribed to him in the articles above:

Captain Shepherd S. Hudson, one of the oldest and best-known sea captains of Atlantic County, was born in Delaware, June 30, 1826. He came to Mays Landing with his father, the late Elisha E. Hudson, in 1832, and his home has been here ever since. The father was a mariner, and at the age of eleven years, in 1837, the year that Atlantic County was organized, the son was made cook for the crew on his father's vessel. There were no public schools in this county in those days. When eighteen years old he was put in command of the sloop *Hornet* and engaged in trade with his father. He was soon in command of larger vessels and has followed the business ever since, over sixty years [at the time this biography was written]. The schooners *Helen Justice*, the *Dove*, the *R. G. Porter*, the *Mary P. Hudson*, and the *S. S. Hudson* are other larger vessels that he has sailed.

On September 21, 1846, Capt. Hudson married Mary P. Ingersoll; b. April 21, 1828; d. August 28, 1891. They had six children: 1. Amanda, who m. Capt. D. F. Vaughn, November 22, 1866, and had two children: Mary C., deceased,

THE VESSEL – COLLISION AND LOSS 51

and Shepherd H., the architect, who m. Lida Eldridge, and lives in Atlantic City. 2. Kate, who m. Melvin R. Morse, October 9, 1871, and had four children: Melvin H., who m. Cora M. Sharp, and has one child: Bessie W., deceased; Amanda V., and an infant deceased. 3. Eva B., d. March 3, 1855. 4. Mina, m. Clarence E. Morse, December 28, 1881, and has two children: Mary L. and Fayette W. 5. Marie, m., June 17, 1880, Capt. Frank R. Davis, deceased, July 4, 1892. 6 Mary S., who lives at home.

During the Rebellion he was in command of a United States transport about Yorktown and Fort Fisher, carrying troops and ordnance for Uncle Sam.

He at present is commander and principal owner of the barkentine *Jennie Sweeney*, which he built at Mays Landing in 1876.

Since his boyhood Captain Hudson has taken an active interest in politics as a Whig or a Republican, but he has never held office except that of Assemblyman, in 1889.

Captain Hudson has not only made the remarkable record of never having lost a vessel during his long service on the high seas, but there stands to his credit the proud record of having saved 51 lives from a wrecked steamer, for which he has never received any medal or public recognition whatever. A more gallant and heroic service perhaps never was performed by man then when this young captain of the schooner *R. G. Porter*, in a gale seven miles off Atlantic City, soon after midnight on Thursday, June 21, 1860, saved 51 out of 71 lives. The last five of the 51 wrecked sailors were saved from a furious sea, when the captain of those he had rescued protested against Captain Hudson's return to the wreck in the high wind perchance to find still others afloat. The skillful manner in which he handled his vessel is worthy of all praise. His crew consisted of E. Smith, mate; John Englison and William Taylor.

The United States steamer *Walker*, under the command of Lieutenant John Guthrie, with a crew of 70 men engaged in the coast survey, was run into at 2.15 o'clock a. m. by the schooner *Fannie* [sic] Captain Mayhew, bound from Philadelphia for Boston with 240 tons of coal. Lieutenant J. A. Sewell of the *Walker* was on the watch. The atmosphere was cloudy and the wind was blowing from the northeast. It was a cold June storm. Both vessels had their lights burning, but neither one discovered the other till too late.

The schooner, long and narrow and loaded, was unable to port her helm to avoid collision. She struck the *Walker* on the port side forward of the paddle box, badly injuring the steamer but doing the schooner no harm. She hung to the steamer a few minutes and then slid off. No man on board was seen or heard. She dropped astern and in ten minutes was out of sight.

The *Walker* was found to be leaking badly and about to sink. The boats were ordered out and the vessel turned toward the shore. To prevent explosion the fires in the boilers were put out and steam blown off. Before the mainmast could be cut away the steamer went down. Besides the crew of 70 men there was one woman aboard, the wife of Lieutenant Sewell. In her night-clothes only she reached one of the boats with 21 of the men, one of them old and sick.

This boat was fastened to a projecting mast by a light line when the *R. G.*

Porter, Captain Hudson, hove in sight. The *Porter* was in ballast from Boston to Philadelphia, and came close to the steamer ten minutes after it had sunk. It was then nearly 3 o'clock in the morning. Men not in the boats, two of which had been smashed in the crash, were clinging to the driftwood and the wreck. The wind was blowing a gale and the sea was rough. All except enough men to man the boats were quickly gotten aboard the *Porter* and made as comfortable as possible.

By 8 o'clock in the morning 46 souls had been saved. The *Porter* had then drifted about five miles to leeward, when Captain Hudson determined to beat back to the wreck if possible to find other members of the crew adrift. The spars could be seen projecting 20 or 30 feet above the surface of the sea. But he persisted, determined to save every living soul possible. Nearing the wreck a black spot was noticed on the angry sea, which proved to be the hurricane deck of the *Walker* with five men clinging to it. One of them was Lieutenant Sewell, who was so exhausted that he had to be lashed to the deck with ropes by his companions. These were gotten aboard about 10.30 o'clock. These five men were the last of the living to escape from the *Walker*. The remaining twenty were lost.

Unable to enter Absecon Inlet in such a sea, Captain Hudson made direct for Cape May, reaching that place at 4 o'clock on that Thursday afternoon, passing around the Point in full view of the big hotels, with colors at half mast. Crowds of people on the beach were startled at the sight and hastened out to welcome the rescued and destitute crew. They provided food and clothing and kindly cared for Mrs. Sewell. Before Cape May was reached Captain Hudson was sent for by Lieutenant and Mrs. Sewell, who after seven hours separation and a very perilous experience were happily united again and saved by the skill and bravery of Captain Hudson. They thanked him most heartily for saving their lives and the gratitude and thanks of the saved is all the thanks or recognition that Captain Hudson has ever received.

From Cape May some of the saved got passage to New York and others to Philadelphia. While a full report of this thrilling event was recorded in the United States Register of that date, up to the present time no medal has ever been struck and no recognition by the United States Government or any department thereof, was ever made of Captain Hudson's brave and successful rescue of 51 out of a crew of 71 precious lives.

In reiteration, attention must be called to the fact that contemporaneous accounts differ slightly in the details of the number of crewmembers on board at the time of the collision, of the number of people who were saved, of the number of people who perished, of the spelling of crewmembers' names, and miscellaneous iota.

Please note that the spelling of Absecom and Absecum evolved into the present day spelling of Absecon.

Robert J. Walker – the Vessel
Aftermath and Conjecture

According to the NOAA report, "Lieutenant Guthrie thought that the steamer might be raised or that the engines and machinery could be recovered. Guthrie was mistaken. The steamer had sunk in approximately 13 fathoms [78 feet; actually 14 fathoms or 84 feet] instead of the 5 fathoms [30 feet] that Guthrie initially thought, and was not thought to be about 12 miles offshore instead of the 5 to 6 miles reported. If there is any criticism of Guthrie, it is that he had no idea where his ship was when it was struck and also that he was not awake and on deck as his vessel had just passed the busy entrance of Delaware Bay and would be approaching progressively more congested waters as it approached New York City."

Skippers had to sleep sometime. They could not stand watch for 24 hours a day. It was a common – indeed, necessary – practice to assign another of the ship's officers to command the vessel so that the skipper could take his "watch below" (nautical slang for "be off duty"). It makes sense that Guthrie would want to be fresh when the *Robert J. Walker* neared New York Harbor and proceeded upriver through the heavily trafficked waterway.

The irony of the situation is that Guthrie had ordered the crew to chop down the mainmast: the mast that was located aft, nearest the stern. Had the mast remained standing, not only could the men still have clung to it and its stays while awaiting rescue, but the mast would have served as a double marker for the wreck site. As James Delgado noted in the quote above, Guthrie did not know the location of the vessel or the depth of water when he scrambled on deck and found the vessel sinking. So he took action that he perceived was necessary to save as many lives as possible. That his quick decision turned out to be the wrong one is no reflection on his character or his capability as a ship's captain. He could not have foreseen that the fallen mast would get tangled in the lifeboat davits. That was purely the luck of the draw.

I mention this scenario not as the critique of a Monday morning quarterback – I have the advantage of historical hindsight – but only as matter of incidental enlightenment.

To Guthrie's suggestion for salvage, Bache replied, "If your desk could be procured containing the papers of the survey, it would be worth $2500 and if the engines or parts of it can be had it would help us materially." Such was not to be.

The NOAA report also suggests that Bache proposed suing the *Fanny* for damages, but that "the advent of the Civil War pushed the affair out of the way." The report then suggests that no official investigation was conducted for the same reason. I take exception to these suggestions. The Civil War did not start until nine months later, in a future that no one could have foreseen. Inquiries start within days after a vessel is loss. Lawsuits are initiated within weeks, or perhaps within a month or so.

I harbor different speculations. Perhaps it was thought that a lawsuit against the *Fanny* could not have been won, and that all it would accomplish would be to impugn Guthrie and the Coast Survey in a public forum. In nearly all cases of collision between a steamship and a sailing vessel, the steamship has been found at fault and held liable because it had unrestricted maneuverability by dint of its engine, while the movements of a sailing vessel were restricted by the vagaries of the wind.

What is more astonishing under the circumstances is that the *Fanny* did not file a suit against the *Robert J. Walker*.

Regarding the lack of an inquiry, the Coast Survey might have realized from the declarations of the survivors that an inquiry would accomplish nothing more than to cast blame against its own, and to no good purpose.

It is also possible that an inquiry *was* conducted, but that the transcript was never archived. Or if it was archived, its location has not yet been discovered. Or perhaps it has been misfiled and therefore not retrievable. Throughout my years of research, I have found that the U.S. Navy cannot locate *half* of the courts-martial and courts of inquiry that the Judge Advocate General has listed on file, even though there are records of their existence and their having been archived at the Washington National Records Center in Suitland, Maryland. Half! Fifty percent! Stuffed with a conglomeration of other reports in a folder in a box on a shelf on a tier in an aisle in a storage facility that rivals in size the warehouse that is shown at the end of the movie *Raiders of the Lost Ark*.

Bache was more pragmatic than he was sensitive to the plight of the living and the dead. He noted in various places in his annual report:

> The progress of the work has been, taking all its branches together, greater than during the year before, but the loss of one of our best steamers by collision at sea has been a sad drawback to the general prosperity of the work. As my estimates for the time of completion of the survey must be materially affected by this loss, I earnestly recommend a special appropriation to replace the steamer at the earliest practicable period. . . .
>
> The loss of the steamer *Walker*, by collision at sea, requires an appropriation to replace her. As the government acts as its own insurer, this is an indispensable item of estimate. The loss of a considerable part of the records of last season's work, and the loss of time from having no steamer to take the *Walker's* place in the Gulf of Mexico, will be sensibly felt in our progress, and I would respectfully urge that another steamer be supplied at the earliest practicable period, so as to enable us to work up again as soon as possible to the former efficiency. . . .
>
> I have elsewhere referred to the wreck of the steamer *Walker*, on the 21st of June of the present year. This disaster, which involved loss of life to twenty of her crew, with the total loss of the vessel and all the records on board, was occasioned by collision with a schooner laden with coal, and occurred about three o'clock in the morning, while the *Walker* was off Absecom, New Jersey, in command of Lieutenant J. J. Guthrie, U.S.N., and on her passage from Norfolk to New York. The officers of the *Walker* and survivors of her crew were rescued from imminent peril by Captain L. J. Hudson [sic], of the schooner *R. G. Porter*, and safely conveyed to May's Landing, on the coast of New Jersey. The steamer sunk in less than half an hour after the collision, which took place about twelve miles from land.

THE VESSEL – AFTERMATH AND CONJECTURE

During slack time after the loss of the *Robert J. Walker*, Guthrie found occasion to reflect on his service aboard the *Levant*, especially when he took an active part in the attack on the Chinese forts. As noted in "Construction and Career," he personally hauled down the Chinese flag from the first of four forts. Now he decided to present the flag to the governor of his home state.

The governor's letter of receipt is worth repeating, not only because of its heading as a Testament to Gallantry, but for its unintentional prescience:

>   Raleigh, Aug. 23, 1859
> "Sir: I have this day received from Capt. A. J. Lawrence a Chinese flag, taken by you [Guthrie] in an assault upon the barrier forts in the Canton river in November, 1856, by the forces of the United States ships *San Jacinto*, *Portsmouth*, and *Levant*, as a present in your name to the State of North Carolina.
>
>   Having been apprised of your desire to make this disposition of the flag, the last General Assembly, by resolutions, authorized me to receive it from you in behalf of the State, and at the same time to express to you the high appreciation of that body of your gallantry on the occasion referred to, and of the evidence of your veneration for the State of your birth.
>
>   Believing that I cannot discharge this pleasing duty in a more respectable manner than by transmitting those highly complimentary resolutions, I herewith enclose a copy of them as transcribed from the statute book. These resolutions, I am well assured: are nonetheless expressive of the sentiments of the people of the State than of their representatives who enacted them; for they have ever manifested a lively pleasure at the honorable distinctions achieved by the sons of North Carolina in every department of the public service. Every distinguished action of the citizens proves useful to the State in the example it affords to the youths of the country, who are thus apprised of the gratifying rewards that ever await a faithful discharge of duty.
>
>   The flag, so gallantly taken by you in the maintainance [sic] of the rights and protection of the persons of American citizens in a distant land, will be placed among the valued treasures of the State, and will be looked upon by posterity, impressing all who may see it with the sentiments of esteem in which are held the brave conduct of the faithful soldier in the service of his country; and to our youths, to whom from time to time the story of its capture may be narrated, will be told that it is a trophy for which the State is indebted to one of her courageous sons who entered the service of the country when a mere boy, and who, without the aid of fortune or the influence of powerful friends, won his way to honorable distinction by his own upright deportment and gallant spirit. Thus, sir, will a valuable lesson be taught them, exciting in their bosoms a laudable ambition to emulate like honorable actions.
>
>   Trusting that your career will prove one of continued usefulness to the country and distinction to yourself, I have the honor to be very respectfully, yours, &c,
>   John W. Ellis.
>   Lieut. John Julius Guthrie, U.S. Navy

Resolutions authorizing the Governor of the State to receive a flag tendered to the State of North Carolina by Lieut. Guthrie, of the U.S. Navy.

Whereas John Julius Guthrie, a lieutenant in the United States Navy and a native of the State of North Carolina, now on official duty at the National Observatory, Washington, D.C., did, on the 20th day of November, 1856, capture and carry off as a trophy of war a Chinese flag from the first of four forts captured in a combined engagement by the *San Jacinto, Portsmouth*, and *Levant*, on the part of the American naval force, and other vessels under the command of Rear Admiral Seymore, on the part of the English, in the Canton River:

And whereas the chastisement inflicted on that occasion was in defence [sic] of American and English citizens residing in the locality, and had the happy effect of securing to them immunity from violence and insult to their persons and property:

And whereas said Lieut. Guthrie has been induced by his friends in the city of Raleigh and elsewhere to express a willingness to tender this flag to his native State, with a desire that she would accept it as an humble evidence of filial sentiments and affectionate recollection: Therefore –

Resolved: That the Governor of the State be authorized and requested to accept the flag thus tendered by Lieut. Guthrie at such time and place and in such a way and manner as may appear suitable and proper.

Resolved further: that he be requested, in behalf of this General Assembly, to express to Lieut. Guthrie its high appreciation of his gallantry on the occasion and this evidence of his veneration for the State of his birth.

Resolved thirdly: That the Governor be farther requested to make such disposition of the flag, when received, as he may think this trophy of her son deserves.

Ratified February 15, 1859.

Guthrie was fortunate not to lose his reputation in addition to his ship. Indeed, he was afterward assigned to the USS *Saratoga* as executive officer. This change in responsibility did not necessary imply that he suffered a reduction in rank or paygrade. He was still a lieutenant. But he was no longer in command of his own vessel. Without a court of inquiry, it is not possible to know whether he was found unfit for command, or whether there were no vessels available in need of a captain.

The *Saratoga* was a sloop-of-war that worked against piracy in the Caribbean Sea until she was decommissioned on June 26, 1860. According to Naval records, after a three-month hiatus the *Saratoga* "Reactivated on 5 November 1860, she sailed from Philadelphia 10 days later to return to the scene of her first cruise [in 1843], the west coast of Africa. On 21 April 1861, she captured slaver, *Nightingale,* off Kabenda, Africa, freeing a cargo of numerous slaves."

Another source claims that "numerous" meant that 961 slaves were landed in Liberia and freed.

"After word of the outbreak of the Civil War reached *Saratoga,* she returned to the United States and decommissioned at Philadelphia on 25 August 1861."

THE VESSEL - AFTERMATH AND CONJECTURE

Saratoga. (Courtesy of the Naval Photographic Center.)

Now, at the age of 46, Guthrie engaged in the most active naval operations of his career. As a Southerner at heart, on July 6, 1861, he resigned from the United States Navy and joined the fledgling Confederate States Navy, in which he retained his rank of lieutenant. He was first given command of a floating battery on the Mississippi River, at Island No. 10. This island was located near New Madrid, Missouri, some 25 river miles downstream of St. Louis, Missouri. He moved on before the famous battle that took place there in 1862.

Guthrie was then assigned to the Confederate gunboat *Chattahoochee*. He was second in command under Catesby ap Roger Jones. The *Chattahoochee* was a bad-luck vessel right from the beginning. Plagued by politics, she existed on paper for six months before she was contracted to a shipbuilder, in late 1861. The Confederates were competent at growing and picking cotton, but they had no expertise in building ships, and almost no familiarity with machinery. Thus the vessel turned out to have too deep a draft for riverine operations, or to escape over the shoals to sea. She was too slow, and her propulsion machinery was unreliable: it broke down constantly, partly due to slack in the cylinder heads. Compounding the problem was poor construction of the boilers: the rivet heads popped loose when high steam was applied. As a result, the *Chattahoochee* lay fallow at Chattahoochee, Florida, unable to engage the enemy or to flee from advancing Union hordes. She was little more than a floating battery that had to be towed upstream and down.

On February 4, 1863, Guthrie took command after Jones was reassigned. Or perhaps Jones departed in frustration, having "commanded" the gunboat since before the keel was laid. In this respect, Guthrie's promotion could be viewed more as punishment than confidence in his ability to handle a warship and her crew, who were dying more from swamp fever than from enemy action.

The recovered section of the *Chattahoochee's* stern. (Courtesy of the Naval Photographic Center.)

On April 7, 1863, the *Chattahoochee* got underway on her own steam. When Guthrie ordered target practice, he was surprised by the accuracy of his gunners at shooting down trees. Even so, not until May 26 did the *Chattahoochee* make an attempt to engage the enemy by passing obstacles that Union soldiers had placed in the river, and by steaming over the Blountstown Bar. In the event, the river was too low for the draft of the vessel. The gunboat lay there overnight in the hope that the water would rise. It did not, so Guthrie ordered a retreat to Chattahoochee.

When the engineers poured water into the boilers, they exploded. Nearby crewmembers were scalded. Some men succumbed to their burns; others jumped overboard to cool their scalded skin in the river, and drowned. The death toll was eighteen. The number of scalded survivors was not recorded.

Guthrie gave the order to flood the magazines because of their proximity to the boilers. This action, plus damage to the hull from the exploding boilers, conspired to cause the *Chattahoochee* to sink. Soon the hull came to rest on the shallow river bottom with her gunwale exposed but the deck under water.

Twelve hours later, the *William H. Young* arrived on site to transport scalded survivors and the bodies of the mortally wounded upstream to Columbus, Georgia. The *William H. Young* returned to the wreck to salvage some of the guns.

The hull was later raised and towed to Columbus for repairs. In the midst of replacing the machinery with that of the CSS *Raleigh*, Union advancement overran the area. The *Chattahoochee* was scuttled in order to keep her out of Union hands. The wreck was discovered in 1963. Part of the hull was raised and put on display at the National Civil War Naval Museum in Columbus. The 30-foot stern section includes the sternpost, one of the two propellers, and part of the propulsion machinery.

THE VESSEL – AFTERMATH AND CONJECTURE

After this tragic mishap, Guthrie served briefly aboard the blockade runner *Advance* (also spelled *A. D. Vance*). The *Advance* has been touted as one of the most successful Confederate blockade runners of the war, having made anywhere between eight and twenty successful runs between Wilmington, North Carolina and either Nassau or Bermuda. (Sources differ widely on the number of runs.) These escapades were attributed to Captain Tom Crossan. It has been claimed that Guthrie was in command on at least one run during Crossan's absence.

The *Advance's* two-year career ended on September 10, 1864, when Crossan was forced to drive the vessel ashore in order to avoid being captured by the USS *Santiago de Cuba*. The crew escaped through surf and sand. Guthrie was not on board at the time of this incident.

Union salvors later pulled the *Advance* off the beach. She was sold in prize court to the U.S. Navy. Renamed *Frolic*, the sidewheel steamer served for many years and in many capacities until she was found unfit for further duty. She was sold in 1883.

Confederate blockade runner *Advance*. (Courtesy of the Naval Photographic Center.)

According to reminiscences that were published subsequent to Guthrie's death, "After the war was over, he moved with his family to Portsmouth, Va. [Virginia], and in the Fall of 1865 was pardoned by the President, (Johnson) being the first officer of the regular service who had received Executive clemency. His disabilities being removed by a unanimous recommendation from the members of Congress."

For a while Guthrie was the captain of a steamship in Georgia. Then "he was appointed by General Grant to the 'Superintendency of the Life-Saving Stations from Cape Henry to Cape Hatteras.'" (From the Chesapeake Bay to mid-North Carolina.)

On November 24, 1877, a major shipwreck disaster occurred off the coast of North Carolina. I gave a long and fully detailed account of this catastrophe in *Shipwrecks of North Carolina: from the Diamond Shoals North*. Here I will provide only a brief synopsis, and focus on Guthrie's tragic involvement.

The USS *Huron* was a two-year-old screw steamer that was categorized as a sloop-of-war (that is, all the guns were on one deck). Although she was armed to the teeth as a warship, on her final voyage she was headed for the Caribbean Sea in order to conduct scientific studies with new navigational equipment. She was southward bound when she ran into a storm of incredible proportions. She bucked a 40-knot wind as she felt her way through pea-soup fog. Somehow the *Huron* got off course, and ran aground off Nag's Head, North Carolina.

Tremendous waves in the surf zone battered the iron hull to pieces. Two of her three masts toppled across the deck, where the rigging created a spider web of lines that entangled sailors who were struggling for their lives as massive combers rolled over the deck. Some men were swept into the sails where they quickly drowned. In short order the lifeboats were carried away and the cabin walls were bashed to splinters. The third mast went by the wayside.

Some men managed to reach shore on floating bits of wreckage. Of the *Huron's* complement of 138 men, only 34 survived the ordeal.

Two days later, the gunboat *Swatara* and the wrecking tug *B. &. J. Baker* arrived at the wreck site. Both vessels anchored offshore, unable to approach the wrecked steamer because of monstrous seas. A surfboat from the *B. & J. Baker* inched its way past the *Huron's* battered remains, but soon got out of control.

Again tragedy struck. "The surf-boat in attempting to make a landing passed the first line of breakers in safety, but at the second she broached to, and was capsized, her whole crew being thrown into the water. It is thought that two men were killed outright, others were drowned, and those who escaped did so by clinging to the boat until they were rescued by life lines thrown from the shore."

Six men died. One of the men who drowned was Captain John Julius Guthrie, who was there in his official capacity to oversee recovery operations. After all his worldwide travels, Guthrie ultimately died in the State in which he was born.

I do not know when Guthrie had the time or the place to marry and beget children, but according to his obituary he was survived by his wife, nee Louisa Sarah Spratley, and seven children: four boys and three girls, whose dates of birth were 1841, 1844, 1849, 1851, 1961, 1861, and 1866.

Guthrie's boat pitch-poling in the surf. (From *Harper's Weekly*.)

Robert J. Walker – the Vessel
Discovery and Identification

The $25 Wreck has been a popular recreational dive site since the 1960's.

Who discovered the wreck is unknown with any degree of certainty. How it acquired its peculiar – and pecuniary – name is part of local lore: a commercial angler who fished on the wreckage, and who caught a piscatorial bounty, later sold the location to one of his compatriots for the princely sum that became the wreck's monetary cognomen.

Be that as it may, the location somehow found its way into the hands of other skippers who operated head boats, enabling these skippers to take their customers to a place that was guaranteed to produce. Eventually, when spearfishing and scuba diving came into vogue off the New Jersey coast, dive charter operators found the site to be equally as productive. It has been a mainstay destination ever since.

That is the unofficial story of the wreck's discovery and subsequence usage. The year in which the original event occurred has not been transcribed, although it has been handed down through oral tradition. Many wrecks were discovered by local anglers in the 1930's, when offshore fishing became a large-scale commercial enterprise.

The method of discovery was usually accidental: it often occurred when a dragger or trawler snagged its net in wreckage. Sometimes, by fancy maneuvering, the net was freed from entanglement. Other times, the net could not be retrieved, constituting a loss of thousands of dollars to the vessel's owner. In either case, the skipper noted the location of the wreck so he could avoid it in the future.

For obvious reasons, these locations came to be called "hangs."

While trawlers and draggers wanted to avoid these "hangs," head boats wanted to fish on them. This because the seabed off the New Jersey coast is a vast desert of sand in which a shipwreck is an oasis.

Sessile organisms such as corals, barnacles, mussels, sea anemones, and crinoids utilize shipwrecks as a substrate on which to attach themselves. Baitfish hide from predators in the wreckage. Larger, predatory fish such as ling, hake, sculpin, sea raven, black sea bass, tautog, and goosefish congregate or make their homes on or inside shipwrecks because they feed on the rich lower lifeforms. Crabs and lobsters feast on the leftovers.

In this manner, each shipwreck evolved into a micro-environment for marine life.

Local knowledge of the wreck probably preceded official recognition. The site was formally acknowledged as a shipwreck on November 9, 1944, when the U.S. Coast Guard cutter *Gentian* pinged the wreckage by means of sonar.

The *Gentian* was designed as a buoy tender. Due to wartime exigencies, many offshore navigational buoys were removed from their stations so that German U-boats could not use them to confirm their position. Because the *Gentian's* primary purpose was temporarily discontinued, she was converted to a survey vessel. She was outfitted with sonar gear, a chemical recorder, a recording fathometer, an underwater camera and a winch to lower it to the bottom, a magnetic submarine detector, loran, wire-drag

A wartime photo of the buoy tender *Gentian*. (Courtesy of the National Archives.)

gear, radar, plus buoys and sinkers to mark significant sites for further investigation.

The *Gentian* was then charged with the goal of locating the wrecks of vessels that had been torpedoed, shelled, and sunk by German U-boats. According to the preface of the *Gentian's* report, "Sixty-seven vessels had been sunk by enemy action and seventeen lost by marine disaster in the District since the war began, and there were numerous pre-war wrecks which had never been located. Thirty-seven of these wrecks were considered menaces to navigation, but many of their positions were not known with any degree of accuracy. Much time and ammunition had been wasted by anti-submarine warfare vessels and planes because of a lack of wreck data."

Sonar is the acronym for "sound navigation and ranging." Armed convoy escorts were equipped with primitive sonar devices that transmitted bursts of sound through the water. When the sound burst struck a solid object, it reflected back to an onboard detector. The object could be a U-boat, a sunken shipwreck, a geological formation, or a whale. More than one wreck was depth-charged to perdition, and not a few rocky shoals and unfortunate cetaceans.

Furthermore, it was believed that Nazi U-boats could hide alongside sunken shipwrecks in order to disguise their presence. In light of modern knowledge this belief appears absurd, but at that time there was no way to be certain that German scientists had not perfected a means of detecting and approximating the distance to a wreck, thereby allowing a U-boat to approach a wreck without fear of smashing into it, and to lie on the bottom next to it.

These were the rationales for the offshore survey. The *Gentian* had a hard row to hoe because the position accuracy in most cases was 1 to 3 miles; in other cases the accuracy was 3 to 5 miles.

In those days, a vessel's position was obtained by means of a sextant that was used to take a sighting of either the sun or another stellar object, plus a marine chronometer that was wound religiously and calibrated with Greenwich Mean Time (GMT), which is now called Universal Time (UT). The astronomical observatory at Greenwich, England was established as the Prime Meridian.

THE VESSEL – DISCOVERY AND IDENTIFICATION   63

The precise time, and the angle between the horizon and the celestial body, comprised part of the formula that was calculated from a book of astronomical tables in a Nautical Almanac. Most mariners took sun sightings precisely at noon, when the sun was highest in the sky. Sometimes, due to rain, snow, or overcast, several days passed between sightings.

My point in giving this abbreviated explanation is to illustrate to my readers why a vessel's position was not known with better precision. After taking a sighting, a vessel's moving position was inferred by taking into account the vessel's compass heading, engine revolutions (speed), and drift (from current and wind): a system of estimation that is known as dead reckoning.

When a vessel was under attack, making avoidance maneuvers, and launching lifeboats, the officers did not have either the time or the inclination to take new celestial sightings and to do mathematics while they were abandoning ship. They were distracted by other responsibilities.

U-boats sank a number of vessels within sight of the New Jersey shore. The tanker *Persephone* lies only three miles from the beach, in 55 feet of water. (It was my first wreck dive.) Other World War Two wrecks rest in the shallows inshore of the continental shelf. It was these wrecks that the *Gentian* was seeking to locate and identify.

In the *Gentian's* report on Wreck No. 839, "Old wreckage was located in the listed position by U. S. C. G. *Gentian* 11/9/44. Wreckage stands 6 feet high in 85 feet of water." The location was given as 39-12-48 N and 74-15-42 W.

839	39-12-48 N 74-15-42 W	Wreckage. Old wreckage was located in the listed position by U. S. C. G. GENTIAN 11/9/44. Wreckage stands 6 feet high in 85 feet of water. (4 N. D. Survey 1/10/45).

The Navy confirmed this information on January 10, 1945, plotted the wreck on nautical charts, and incorporated it into the Wreck Information List of 1945, which was classified as Restricted. The Navy updated this list in 1957, and retitled it the Navy Wreck List.

In the 1950's, the U.S. Coast and Geodetic Survey conducted wire-drag operations off the coast of New Jersey, in search of shipwrecks that could possibly pose a hazard to navigation: mostly World War Two wrecks whose large hulls and substantial structure and masts might rise close to the surface. One of the wrecks they searched for was Wreck No. 839, but the wire-drag failed to snag it.

An item that was described as an obstruction with a nearby position was posted in the Navy's Confidential list of Non-Submarine Contacts. According to the Preface, "The publication is designed to furnish ships with information to aid in the prompt identification and evaluation of fixed and repeatable SONAR and MAD contacts. It contains as a list all known subsurface objects in the area covered." (MAD is the acronym for "magnetic anomaly detector.") Although number 839 is not listed as such, an obstruction that is given as number 0381 might refer to Wreck No. 839; the approximate position is given as "39 12 00" and "74 15 00."

Decades later, entries on the Wreck Information List and the Navy Wreck List were incorporated into NOAA's Automated Wreck and Obstruction Information System

64 THE VESSEL - DISCOVERY AND IDENTIFICATION

```
9849    39 10 00    72 52 00    OBSTRUCTION BOMB
0122    39 10 00    73 07 00    ISABEL B WILEY     SCH   06 02 18     776
0380    39 10 18    73 20 30    EDWARD H COLE      SCH   06 20 18    1791
3913    39 11 00    71 34 00    PENISTONE          LGO   08 11 18    4139
0560    39 11 48    74 31 00    WETHEA             YCT   10 01 45     200

0381    39 12 00    74 15 00    OBS
8394    39 13 42    74 14 03    C F PRICHARD
0333    39 14 45    74 09 06    SAN JOSE           LGE   10 23 37     861
0356    39 14 45    74 23 00    UNKNOWN            CGO   01 17 42    3358
0334    39 15 00    72 30 00    RIO TERCERO        CGO   06 22 42    4864

0561    39 17 30    74 21 23    DARIEN
1635    39 17 30    74 26 30    UNKNOWN            LGE   05 02 48     924
0332    39 18 12    74 15 54    LEMUEL BURROW      TWR         55
0331    39 19 36    74 13 12    FALL RIVER         CGO   03 14 42    7610
0582    39 19 36    74 17 57    UNKNOWN                               1759
```

In the Non-Submarine Contacts list, the closest position to Wreck No. 839 is number 0381.

(AWOIS). The location was corrected to 39-13-28.5N and 74-17-17.25W. The AWOIS list also claimed that the wreck was that of a World War One freighter.

This unsupported identification is not as absurd as it sounds. Most people today are unaware that the Kaiser's U-boats ravaged shipping on the eastern seaboard in 1918. They sank nearly a hundred vessels by gunfire, torpedoes, mines, and bombs (which were placed onboard after a German demolition party boarded and ransacked the vessels). One of the largest victims was the U.S. armored cruiser *San Diego*, which struck a mine some 10 miles south of Fire Island, New York.

The *Chaparra* and *San Saba* lie in 80 feet of water some 30 miles north of the *Robert J. Walker*: in the approximate depth but at the wrong location. So it was not out of bounds for surveyors to speculate that the broken-down hull was a relic from the Great War.

Years after that, recreational diver and dive boat operator Tony Vraim provided loran-C numbers for publication in the AWOIS list: 26929.1 and 42939.3.

Nowadays, with the advent of satellites and the Global Positioning System, plus the termination of loran, old-time location coordinates that were given in latitude and longitude have evolved into GPS numbers that are similar and (hopefully) more accurate: 39-16.230 and 74-17.269.

And there she lies.

The AWOIS listing for the $25 Wreck.

```
RECRD       2480         VESSLTERMS   UNKNOWN          CHART    12300         AREA       C
                         CARTOCODE    0100             SNDINGCODE              DEPTH      0

NATIVLAT    39/13/28.50  NATIVLON     074/17/17.25                             NATIVDATUM 6
LAT83       39/13/28.91  LONG83       074/17/15.76                             GPQUALITY  Low
LATDEC      39.224697222222  LONDEC   74.287711111111                          GPSOURCE   NA

History     02480
            DESCRIPTION
            178 ANTHONY VRAIM, DIVERS; OBSERVED SUNKEN WWI FREIGHTER; LORAN-C
            9960-X-26929.10, 9960-Y-42939.30 (ASF CORRECTED) POS.39-13-28.5N,
            74-17-17.25W.

            SURVEY REQUIREMENTS
            LIMITED

            REFERENCE:              YEARSUNK              SYSTEMNUM         2388
```

Recreational Divers Triumphant

In all the time since its initial discovery, nothing was ever seen on or recovered from the wreck to identify its origin. Or so it seemed. In retrospect, it turned out that paddlewheels were seen and portholes were recovered. Together these facts provided clues to the wreck's identity when they were considered in the proper light.

Now, a great deal has not only been seen, but measured: data that have provided strong circumstantial evidence that lead to the wreck's identity.

As I have often said and written, many shipwrecks are identified not by an artifact with the vessel's name stamped, embossed, cut, carved, or printed on it, but by a preponderance of evidence. So it is in the instant case.

There seems to be little doubt that the $25 Wreck is the *Robert J. Walker*.

The path to the wreck's true nature was a long, complex, and expensive ordeal that involved a number of people who each added pieces to the puzzle until it formed a picture whose image made sense.

The inspiration arose from James Delgado, director of the Marine Heritage Program for the National Oceanic and Atmospheric Administration, or NOAA (pronounced like the name of the first skipper in recorded history to wreck his ship, Noah; in case you have forgotten your *Bible* studies, his animal laden cargo vessel was the *Ark*).

In Delgado's report ("Identification of the Wreck of the U.S.C.S.S. *Robert J. Walker* off Atlantic City, New Jersey"), he became the only NOAA official in the history of the Administration to ever give credit where credit was due: "New Jersey has an active corps of wreck divers, many of whom invest considerable personal sums to outfit dive expeditions to locate and identify the many wrecks off the shore. Some collect artifacts, others do not. A number of these divers have donated their finds to the New Jersey Maritime Museum, a non profit [sic] educational institution located in Beach Haven, New Jersey. Others retain their finds in personal collections. Without the attention paid to this wreck by New Jersey Wreck divers, its presence and ultimate identification as *Robert J. Walker* would not have occurred."

Delgado started his search for the location of the *Robert J. Walker* by reviewing nautical charts in the area in which she was reported to have sunk. Although numerous shipwrecks were marked on the chart, none was annotated with names. He then reviewed a multi-beam sonar survey that NOAA had conducted in 2004. The dimensions of one target approximated those of the *Robert J. Walker*. More data were needed in order to ascertain the nature of the target in question.

Delgado tasked Joyce Steinmetz with the job of researching local sources of wreck information, to determine if the site was already known and commonly fished or dived. Steinmetz was an engineer who had switched occupations in midlife because she wanted to be a marine archaeologist. She was currently attending East Carolina University as a graduate student in her newly chosen profession. She was also a fervent wreck-diver, and had been one for more than three decades.

An Internet search quickly found a website with a wreck description that she found intriguing.

Gene Peterson owns and operates a dive shop known as Atlantic Divers. He maintains a website on which local shipwreck destinations are described. He is a long-time diver who has dived on all the wrecks in the vicinity of Atlantic City (plus numerous other wrecks off the eastern seaboard in U.S. and Canadian waters).

THE VESSEL – DISCOVERY AND IDENTIFICATION

Under the heading "Mason's Paddle Wheeler – Paddle Wheelers' Mystery," Peterson wrote: "In 1892 the paddle wheel steamer *Florida* foundered off Absecon Shoal, while being towed north to a salvage yard in Cow Bay, New York. Atlantic City was a new resort destination frequented by rail passengers and some large resort hotels were dotting the sandy outer island. Much vacant beach still remained awaiting the boom in this pre-1900 era.

"After a few months the remains of the derelict wreckage became a hazard and was detonated with explosives by the U.S. Navy salvage tug *Nina* shortly afterwards. This site remained undisturbed for nearly eighty years.

"The remains of two other paddle wheelers remain close to this area where the *Florida* sank. Another very small possible paddle wheeler locally known as the Muddigger is just southeast of the presumed *Florida*, and Mason's Paddle Wheeler, a well-known site has yet to be positively identified.

"In the early seventies the wreck was discovered by a local fisherman and the loran coordinate was sold for $25 dollars [sic] to a local party boat. Hence its original name, the $25 Dollar Wreck [sic].

"Captain Ed Boyle of the original Atlantic City dive boat *Gypsy* began taking charters to the wreck, discovering barrels, square portholes, a large toppled engine with an upright bow and two paddle wheels in the debris. The starboard paddle was standing vertical and the port lays on its side in the sand. Visibility was often limited at that time, because a sewage outfall pipe north of the wreck was still in operation and the wreck remained infrequently visited. The untreated outfall was capped in the mid eighties and soon visibility greatly improved.

"On a dive in the late eighties Atlantic Divers discovered a barrel with white china labeled Mason on the bottom. Because of the previous name's bad reputation [due to poor visibility], Atlantic Divers rechristen[ed] the wreck Mason's Paddle Wheeler to stimulate more exploration of the site. Soon it became a popular dive and much discovery continued. A diver recovered a large brass steam vent with a thermometer enclosed. Several bottles, and more pieces of china have been uncovered since that time and numerous copper pipe lay ambiguously in the debris. Today the water is clear over the wreck with a healthy abundance of marine life. More needs to be uncovered to verify its identity."

Steinmetz then interviewed Eddie Boyle. Boyle was a long-time diver and dive boat skipper who ran the *Gypsy* on weekends as far back as the 1960's, and for decades afterward. During his lifetime, Boyle must have taken thousands of divers (including this author) to wrecks off Atlantic City, where the *Gypsy* was docked. He later teamed up with Tony Vraim, who sometimes ran the boat for him. Vraim was also a long-time diver; he started diving in the early 1970's.

Boyle worked fulltime in construction as a pipe coverer. Vraim was a licensed funeral director.

Boyle confirmed Peterson's description of the wreck, and added his story of how the wreck received its name.

Boyle (verbatim as written): "Back in the 50's and 60's we had to line up land ranges to get on a wreck. Johnny Shaw was a lobster fisherman, who had a lot of good ranges. Nobody knew what anything was. They were just referred to as snags. Johnny Shaw sold the ranges to the $25 wreck to George Black a party boat fisherman for $25.

THE VESSEL - DISCOVERY AND IDENTIFICATION 67

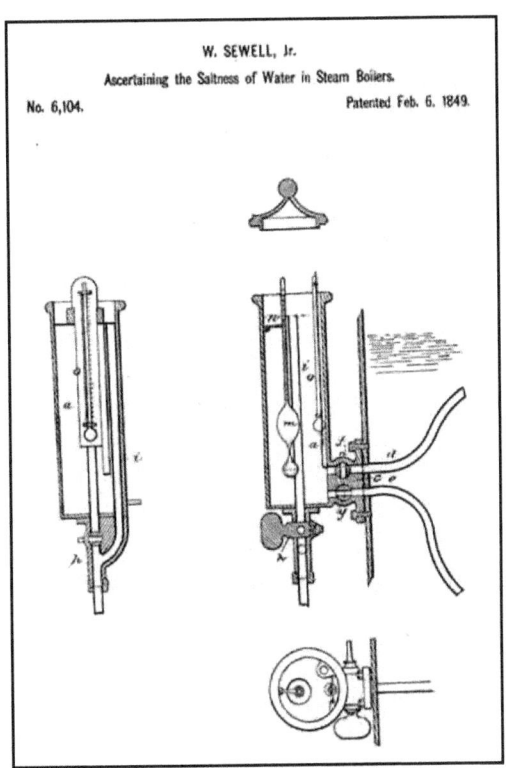

Dave Keller found, photographed, and researched this bronze instrument for "Ascertaining the Saltness of Water in Steam Boilers." Because of the 1849 patent date, the instrument must have been installed during one of the *Robert J. Walker's* maintenance inspections, or when her boilers were replaced. Keller also found a contemporary advertisement for William Y. McAllister, which was located at 728 Chestnut Street, Philadelphia, Pennsylvania. As shown in the diagram above, the graduated gauge that is pictured below fit inside the cylindrical casing.

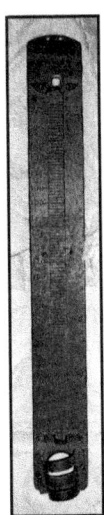

"The first day George was on the wreck and other party boat captain Frank Deebold caught George and got the ranges. The next few days Deebold would get on the wreck first and the other party boat captain would kid George about paying $25 for a wreck for Deebold, and then they started referring to it as the $25 wreck.

"Then some divers claimed it was paddle wheel. It never looked that way to me. I did get a couple of square brass portholes off it. One fellow diving from my boat brought up a cannon ball.

"Before diving got popular, nobody knew what they were fishing on. The divers identified most of the wrecks that are out there."

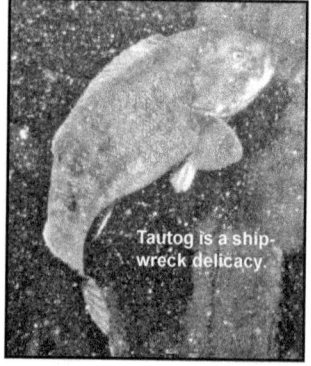

Tautog is a shipwreck delicacy.

Steinmetz paid a visit to Peterson at his shop. He was able to provide additional information about the layout of the wreck, and about artifacts that had been recovered from it. She told him about her suspicions of the wreck's possible identity, and asked if he wanted to be credited for the information that he provided to help identify the site. He told her that he did not want his name associated with NOAA in any way, and that he wanted nothing to do with the identification project.

Peterson had good cause to be wary of NOAA. He was on my *Monitor* expedition in 1990, and he was acting dive master in my behalf when I was in the water. In the latter capacity he had to argue vehemently with NOAA's onboard observer when she called Marine Fisheries and issued instructions to find some excuse to shut down our diving operation. Marine Fisheries dispatched a law enforcement officer to the dive site. Peterson warned the boat driver to maintain a safe distance from our drifting dive boat because of safety concerns, but with the onboard observer's consent the Marine Fisheries boat ran me over while I was decompressing. (Read the full story in *Ironclad Legacy: Battles of the USS Monitor*.)

Peterson knew how hard NOAA had tried to prevent public access to the *Monitor*. He knew that it had taken me six years and two lawsuits to obtain the first permit to dive on the wreck, then another two years and two more lawsuits to ensure permanent public access. He knew that NOAA's attitude about public access had not changed in the intervening years. He knew that NOAA was trying to expand the borders of all the National Marine Sanctuaries in order to control more underwater territory and to impose strict rules and regulations against public access.

My readers can understand why he was antagonistic toward NOAA, and why he did not wish to be associated with the despotic government agency.

Nonetheless, in Delgado's report, Atlantic Divers was credited with furnishing the crucial information that led to the wreck's ultimate identification. With this fait accompli, Peterson has allowed me to tell the full story of his involvement, and to emphasize the fact that he insisted on not taking credit for his unintentional participation.

Steinmetz acquired the GPS coordinates that local divers used to access the wreck. They corresponded with the location of the target that Delgado had picked out from NOAA's 2004 multi-beam scan survey.

With this information in hand, Delgado asked NOAA scientist Vitad Pradith to correlate the historical material with current documentation. According to Delgado's

THE VESSEL ~ DISCOVERY AND IDENTIFICATION

Report: "The information helped define a search area for an updated multibeam survey with higher resolution equipment than that available in 2004."

The statement above is somewhat less than accurate, even misleading, in that the "search area" was in fact a precise location: a pinpoint GPS coordinate given as 39-13.230 and 74-17.269. The wreck did not need to be searched for or found; its position was already known with perfect accuracy. Delgado's statement gave credit to NOAA where no credit was due.

The next step for NOAA was to conduct a follow-up multi-beam sonar survey. For this purpose, the NOAA vessel *Thomas Jefferson* was detached from important duties in connection with the aftermath of Superstorm Sandy in order to confirm the location of a wreck whose position was already know with precision. NOAA employees were so certain that the coordinates were correct, and that because of their descriptions the wreck was actually that of the *Robert J. Walker*, they came prepared to hold a memorial service over the site on the day of the survey: June 21, 2013, which coincidentally happened to be the 113th anniversary of the sinking of the vessel.

It may come as no surprise that NOAA experienced no difficulty in locating the wreck: it lay exactly where recreational divers told NOAA it would be found. A previously purchased wreath was dropped dramatically over the wreck, and a ceremony was filmed for the purpose of self-promotion.

The NOAA website claimed that this wreath was "placed" on the water, not dropped.

Photo courtesy of NOAA.

As expected, the wreck's dimensions that were scaled off the multi-beam sonar image closely matched those of the vessel according to construction statistics. This further reduced any doubt that NOAA may have had about the information that recreational divers had provided.

NOAA commenced diving operations the following day. Another NOAA vessel – the *SRVx* – was detached from vital hurricane aftermath duty so that NOAA's head honchos could make recreational dives on the wreck while some working personnel took in-water measurements.

On board to wallow in the limelight was the director of the Office of National Marine Sanctuaries, Dan Basta, who was playing hooky from his office in Washington, DC. Also off station was David Alberg, whose official purview was North Carolina, where he was superintendent of the Monitor National Marine Sanctuary.

All doubt about the wreck's identity was erased after two days of diving, and the site was officially accepted as the *Robert J. Walker*. Nonetheless, NOAA did not make a public announcement until after the underwater survey evidence was reviewed and corroborated the way it is done in the recreational diving community.

NOAA listed the indicative clues thus (ellipses denote the insertion of illustrations or photographs; brackets denote my explanatory insertions):

The wreck is in the right area. Estimates at the time placed the loss 12 miles offshore, on what was truly a dark and stormy night. The site is 10.5 miles from shore. [This placed the wreck in international waters.]

The wreck was the only unidentified steamship wreck in the area – all other sites had been identified by the New Jersey diving community. [Except for the Muddigger.]

The wreck is pointed toward shore, and on a straight line to the Absecon Lighthouse, as would be expected since *Robert J. Walker's* crew were heading for the lighthouse after the collision while the ship was sinking."

[The heading of the wreck was irrelevant. Although the vessel was steered toward shore under power, once the boilers were blown off to prevent them from exploding when cold seawater poured into the machinery spaces and inundated the hot exteriors of the boilers, the vessel went adrift. From that moment until she settled beneath the surface, her heading was subject to the vagaries of current and gale-force winds.]

The construction contract for *Robert J. Walker* specifies a vessel of 132 [sic] feet and a beam (width) of 24 feet 6 inches. The wreck has the same dimensions.

The wreck has two paddlewheels, one on each side. The width of *Walker's* paddlewheel hubs show it had the same width – six feet.

The wreck is an iron-hulled, riveted steamer with T-bar frames (ribs). The contract for building *Robert J. Walker* stipulated it be built with iron hull plates eight feet in length and 5/15th of an inch thick, double and single riveted with 10/16th of an inch headed rivets. The frames were 10-lb T bar.

The wreck had rectangular brass portholes. As shown in this 1852 painting of *Robert J. Walker* is [sic] had rectangular portholes with glass.

The wreck has the same type and size of engines that *Robert J. Walker* did. They are two horizontal, half beam, condensing engines of the 'Lighthall Patent.'

The Lighthall Lever Half-Bear Engine, patented on October 23, 1849 (Patent 6811) by William A. Lighthall of Albany, New York, is illustrated here:

An 1852 survey of the *Robert J. Walker* machinery reported that the steam cylinder of the engines were 2 feet, 9 inches in diameter; that is the dimension of the cylinders on the wreck.

These photographs of the wreck's machinery are keyed to show where they would fit on the engine plans of *Robert J. Walker*. . . .

The boilers, lying just behind the engines, had not survived intact, but their basic shape remains, and matches *Robert J. Walker's* boilers, shown here in an 1852 survey of the steamer's machinery: . . .

All this evidence is admittedly circumstantial, but as I noted above, most wrecks are identified by a preponderance of evidence. The evidence here is certainly preponderant.

As a point of interest, however, note that when NOAA compared the engine on the wreck site with the engine in the diagram in order to confirm the wreck's identity, it compared two different engines. The *Robert J. Walker's* engine was installed in 1847, whereas the engine that is shown in the patent application was dated 1849 – nearly two years after the *Robert J. Walker* went to sea.

Keep in mind that the process of wreck identification is not as strict as it is in a court of law, where guilt must be established beyond all reasonable doubt. In the instant case there is so little doubt that even if the identity were on trial, I suspect that an unbiased jury would issue a verdict of guilty in the first degree, even in light of the engine's temporal displacement.

Monster from the ID Announcement

NOAA made its official announcement on August 27, 2013:

> More than 153 years after it was lost in a violent collision at sea, government and university maritime archaeologists have identified the wreck of the ship *Robert J. Walker*, a steamer that served in the U.S. Coast Survey, a predecessor agency of NOAA.
>
> The *Walker*, while now largely forgotten, served a vital role as a survey ship, charting the Gulf Coast – including Mobile Bay and the Florida Keys – in the decade before the Civil War. It also conducted early work plotting the movement of the Gulf Stream along the Atlantic Coast.
>
> Twenty sailors died when the *Walker* sank in rough seas in the early morning hours of June 21, 1860, ten miles off Absecon Inlet on the New Jersey coast. The crew had finished its latest surveys in the Gulf of Mexico and was sailing to New York when the *Walker* was hit by a commercial schooner off New Jersey. The side-wheel steamer, carrying 66 crewmembers, sank within 30 minutes. The sinking was the largest single loss of life in the history of the Coast Survey and its successor agency, NOAA.
>
> "Before this identification was made, the wreck was just an anonymous symbol on navigation charts," said Rear Admiral Gerd Glang, director of NOAA's Office of Coast Survey. "Now, we can truly honor the 20 members of the crew and their final resting place. It will mark a profound sacrifice by the men who served during a remarkable time in our history."
>
> Built in 1847, the *Walker* was one of the U.S. government's first iron-hulled steamers, and was intended for the U.S. Revenue Service, the predecessor of the United States Coast Guard. Instead, the *Walker* and some of its sister steamers were sent to the U.S. Coast Survey.
>
> Admiral Robert J. Papp, commandant of the Coast Guard, said that *Walker* represented the transition from sail to steam for government vessels, "reflecting the enduring need of the United States to harness the power of new technology to promote its maritime interests."
>
> "Coast Guardsmen are always saddened by the loss of life at sea and especially so when those lost were working to make the lives of other mariners safer by charting the waters of the United States," Papp said.
>
> The U.S. Coast Survey is NOAA's oldest predecessor organization, established by President Thomas Jefferson in 1807 to survey the coast and produce the nation's nautical charts. In 1860, as the Civil War approached, the Coast Survey redoubled efforts to produce surveys of harbors strategically

important to the war effort along the Gulf and Atlantic coasts.

The *New York Herald*, in reporting the *Walker's* loss on June 23, 1860, noted that a "heavy sea was running, and many of the men were doubtless washed off the spars and drowned from the mere exhaustion of holding on, while others were killed or stunned on rising to the surface by concussion with spars and other parts of the wreck."

The *Walker* wreck site initially was discovered in the 1970s by a commercial fisherman. The wreck's identity has been a mystery despite being regularly explored by divers. Resting 85 feet underwater, the vessel's identity was confirmed in June as part of a private-public collaboration that included research provided by New Jersey wreck divers; Joyce Steinmetz, a maritime archaeology student at East Carolina University; and retired NOAA Corps Capt. Albert Theberge, chief of reference for the NOAA Central Library.

While in the area to conduct hydrographic surveys after Hurricane Sandy for navigation safety, NOAA Ship *Thomas Jefferson* sailed to the wreck site and deployed its multibeam and sidescan sonar systems. Hydrographers searched likely locations based on analysis of historical research by Vitad Pradith, a physical scientist with NOAA's Office of Coast Survey.

A NOAA Maritime Heritage diving team, on a separate Hurricane Sandy-related mission in the area, was able to positively identify the *Walker*. Key clues were the size and layout of the iron-hulled wreck, and its unique engines, rectangular portholes, and the location of the ship, which was found still pointing toward the Absecon lighthouse, the final destination of a desperate crew on a sinking vessel.

"The identification of *Walker* is a result of excellent collaboration with the local community," said James P. Delgado, director of maritime heritage for NOAA's Office of National Marine Sanctuaries. "We look forward to working with our local partners to share *Walker's* story with the public in a manner that both promotes educational dive tourism and protects this nationally significant wreck and gravesite."

NOAA's intent is not to make the wreck a sanctuary or limit diving, but to work with New Jersey's wreck diving community to better understand the wreck and the stories it can tell.

"We want to enhance the dive experience and support the dive industry with enhanced access to this wreck," Delgado said. "New Jersey is home to some of the most accomplished wreck divers who not only understand history and wrecks, but who have also been in the forefront of wreck exploration. We look forward to working with them on the *Walker*."

At this point, the site that had been known as the $25 wreck to local anglers and divers for more than half a century, was officially designated the *Robert J. Walker* – and with a great deal more fanfare than other wrecks received when they were identified by recreational divers, who were not in the habit of calling attention to themselves outside of their small but active community.

NOAA's identification was part of a plan on a grand scale. Or perhaps "plan" should be called "scheme." This attribution will become abundantly clear in Part 2.

Robert J. Walker – the Vessel
Exploration and Mapping

The NOAA Exclusion Principle

Joyce Steinmetz was a teenager when I first met her at Dudas' Diving Duds, a dive shop in West Chester, Pennsylvania. She started scuba diving at a young age, and kept scuba diving forever more. Throughout the years our paths constantly crossed and intertwined. We met on dive boats, at dive club meetings, and at dive conferences. Once we met accidentally at the Independence Seaport Museum library. I was spending the day there doing shipwreck research. She walked in during an extended lunch break from her job. She was also a shipwreck researcher: one who visited the National Archives to conduct primary research on East Coast shipwrecks in which she was interested. She even went to Germany to research the cargo of a local wreck known as the Lead Wreck.

We never worked together. She had her projects and I had mine. But we shared information whenever one of us discovered something and thought that it might be useful or of interest to the other. Occasionally we talked on the phone about our various shipwreck research projects.

Therefore, there was nothing unusual about her calling me to tell me about the identification of the *Robert J. Walker*, based on the location of the wreck, it being a paddlewheeler, and measurements that she had taken of several of the components. She told me about NOAA's involvement, and how NOAA was going to sponsor a full investigation of the site. She asked me to join her on the boat and under water during the next diving season.

I tactfully declined without telling her my reason.

NOAA would never let me have any involvement whatsoever with a NOAA project. NOAA's arrogant overlords hated me with a passion. I had been on NOAA's shit list since 1984, when I first requested permission to dive on the Civil War ironclad *Monitor*, which had been designated unlawfully as a National Marine Sanctuary that lay in international waters off the coast of North Carolina.

What followed was eight years of legal wrangling that culminated in four federal lawsuits, all because NOAA did not want anyone diving on a shipwreck that the Administration's tyrants believed was their own personal property. NOAA denied public access, even though it was Congressionally mandated in the Marine Protection, Research, and Sanctuaries Act. I won the second lawsuit, in part because NOAA's prime witness committed perjury on the stand in order to hide pertinent truths from the judge. He was subsequently fired for failing to help win the case for NOAA.

After diving on the wreck in 1990, NOAA denied my next permit application on trumped-up grounds. (This application was identical to the one that won in court.) NOAA administrators were seething over the loss of what they perceived to be their private domain. They did not want encroachment by the unwashed public.

I filed two more lawsuits against NOAA. Finally, in 1992, against NOAA's rabid wishes, Congressional intervention forced NOAA to adopt a policy of open public access. The *Monitor* was open for all to see and enjoy!

NOAA despots passed down their hatred to incoming personnel, brainwashing them so that they could hate me too. You can read all about it in *Ironclad Legacy: Battles of the USS Monitor*.

Ironically, despite this ongoing loathing of me personally, NOAA used the books in my Popular Dive

In surveying the *Monitor*, I used two methods for demonstrating scale: a knife next to the scuttle, and PVC pipe divided into foot-long lengths by strips of electrical tape.

Guide Series as their prime source of East Coast shipwreck information and location. (I will expound upon this topic in Part Two.)

I kept sniping at NOAA's unethical practices in a constant letter campaign, periodic warnings to Congress, then in my quarterly newsletter, which reached thousands of interested parties. Matters came to another head in 2008, when I published *Shipwrecks of Massachusetts: North*. In a chapter entitled "The Stellwagen Bank Robbery," I told the sordid tale of how NOAA refused to release public shipwreck information to the public, and how the Administration went out of its way to prevent anglers and divers from accessing the wrecks. NOAA even refused to honor requests pursuant to the Freedom of Information Act: only one of its many illegal actions.

NOAA had set its sights on controlling all the wrecks off the State of Massachusetts, a secret that I exposed in the book. My exposé galled NOAA personnel to no end. Worse yet, I provided the information that NOAA was withholding: GPS coordinates, wreck descriptions, and historic chronicles. Now a whole new generation of NOAA sycophants could hate me.

The ultimate reinforcement of my thesis against NOAA appeared in 2013: a book entitled *NOAA's Ark: the Rise of the Fourth Reich*. The book contained 260 pages of NOAA's lies, deceptions, and administrative abuse. I was writing the book at the time of Steinmetz's call. According to the back cover blurb:

> The title says it all.
> The subtitle leaves nothing to the imagination.
> As the cover text clearly denotes, this book is a history of outright lies, deceptive practices, and gross administrative abuses that have been perpetrated by the National Oceanic and Atmospheric Administration throughout its existence. Much of the book focuses on the National Marine Sanctuaries Program, but fraudulent activities in other NOAA agencies are covered as well: past as well as present.
> The narrative starts with the Civil War ironclad warship *Monitor*, which was designated unlawfully as the first National Marine Sanctuary. A brief account of four federal lawsuits, which ultimately led to Congress forcing NOAA to permit public access to the site, is followed by NOAA's recent scheme to expand the boundaries of the Monitor National Marine Sanctuary

THE VESSEL – EXPLORATION AND MAPPING 75

in order to annex every shipwreck off the coast of North Carolina – and beyond.

The Stellwagen Bank Robbery relates NOAA's plot to expand the Stellwagen Bank NMS to include all the fishing waters off the State of Massachusetts. This expansion goes hand in hand with NOAA's sordid history of preying upon commercial anglers by citing them with exorbitant fines for alleged violations that were never proven in court – and then using the proceeds as perquisites for NOAA's law enforcement personnel: personal credit cards, free vehicles, and around-the-world all-expenses-paid junkets for NOAA's judges and prosecutors.

NOAA representatives have knowingly misled the public at so-called scoping meetings. Worse, they have deceived and lied to Congress by submitting false and distorted information in various action plans: all of which are designed to increase NOAA's authority and submerged land holdings.

NOAA wants to expand the boundaries of its West Coast sanctuaries to create a huge conglomerate that will control all the waters off the State of California – and beyond.

If NOAA gets its way, public access to National Marine Sanctuaries will be either totally disallowed or severely restricted. Prohibitions against sportfishing and recreational diving will result in economic catastrophe as charter boats, dive shops, tackle shops, restaurants, and motels are forced out of business by the loss of tourism.

NOAA is a juggernaut that is totally out of control. NOAA's plans for expansion are unlimited. NOAA has reduced its core responsibilities in order to pursue a self-serving goal of empire building. This is NOAA's story.

Even absent my confrontational history with NOAA, the appearance of this book before underwater investigations commenced, was bound to put me in Dutch with NOAA – especially with certain career employees who had worked for NOAA at the time of my court cases, and who had maintained their enmity over Congressional muzzling at my behest.

There was no way that NOAA would allow me to participate in dive trips to the *Robert J. Walker*, in any capacity. No way, no how. Besides, NOAA wanted to garner all the recognition for itself. NOAA certainly did not want nosy reporters interviewing me during the project, and unearthing its sordid past and present crimes against freedom that my presence would invite.

Despite thousands of pages of court documents, despite reams of newspaper articles about my precedent setting case, despite NOAA's library containing my shipwreck reference books, nowhere on the NOAA website did my name appear – not even on its *Monitor* pages. NOAA delusively stated that it allowed recreational diving on the *Monitor* as if it did so willingly. Although my court cases are part of NOAA's history, NOAA neglected to mention them at all.

I reiterate: the chances that NOAA would let me work on the project were slim to none, and Slim left town. In the event, when the Mapping Project was organized and divers were asked to join the project, I was not invited to be one the mapmakers. I told you so!

76 THE VESSEL – EXPLORATION AND MAPPING

Cast of Characters

Two experienced recreational divers were appointed to oversee the mapping of the wreck: Dan Lieb and Steve Nagiewicz.

Lieb possessed exceptional skill in drawing. He had mapped other shipwrecks on and off the New Jersey shore. He had identified more than a dozen local shipwrecks. He was the president and co-founder of the New Jersey Historical Divers Association. And he had provided accurate sketches of shipwreck land ranges for my New Jersey shipwreck books. He was largely responsible for obtaining volunteer divers from the recreational diving community to do the actual underwater survey work.

The New Jersey Historical Divers Association was organized informally in 1992. Two years later it began to exhibit shipwreck artifacts, and its members started to give lectures and slide presentations in the local community. The NJHDA was incorporated as a non-profit organization in 1995. According to its website, the corporation existed for the following purposes:

1.) To preserve New Jersey's shipwreck and Maritime history.
2.) To research and record the many unknown, lost and misnamed shipwrecks, as well as other potentially historically significant sites.
3.) To document findings and present these findings to the public by means of exhibits, lectures, video presentations and printed publications.
Our nonprofit status has made it possible to receive financial assistance for our expedition, conservation and publishing needs.

Delgado made the right call when he chose Lieb and the NJHDA for the project, especially as NOAA held no such lofty goals with regard to shipwrecks. NOAA's pri-

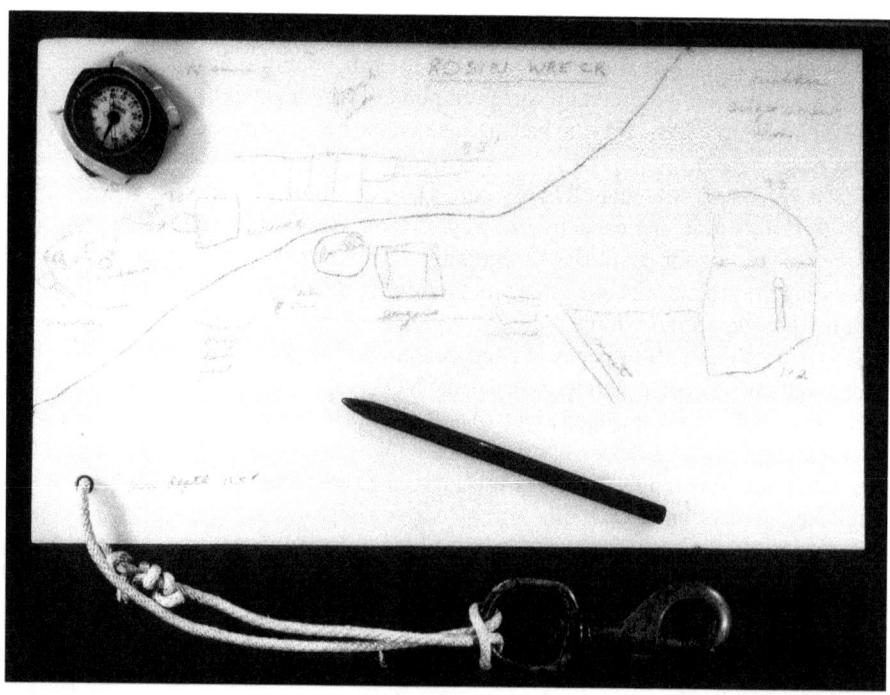

THE VESSEL – EXPLORATION AND MAPPING

mary goal was to *control* shipwrecks.

Nagiewicz was a local boy, born and bred in Atlantic City. He was a science teacher at a local school. He also owned and operated a dive charter boat on weekends. He was an essential asset to the project because he obtained the backing to finance it. NOAA contributed no money or financial support of any kind. Nagiewicz also managed the remote sensing part of the project. Although we had been friends for many years, I did not feel the same after he copied the title of my *Texas Tower* article, "Cold War Relic," as well as the format and some of the contents, without crediting me as his inspiration.

Steinmetz was a major participant in the underwater work, and deservedly so.

Herb Segars, a long-time underwater photographer with numerous magazine publications to his credit, snapped pictures of the wreck and of divers with their measuring tapes. He and I had met infrequently throughout the years, when we both gave presentations at the same dive symposium.

Vince Capone was the owner of Black Laser Learning. As one of the top side-scan sonar operators in the world, he taught side-scan technology to people everywhere. In 1990, he participated in my *Monitor* expedition. He did not dive, but he captured side-scan images of the wreck the way it appeared at the time, before the propeller collapsed and before NOAA conducted its expensive recovery operations of the engine and turret. I presume that he neglected to mention our past working relationship to NOAA.

And last but not least of the major players (or workers) – in fact, he was indispensable – was Captain Paul Hepler, whose charter dive boat *Venture III* was employed to transport divers and support personnel to the wreck site. The 46-foot crew boat was licensed to handle up to twenty-four passengers.

Although NOAA made it sound as if the mapping project was solely a NOAA undertaking, NOAA actually had very little to do with it. The divers were volunteers, and

---

For many years I conducted wreck surveys with the slate that is shown on the opposite page. I made the survey slate out of white plastic which I cut to a convenient carrying size, then affixed a pencil holder (on the back), compass, and lanyard (which I clipped to a D-ring on my tank harness for carrying to and from the bottom, and slipped onto my wrist while I was surveying). I made this drawing of the Rosin Wreck in 1992 as I swam along the wreck. After the dive, I redrew my rough sketch while the details were still fresh in my memory. The reverse side of the slate was used for observational notes and close-up sketches. This kind of survey slate has become the accepted tool for drawing wrecks on the bottom. I recorded depths by placing my depth gauge where I wanted to determine heights above the seabed, or rise. I also took photographs of key features on the same dive. After the film was processed, I was able to correlate the photographs with my drawing in order to create an overall description of the site. This is the same process that the mapping crew used on the *Robert J. Walker*.

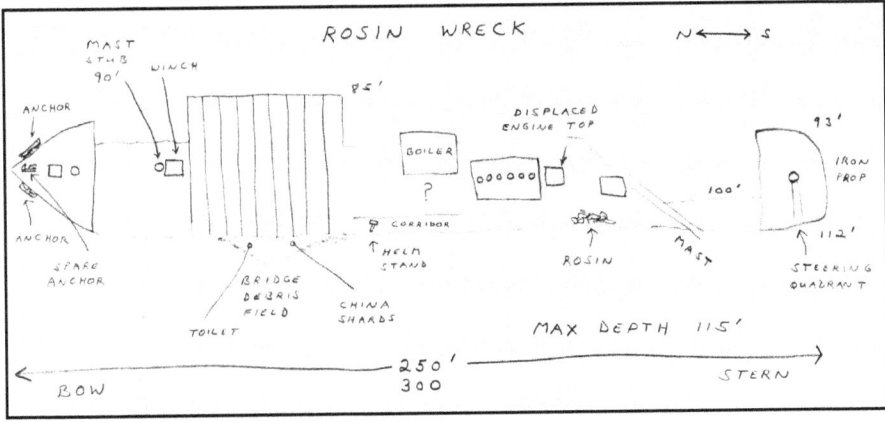

money to pay the charter fee and other expenses was donated. By claiming that NOAA "supported" the project, NOAA gave the impression that it "funded" or "paid for" the project. NOAA's "support" was mostly logistical in appointing volunteer leaders, who then obtained recreational divers to work on the project.

Fluke and flounder inhabit the wreck in large numbers: a great lure for anglers and spearfishing divers.

Granted that James Delgado was responsible for initiating the project, NOAA's only other major involvement was in having a couple of NOAA staff members share some of the work load. I knew one of them personally, and did not think much of his (dis)ability as an archaeologist. He claimed that a wreck known as the Toy Wreck, in the Stellwagen Bank National Marine Sanctuary off the coast of Massachusetts, was the coastal steam freighter *Pentagoet*, which sank in the Portland Gale of 1898. When I surveyed the wreck, I found no signs of machinery of any kind, not even a donkey boiler (or a windlass). There was no engine, no boiler, no bedplates, and no piping – in short, nothing that would lead one to surmise that the site was the wreck of a steamship.

After I published my findings in 2008, and after he purchased a copy of my book of findings from my website, he *still* persisted in his absurd belief. Worse yet, now – eight years later – NOAA not only continues to promote the site as the long lost *Pentagoet*, but the Administration is contemplating nominating the site for inclusion on the National Register of Historic Places, because they believe that the wreck "could possess potential historical importance."

That's NOAA for you!

In another instance of newsmanship, NOAA claimed that the *Robert J. Walker* mapping project took place "over the span of about 10 weeks." This statement may be true in a way, if the time from the first boat trip to the last was ten weeks apart. But it leads people to believe that the project entailed seventy days of hard work.

Except for a preliminary dive in June 2014, all the diving, mapping, and underwater photography was done during a four-day period in August 2014, when the volunteers took vacation time from their full-time jobs. A couple of other single day trips were made to conduct remote scanning operations. The actual on-the-wreck time totaled seven days or so.

According to the headline of one NOAA publication, the mapping project was conducted "with a little help from our friends." The word "little" belittles the enormous effort that the volunteers put into the project. In fact, the volunteers conducted the *whole* project for which NOAA took the credit.

In the body of the article, NOAA stated that it "enlisted the help of a group of New Jersey divers to survey the wreck." The word "enlisted" was carefully chosen so the public might believe that NOAA "hired" the divers, and paid them.

Then, "The New Jersey Historical Divers Association provided a team of scuba divers trained as amateur archeologists who measured, mapped and drew the wreck of the *Walker*." Partially true, except that not *all* were trained as archaeologists; and except

THE VESSEL – EXPLORATION AND MAPPING

that the carefully chosen word "provided" implies "hired," again making it seem as if NOAA funded the project.

In non-NOAA publications, it was noted that the mapping project was "privately funded," something that NOAA neglected to mention.

In reality, Lieb and Nagiewicz and the other volunteers could have effectuated the entire project by themselves, without any NOAA presence whatsoever. At least the NOAA presence was not obstructive, as it was on my various *Monitor* expeditions.

NOAA's article did give some credit: "Playing a major role in this effort were several partners, in particular the Richard Stockton College Marine Science Field Station, which used state-of-the-art side-scan and multi-beam sonar and remotely operated vehicles (ROVs) to map and record video of the wreck. The exercise provided an opportunity for students interested in marine archaeology to get hands-on experience using this equipment in the field.

"Other expedition partners included Black Laser Learning [Vince Capone], which teaches clients including the U.S. Navy how to use and interpret sonar data; Revel Resorts of Atlantic City, which provided lodging and food for the divers; the National Marine Sanctuary Foundation, which funded the cost of the dive boat and mooring; and the Office of National Marine Sanctuaries, which provided several marine archeology advisors. Other NOAA staff also contributed knowledge and historical information on the wreck."

Note that the National Marine Sanctuary Foundation is *not* a NOAA agency, nor is it in any way affiliated with NOAA. It is a private, non-profit, and tax exempt organization that supports NOAA.

The names of the college students I obtained from a non-NOAA article in a Richard Stockton College publication: Walter Poff, Chelsea Shields, and Jamie Taylor. Emily Burnite was also mentioned, but she was never on the boat; she must have helped in "laboratory" work, perhaps by interpreting field-school images. Project faculty members were Steve Evert, manager of the college's field station, and Peter Straub, who manned "the controls of the remotely operated vehicle." All in all, this team accumulated a great deal of useful data, and accomplished much-needed work.

Other divers were my long-time technical diving buddy and FBI agent Mike Pizzio, who took underwater photographs; Al Vogel, who also took pictures; Joe Fiorentino; Mike Haas; Mike Lavitt; Matt Nigro, Harry Roecker, and Shawn Sweeney.

Divers generally made two diver per day, with bottom times in the range of thirty minutes.

Topside personnel – not mere bubble watchers but active participants – were Ruth Hepler and Ronnie Segars, plus expedition doctor Matt Partrick.

Also, James Del-

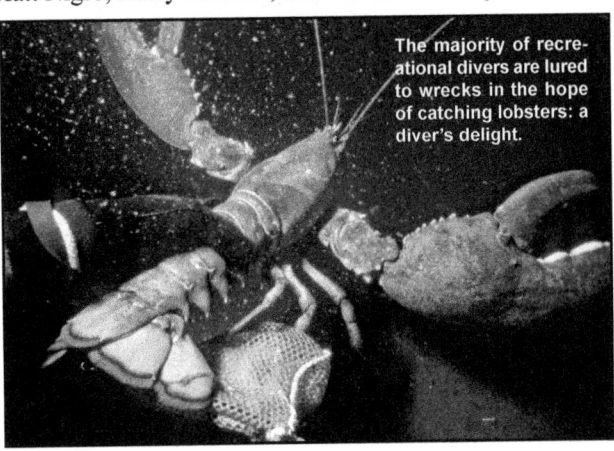

The majority of recreational divers are lured to wrecks in the hope of catching lobsters: a diver's delight.

80   THE VESSEL – EXPLORATION AND MAPPING

Above is an enlargement of the W. E. Martin painting of the *Robert J. Walker*. It clearly shows rectangular portholes like those that were recovered by recreational divers more than four decades ago. These portholes constituted another piece of evidence that helped to identify the $25 Wreck as the lost Coast Survey vessel.

The porthole that is shown on the front cover was donated to the New Jersey Maritime Museum by Eddie Boyle. He used to dive on the wreck in the 1970's. I learned about the provenance of this porthole barely one month before this book went to press. I remembered that in the 1970's my long-time dive buddy Joel Entler recovered a rectangular porthole from the $25 Wreck. I had not spoken with him in several years, so I called him to ask if the porthole was still in his possession. His answer came as a complete surprise.

Entler told me that he gave the porthole to Boyle!

The museum is hoping to obtain additional artifacts from recreational divers, to put on display with the porthole. This will probably never happen.

Recreational divers know that NOAA is a switch hitter. On one hand NOAA makes promises in order to achieve a result that is beneficial to itself or that is in keeping with its goals of aggrandizement and control; on the other hand NOAA has no intention of keeping those promises.

James Delgado has pledged to write a letter which will guarantee that NOAA will never assert ownership over any $25 Wreck artifacts that the museum accessions. So far that letter has not been produced. For fear of prosecution by either NOAA or the Navy, recreational divers are not likely to reveal that they have ever recovered such artifacts.

THE VESSEL - EXPLORATION AND MAPPING

gado went out on the boat for a couple of days. He may have provided encouragement and moral support but did not dive.

When all is said and done – no matter who did the work and who took the credit – the project was a resounding success.

Wreck Description

Dan Lieb described the site in the *NJHDA Journal*, Volume 8, Number 4. This is the official organ of the New Jersey Historical Divers Association. He is the editor-in-chief of the journal. He gave me permission to quote his first-hand description:

> The wreck site of the *Robert J. Walker* lies ten nautical miles out of Absecon Inlet, Atlantic City, New Jersey. She lies in 85 feet of water on a sandy bottom in a slight depression. Detritus from the inlet and other natural processes causes the wreck site to "silt up" and have a muddy bottom from time to time. This muddy bottom can clear out depending on the currents at any given time of year. Diving the wreck can either be a pleasure as it was when divers mapped the site in August of 2014, or a chore groping in the dark as it was during a preliminary dive just two months earlier.
>
> The bow has a heading of 313 degrees and is lying on its port side. A relatively small anchor is lodged between some frames and there is a coil of anchor chain still remaining on the deck. An anchor, almost completely buried in the sand, lies to port. A large anchor lies just aft of the bow wreckage lying on top of what may be a hatch combing. A few yards aft of the bow lies another anchor.
>
> Further aft is a set of tanks that may have been used in conjunction with the vessel's boilers. Directly aft of these are the boilers arranged side by side. Port and starboard of the boilers are the remains of the vessel's hull protruding just above the sand bottom.
>
> Directly aft of the boilers are the steam engines listing to starboard. The starboard engine is relatively intact while the port engine is completely destroyed. Heavy pieces weighing tons are flipped and turned around. The cause for this is speculative, but may indicate a botched salvage attempt or impact with commercial fishing equipment. Commercial fishing gear is on the site today, and other area wrecks also show impact with fishing gear. A nearby wreck, also a paddle wheeler, has a clam dredge lodged in its fragile paddle wheel assembly and clearly resulted in its destruction. I speculate that mechanism commercial fishing practices have resulted in the premature degradation of this wreck.
>
> Well aft of the engines and protruding above the bottom is the stern of the vessel. Frames, hull plates and the remains of the steering mechanism are exposed.
>
> The sea life includes many of the regular Mid-Atlantic Seaboard species from free-swimming species such as fluke, seabass, blackfish [tautog] and cunner [bergall]. We observed several lobster and fluke on the site that we encountered each day. In fact, some of the fluke, traveling in pairs, we safe [sic] as church [sic] from us as we performed our tasks – much as we may have

been tempted.

Few sponges and mussels were encountered on the wreck, and I did not notice any starfish. However, what struck me was the large amount of hydroids and coral that in some places so encrusted objects and features that it was nearly impossible to take an exact measurement. In fact, the wreckage appeared more white in color than anything else.

In addition to obtaining an overall physical description of the site, divers stretched guidelines across the wreck, and used tape measures and folding rules to gauge the lengths and widths of contiguous structures, the distances between disarticulated pieces of wreckage, and the sizes or diameters of individual members such as paddlewheel hubs. Elevation data were also obtained: that is, the height above the seabed of exposed portions of the wreck. This latter information was necessary in order to draw a perspective illustration of the disparate remains (which I was not permitted to publish).

This was a daunting task that required a great deal of time and attention to detail so that every discrete member that was exposed above the sand could be recorded for posterity.

NOAA promised to collate the data from the mapping project and use it to create a map of the site that would be put on a plastic slate and given freely to recreational divers. So far this has not happened.

Hydroids above and coral to the right. Although these organisms resemble flowers, they are members of the animal kingdom and not the plant kingdom. They are called filter feeders. They live by straining microscopic organic material from seawater - the same as clams, oysters, barnacles, and similar shellfish.

Robert J. Walker – the Vessel
Nomination and Future

Portent and Pretension

James Delgado has made a number of statements about current events on the *Robert J. Walker*. All were complimentary. Some of them are worth noting. For example:

"The identification of the *Walker* is a result of excellent collaboration with the local community. We look forward to working with our local partners to share *Walker's* story with the public in a manner that both promotes educational dive tourism and protects this nationally significant wreck and gravesite. We want to enhance the dive experience and support the dive industry with enhanced access to this wreck. New Jersey is home to some of the most accomplished wreck divers who not only understand history and wrecks, but who have also been in the forefront of wreck exploration. We look forward to working with them on the *Walker*."

Here is another: "The New Jersey coast is littered with many wrecks, but fortunately there's an exceptional group of sport divers, wreck divers, who regularly go out there, sleuth, try to discover more and it was thanks to some of those divers' reports and in particular Captain Eddie Boyle, one of the pioneer dive boat captains on the old *Gypsy*."

And: "What we want to do is with this one ship in particular, this is a perfect opportunity for us to work hand in hand with the wreck diving community. There's some great folks out there that do a tremendous amount of work. There's folks who researched this history. Gary Gentile has written incredible books about the wrecks of New Jersey."

At this point I need to remark that Delgado is the only NOAA employee who has ever said anything nice about me and my accomplishments. He also mentioned me and my books in the Sources for his Report on the *Robert J. Walker*.

Now read this response to concerns from recreational divers who feared that NOAA was going to prevent any more diving on the wreck: "Here's what we would like to get out to you folks: 1. We are NOT going to make the wreck a sanctuary. 2. We are NOT going to restrict access to the wreck. 3. We want to work with the community to enhance the dive experience on the wreck. That could include placing a mooring buoy just below the surface, better marking it on the charts, sharing the history and making a wreck dive slate, available at no cost to the dive community. Charter boats, and others like the one I've attached for a wreck at Thunder Bay [Michigan]. 4. Create a memorial on the beach in Atlantic City to the ship's crew. 5. Work to create an exhibit with artifacts folks might like to donate in a local museum or museums on the coast to tell more of the story of *Walker*."

I have no reason to doubt Delgado's sincerity. But in the same missive (to Gene Peterson at Atlantic Divers) he noted, "I'm a fairly recent addition to NOAA." Therefore, I am prepared to let him slide about not understanding NOAA's hidden agenda to control every shipwreck on the bottom of American coastal waters, including those that lie in international waters beyond the three-mile territorial limit of American jurisdiction.

NOAA has played this flimflam before. It lets a subordinate pledge allegiance to local anglers and divers about not curtailing their activities. Then it does just the opposite. The subordinate may be part of the scam, or he or she may be caught unawares by the sudden turnaround in policy. In either case, all he can do is shrug his shoulders and claim that he did not have any say in the matter, that the program change was made higher up the hierarchical ladder, perhaps at the top rung.

I do not mean this planned subversion to reflect on Delgado's character or to impugn his integrity. He admitted that he is a NOAA neophyte, and therefore he might not be aware of the machinations that NOAA has conducted in the past, and that NOAA has planned for the future.

Restrictions Applied

Despite Delgado's promises, NOAA wasted no time in formulating restrictions for the wreck site – a wreck site over which it had no legal control.

The only reason that NOAA did not make the *Robert J. Walker* another national marine sanctuary was that it was forbidden to do so by Congress. Congress had passed a resolution that stopped NOAA from creating any more marine sanctuaries. As you will read later in the book, in order to circumvent the wishes of Congress, NOAA adopted a policy of expanding the boundaries of existing sanctuaries, in some cases as much as a thousand-fold.

As a stop-gap measure for exerting control over the wreck site, NOAA nominated the *Robert J. Walker* for inclusion on the National Register of Historic Places. Such a pretentious designation offers a modicum of protection to buildings and other properties because they may not be torn down or allowed to fall into disrepair. Nor are they allowed to be modernized or modified in any way that would alter the characteristics of their originality.

In other words, they must be preserved exactly as they are, under threat of civil suit for failure to comply with the regulations of historic preservation. No one seems to have realized that these antique buildings do not meet modern building standards or fire codes, and certainly could not pass inspection or receive an occupancy permit without extensive repairs or restoration. Despite these hazards to human life, safety code violations are overlooked so that the owner may keep the structure "as is."

Inclusion on the NRHP is a promotional scheme that owners can use to increase tourism. It also serves as an inducement to preservation societies and government agencies to donate grant money and allocate funding for the benefit of the owner. I call the NRHP the National Cash Register of Historic Places.

There can also be a downside to inclusion on the Register. For example, the City of Philadelphia decided to create an historic district in order to cater to the tourist trade. Philly commissioners selected a block to be restored to the way it appeared during the time of the city's founder, William Penn. The City did not own the buildings on the block; it owned only the street.

The street was paved with the original red bricks which were in a sad state of disrepair. At one time the buildings presented a matching red brick façade, but after two hundred years of renovations they no longer appeared as they did in Revolutionary

THE VESSEL – NOMINATION AND FUTURE

times. The City refurbished the bricks in the street, but forced private owners to pay for the restoration of their property. Each owner was forced to shell tens of thousands of dollars out of his own pocket.

When I investigated the construct of Nerp, I found that they conducted no investigations to determine the historic quality of a site. They merely processed applications. There were no standards or guidelines for eligibility. The merits were left entirely to the nominators to research and document. Once Nerp determined that an application conformed to its guidelines for applicability – that is, all the blanks in the nomination form were filled in correctly, the t's were crossed, the i's were dotted, and the paperwork was complete – it rubberstamped the nomination, and the rest was history (or historic preservation).

You could nominate your neighbor's eyesore garage as an historic building and Nerp would grant it protective status as long as you described the structure with sufficient academic pomposity and infused the text with a number of bombastic phrases and buzz words – and they would never know the truth.

What is the value of acceptance as an historic site if no qualifications are required for granting such a status other than a nominator's knack for composing highfalutin language?

If the nomination is such a giveaway, then it follows that a site that is listed on the Register is no more significant than that of a person whose name is published in the telephone directory, because no one ever gets turned down.

One do-gooder conservation group nominated some World War Two army barracks for inclusion on the Register. Nerp duly accepted the application and approved the designation. The U.S. Army was later sued because it failed to maintain the structures when they were in dire need of repair.

When the case came to trial, the base commander testified that he had been allocated $80,000 for upkeep of the base. He decided to use the money to renovate the base's hospital facilities so that patients could receive better care, rather than squander the money on a group of unoccupied buildings that had no useful function or military application.

In another instance, two aging schooners in Maine graced (or disgraced, as the case may be) the waterfront in Wiscasset. They were on the Register, but no one bothered to maintain the structures. The *Hesper* and *Luther Little* gradually fell apart until they were nothing more than a blot on the seascape. The city council voted to have them removed. Wreckers were hired to demolish the hulls and haul the debris to a trash dump.

A similar situation is occurring in another part of Maine. The National Park Service nominated the *Cora F. Cressy* a quarter of a century ago, then proceeded to neglect the grounded schooner. The wreck has slowly disintegrated over the years due to the total lack of conservation. It will not be long before the hulk must suffer the fate of the *Hesper* and *Little Luther*. (For more details on all three vessels, see *Shipwrecks of Maine and New Hampshire*.)

Perhaps just as bad is the case of the *Portland* and other shipwrecks that NOAA has placed on the Register. By law the owners must keep the structures in good repair. Because the *Portland* and nearby nominated wrecks lie within the borders of the Stellwagen National Marine Sanctuary, NOAA is obligated to keep the wrecks in their orig-

THE VESSEL – NOMINATION AND FUTURE

The postcard photograph at top right shows how the *Hesper* and *Luther Little* appeared in the 1960's.

I took the picture at bottom right in 1997, a year before the Wiscasset schooners were demolished and removed to a trash dump.

In all the time of their existence, no NOAA archaeologists bothered to survey the site. Instead, NOAA nominated for inclusion on the National Register of Historic Places several schooners that were sunk in more than 300 feet of water in Stellwagen Bank NMS, where they could neither be archaeologically examined or in any way preserved for posterity. If NOAA truly cared about information that sunken vessels could provide, it would have examined the exposed and easily reached schooners in Maine. That NOAA did not do so proves that its goal is not to study wrecks, but only to control them.

inal condition.

Yet there is no way to maintain the condition of a shipwreck in 430 feet of water. NOAA has been able to do nothing more than occasionally deploy a waterproof video camera to observe the rate of deterioration. Thus NOAA is violating the law by not shoring up collapsing decks and bulkheads, and by letting the hull rot away.

A visit to the Nerp office in Washington, DC revealed more shenanigans. In going through some accepted nomination forms, I found a number of so-called historic sites that were "address restricted." This means that Nerp would not reveal the location of the site. In other words, the Register contains historic properties whose locations are concealed from the public. When I filed a request for the locations pursuant to the Freedom of Information Act, my request was denied; my appeal was also denied.

At the DC office I asked for photocopies of nine nomination forms. The staff was able to find only one. They had no idea where the other eight forms were filed. They still have not found them. They are either lost or misfiled among 80,000 other nomination forms.

For NOAA, placement of the *Robert J. Walker* on the National Register of Historic Places was, first, propaganda whose purpose was to draw attention to NOAA's façade of "preservation." Second, it gave NOAA a measure of control over the wreck. And third, it was a foot in the door to eventually create an all-inclusive marine sanctuary off the coast of New Jersey: one which will comprise strict rules and regulations against fishing and diving.

Readers should heed this dire warning. NOAA is not as benevolent as it appears by the false front that it puts before the public. As the Indians would say, NOAA speak with forked tongue. NOAA *says* that it has no intention to make the *Robert J. Walker* a marine sanctuary. What NOAA *means* is that it has no intention *now*. Or at least, NOAA wants to public to *believe* that it has no such intention. But intentions can change or be concealed.

For now, the most that NOAA could get away with was to prevent the collection of souvenirs. That is, NOAA may take souvenirs but not anyone else.

Fictitious Interpretation

The U.S. Navy has been the leader in making unwarranted interpretations of Constitutional law, in order for a handful of civilian employees to control tens of thousands of wrecks across the world. As this is being written, the Navy is attempting to usurp more than 17,000 wrecks from the public domain, including aircraft and privately-owned tankers and freighters. (For details, see *The Great Navy Wreck Scam: Being a History of Double Dealing, Double Standards, and Unethical Actions*.)

NOAA has followed the Navy's presumption with regard to the wreck of the *Robert J. Walker*. The Navy, and now NOAA, refer to Article IV of the Constitution of the United States as grounds for their unjustified possession of wrecks that were owned by the government at the time of their loss but which were subsequently abandoned in

The postcard photograph at top left was taken shortly after the schooner Cora F. Cressy was docked permanently at her final destination.

I took the photograph at bottom left in 2015.

The National Park Service nominated the wreck for inclusion on the National Register of Historic Places in 1990, then left it to rot. Soon it will have to be dismembered and the timbers burned or taken to a trash dump, because the NPS did nothing in a quarter of a century to preserve the aging wood. Official sanction did not do anything to "preserve" the wreck. Nor can official sanction *ever* "preserve" a wreck.

fact by the government's lack of effort to salvage them.

I will quote Article IV in full so that my readers will not think that I excluded pertinent information.

> Section 1. Full faith and credit shall be given in each state to the public acts, records, and judicial proceedings of every other state. And the Congress may by general laws prescribe the manner in which such acts, records, and proceedings shall be proved, and the effect thereof.
>
> Section 2. The citizens of each state shall be entitled to all privileges and immunities of citizens in the several states.
>
> A person charged in any state with treason, felony, or other crime, who shall flee from justice, and be found in another state, shall on demand of the executive authority of the state from which he fled, be delivered up, to be removed to the state having jurisdiction of the crime.
>
> No person held to service or labor in one state, under the laws thereof, escaping into another, shall, in consequence of any law or regulation therein, be discharged from such service or labor, but shall be delivered up on claim of the party to whom such service or labor may be due.
>
> Section 3. New states may be admitted by the Congress into this union; but no new states shall be formed or erected within the jurisdiction of any other state; nor any state be formed by the junction of two or more states, or parts of states, without the consent of the legislatures of the states concerned as well as of the Congress.
>
> The Congress shall have power to dispose of and make all needful rules and regulations respecting the territory or other property belonging to the United States; and nothing in this Constitution shall be so construed as to prejudice any claims of the United States, or of any particular state.
>
> Section 4. The United States shall guarantee to every state in this union a republican form of government, and shall protect each of them against invasion; and on application of the legislature, or of the executive (when the legislature cannot be convened) against domestic violence.

The words to which the Navy and NOAA allude are in Section 3, paragraph 2: "The Congress shall have power to dispose of and make all needful rules and regulations respecting the territory or other property belonging to the United States."

This sentence deals with real estate, not personal belongings. In this case, the word "property" is equivalent to "land" or "building lots" or, obviously, "territory." The Navy has intentionally misrepresented the whole tenor of the Article of which this sentence is a part. The Article has nothing to do with personal effects, and it says nothing at all about vessels or shipwrecks.

When a person buys a boat, he says, "I bought a boat." He does not say, "I bought a piece of property." He says "I bought a piece of property" when he purchases a woodland plot, or vacant lot, or hunting grounds, or a house, or a gas station, or a building, or a shopping mall, or, most obviously, beachfront property or commercial property. The word "property" had the same meaning in Revolutionary times that it has today. It meant land. Not in the framers' wildest imagination was "property" ever meant to mean a shipwreck.

The Navy hopefuls have twisted the meaning of this sentence to mean what they want it to mean for the purposes of that handful of civilians who work for the Naval History and Heritage Command (the imaginative and pompous name of the Naval Historical Center).

Understand that the newly ordained Naval History and Heritage Command occupies little more than a few rooms in a dilapidated building in the Washington Navy Yard, in Washington, DC. Likely, the number of active and retired Navy personnel who have even *heard* of the NHC or the NHHC define a tangent that approaches zero. Most people do not know that the Center exists. Yet its handful of civilian control freaks – literally a handful – seek to take possession of tens of thousands of sunken wrecks, only to let them rot and rust away.

Rest assured that the Navy has no intention of preserving these wrecks. The word "preserve" is a political euphemism for "control."

The proof of the Navy's misconstruction and perversion of the intent of the Constitution's framers is made evident by what the Navy calls the "Sunken Military Craft Act." This was not an Act of Congress, but a rider that was surreptitiously sneaked into the "Ronald W. Reagan National Defense Authorization Act for Fiscal Year 2005," where it was buried among some 3,000 pages of funding appropriations that were absolutely essential to the defense of the United States. Probably none of the representatives knew of the rider's existence, as it was not attached to the Act until the last minute before the Act came up for vote.

That was the only way the self-serving NHC could get its personal piece of legislation enacted. If the Navy truly believed its own guff – that Article IV required an Act of Congress to abandon unwanted vessels and other non-territorial "property" – then there was no need to seek additional legislation. The very fact that the Navy resorted to subterfuge and unethical tactics to ram through a piece of legislation that Congress would not have passed had the rider been submitted as a standalone Act on which the representatives could ponder and investigate before voting – is proof of the lack of validity of the Navy's stance.

If the Navy wannabes truly believed that Article IV bequeathed ownership of wrecks to them, there would be no need for the "Sunken Military Craft" rider. It would be unnecessary and redundant. And the same goes for the current legislation that the handful of power-mongers are trying to have passed in their behalf.

If Congress had to take affirmative action on every piece of government "property" other than land acquisitions, then no government employee would ever be allowed to throw anything away without Congressional approval. He would have to submit a formal application to Congress so that august body could conduct meetings and hearings on whether to formally abandon a broken fax machine or other piece of so-called property.

The list would include not only vessels but vehicles, desks, chairs, filing cabinets, worn-out auto parts, spent cartridges, non-working clocks, torn uniforms, crumpled paper, dried up pens, even pencils and paperclips, and hundreds of thousands of other items that are thrown into the dumpster or wastepaper basket every day. Can you imagine a clerk asking Congress for approval to put a worn out pencil stub in the trash can? Such a situation is absurd. Yet that is what the NHC would have the world believe.

And the NHC itself does not even believe it. Otherwise, to reiterate, the civilian corps would not need to pass additional legislation.

The coin a cliché, haste makes waste. The civilian despots who work for the Heritage Command drafted their rider so fast, in order to smuggle it into the appropriations bill unannounced, that it was deficient with respect to the amount of control that they wanted to possess.

The "Sunken Military Craft" rider applies only to Navy vessels that were in commission at the time of their loss. It does not apply to Navy aircraft, nor to the commissioned vessels of any other military service, and certainly not to non-military service vessels such as the *Robert J. Walker*. That is why they – the civilian control freaks – are now trying to pass new legislation that would grant them control over more than 17,000 wrecks worldwide. And, again to reinforce my point, not just bona fide Navy vessels, but aircraft and merchant vessels.

Presidential Sanction – Not!

The Navy, and then NOAA, next rely on a statement that supposedly was made by President Bill Clinton. Because the language in the "statement" clearly parrots that of the NHC civilians who want to control every wreck in the underwater world, it appears to have been written by them, then passed along to a Presidential aide for inclusion in Clinton's so-called statements. It reads:

> Thousands of United States Government vessels, aircraft, and spacecraft ("State craft"), as well as similar State craft of foreign nations, lie within, and in waters beyond, the territorial sea and contiguous zone. Because of recent advances in science and technology, many of these sunken Government vessels, aircraft, and spacecraft have become accessible to salvors, treasure hunters, and others. The unauthorized disturbance or recovery of these sunken State craft and any remains of their crews and passengers is a growing concern both within the United States and internationally. In addition to deserving treatment as gravesites, these sunken State craft may contain objects of a sensitive national security, archeological, or historical nature. They often also contain unexploded ordnance that could pose a danger to human health and the marine environment if disturbed, or other substances, including fuel oil and other hazardous liquids, that likewise pose a serious threat to human health and the marine environment if released.
>
> I believe that United States policy should be clearly stated to meet this growing concern.
>
> Pursuant to the property clause of Article IV of the Constitution, the United States retains title indefinitely to its sunken State craft unless title has been abandoned or transferred in the manner Congress authorized or directed. The United States recognizes the rule of international law that title to foreign sunken State craft may be transferred or abandoned only in accordance with the law of the foreign flag State.
>
> Further, the United States recognizes that title to a United States or foreign sunken State craft, wherever located, is not extinguished by passage of time, regardless of when such sunken State craft was lost at sea.

International law encourages nations to preserve objects of maritime heritage wherever located for the benefit of the public.

Those who would engage in unauthorized activities directed at sunken State craft are advised that disturbance or recovery of such craft should not occur without the express permission of the sovereign and should only be conducted in accordance with professional scientific standards and with the utmost respect for any human remains.

The United States will use its authority to protect and preserve sunken State craft of the United States and other nations, whether located in the waters of the United States, a foreign nation, or in international waters.

The President is entitled to his beliefs, and he can make as many statements as he wants, but neither his beliefs nor his statements constitute law. None of them has any validity outside of his personal philosophy, or the personal philosophy of those who convinced him to repeat their sentiments. Only Congress can pass such laws.

In point of fact, Clinton never vocalized the fortuitous statement that is attributed to him. By that I mean that he neither uttered nor articulated those words. The "statement" was shoehorned into an entire book full of statements that are attributed to Clinton, most likely by the control freaks at the Naval Historical Center: those who have the most to gain from the statement. Perhaps they bribed Presidential staff members to insert the self-serving quote in Clinton's book of statements. With so many world-saving issues that arose during his Presidency, it is highly doubtful that he even knew or cared about sunken rotting and rusting wrecks.

In summation, the Navy and NOAA's specious testimonials stand on soft ground that lacks support for the foundation of a law.

Nonetheless, NOAA, like the Navy, is crooning the same tune and trying to flummox people into believing that the alleged Clinton statement possesses Congressional authority. For example, on NOAA's website it poses the following questions and answers:

> What laws protect the *Walker* from looting and unwanted salvage to ensure that it is being properly protected and managed?
>
> As the U.S. Government owns the *Walker*, laws regarding the protection and management of Government property apply, including, but not limited to: the National Historic Preservation Act (NHPA) (16 U.S.C. § 470); and laws regarding the destruction or theft of U.S. Government property (18 U.S.C. § 641 *et seq.*). Under the maritime law of salvage, public and private owners have the right to deny salvage. In addition, U.S. sovereign wrecks are immune from arrest under the law of salvage without the consent of the U.S. Government, and in this instance the Department of Commerce (DOC) National Oceanic and Atmospheric Administration (NOAA) as the management agency (See the next Q&A). As such, the law of salvage and authority of federal Admiralty courts may also provide protection of the *Walker* from looting and unauthorized salvage.
>
> Is [sic] the Department of Commerce (DOC) and the National Oceanic and

Atmospheric Administration (NOAA) responsible for protecting and managing the *Walker*?

Yes. The USCSS *Walker* was managed by the U.S. Coast Survey when it sank. Since then, the wreck has neither been abandoned nor been designated surplus property by the United States. As the Coast Survey is now part of NOAA, DOC/NOAA is the federal agency that manages the *Walker* on behalf of the U.S. Government. Because the *Walker* is a historic shipwreck, DOC/NOAA also has a responsibility under the NHPA to consider it for listing as a "historic property" on the National Register and to develop a plan for its management and preservation. The wreck will be prominently marked on official U.S. nautical charts and other notices. NOAA will ask the fishing community to try to avoid trawling or dredging near it; NOAA will also work with others to avoid any activities that might harm the wreck site and therefore make it less of a diving attraction as well as an historic site.

The above two paragraphs are pure fluff. Note that NOAA has elected itself as the owner of the *Robert J. Walker*. The *Robert J. Walker* belonged to the U.S. Coast Survey, which operated under the Department of Transportation. NOAA operates under the Department of Commerce. One Department does not have the authority to confiscate the property of another Department, even though that property had been abandoned by the other Department. Yet without Congressional authority, NOAA has nominated itself as the guardian of the *Robert J. Walker*.

Elsewhere, NOAA used the term "looter" as a pejorative that applied to recreational divers. Keep in mind that a looter is someone who took something that you would have taken if you had found it first.

Now consider this question and answer:

What, if anything, does NOAA plan to do about artifacts divers have collected off the wreck over the years?

NOAA's site management plan is prospective and will focus on future activities. NOAA is not seeking any action against persons who recovered artifacts before the public knew it was U.S. Government property. NOAA recognizes that some divers and artifact collectors want to contribute to the scholarship of our nation's maritime heritage through the artifacts in their possession. In regard to those artifacts, NOAA would like to explore setting up an arrangement with a museum of public access, such as the New Jersey Maritime Museum, where people can donate their *Walker* artifacts for conservation and public display. In addition to sharing the story of the *Walker*, this exhibit would recognize the role of wreck divers in locating and identifying the wreck as well as helping tell its story.

This statement is gratuitous because it neglects to mention that the Statute of Limitations has long since expired on rescued artifacts. It is NOAA's way of making the public believe that it does not hold a grudge against recreational divers who recovered artifacts years or decades ago, while failing to note that it has no authority to take action against them anyway.

THE VESSEL - NOMINATION AND FUTURE

When all is said and done, the Navy's and NOAA's position with regard to wrecks in general and to the *Robert J. Walker* in particular is unsupportable. They can claim that the Constitution grants them ownership of abandoned wrecks of their choice, but their claim is not a truism; it is a self-serving assumption.

Uncertain Future

A big shipwreck war is raging in America. The contenders in this war are NOAA and the Navy. Both the Administration and the Department are engaging in parliamentary fisticuffs to take control of all the wrecks in the world.

NOAA's rabbit punches come in the form of creating new sanctuaries; or, if that process is denied by Congress, of expanding the boundaries of existing sanctuaries.

The Navy is hitting below the belt by slipping riders into crucial pieces of legislation; or, when that fails, by writing all-inclusive resolutions to empower the so-called Heritage Command with total control over wrecks all over the globe.

The problem that these power plays pose for the wrecks is that neither NOAA nor the Navy has any plans to conserve them. They each make grandiose statements about "preservation," but neither one has ever attempted to preserve a wreck. As I noted elsewhere, the word "preserve" is a euphemism for "control."

NOAA is content to let shipwrecks rust and rot away. This statement is not an idle sentiment on my part. NOAA has proudly stated that it fully intends to let the *Robert J. Walker* collapse. Consider this NOAA question and answer:

> Is there a ban on recovery of artifacts or will NOAA permit recovery of artifacts?
>
> As a matter of policy and practice, *in situ* preservation – leaving artifacts in place – is the preferred option for preserving the wreck for the public interest in this wreck as a destination for diving and bottom fishing, as a memorial for the lives that were lost when it sank, and the archaeological and historical value of the site. *See*:NOAA Guidelines for Research, Exploration and Salvage of RMS Titanic, 66 Fed. Reg. 18905, April 12, 2001 for guidelines on exploring and researching a shipwreck that is also a grave site. As the *Walker* rests at a depth of 85 feet in a mud hole, partially covered by silt, the wreck appears to be sufficiently preserved *in situ* while still accessible to the public. NOAA's management plan will facilitate continued diving and fishing activities in a manner consistent with historic preservation law and policy and to enhance the diving and interpretive experience.

How does this self-serving policy constitute preservation? NOAA's posture is tantamount to letting the wreck continue to fall apart, except that the notion is expressed in terms that make it seem as if NOAA is taking affirmative action to conserve it.

To actually "preserve" the *Robert J. Walker* – that is, to prevent the hull from deteriorating any farther than it already has – NOAA must stabilize the rusting process by installing sacrificial anodes made of zinc, magnesium, or aluminum: a system of stopping the wastage of metal that is known as cathodic protection. Existing wood must be coated with heavy-duty anti-fouling paint.

The blue woolen blankets were likely exposed by deep ground swells from the passing of Superstorm Sandy. Unless they are either reburied or recovered, they will soon rot away or be consumed by micro-organisms.

What does NOAA want to do instead? It is going to "establish a baseline" of the wreck's present condition, so it can monitor the rate of disintegration and collapse. This is like watching the paint peel off an historic building, taking pictures of termite progress, letting rainwater seep through the roof where the shingles have fallen off, observing the plaster peel off the walls, noting the floorboards curl up and break apart.

Everyone knows that buildings fall down if they are not rigorously maintained. How many readers live in homes that were never maintained? Every homeowner knows that worn shingles must be replaced, leaks must be stopped, old plumbing must be repaired, walls must be repainted, and so on and so on. No homeowner sits back and relaxes while his house collapsed around and on top of him. But that is what is meant by in situ preservation.

The real definition of "in situ preservation" is "allowing deterioration."

This is not preservation. This is merely acknowledgment of slow and uncontrolled destruction. That is NOAA's policy for so-called preservation. NOAA seems to believe that sunken shipwrecks can be preserved by means of bureaucratic fiat. This attitude is as ridiculous as requesting Congress to repeal the law of gravity.

Note, too, that the *Robert J. Walker* is not a grave site. A wreck site must contain human remains in order to qualify as a grave site. There is no documentation that states that any crewmembers were left inside the vessel when she sank. Nor is there any evidence of human remains on the wreck. NOAA has contrived the implication of human remains from whole cloth instead of a bona fide shroud.

In the Introduction to *U.S.S. San Diego: the Last Armored Cruiser* (1989), I wrote:

> A shipwreck is a time capsule: a fragment of history buried in the sea, a temporary repository of the remnants of a bygone age. The wood or steel hull is a transient abode that precariously extends the life of man's handiwork only slightly beyond the date of disaster and human suffering. This does not mean that the objects contained within are granted eternal life, for the sea is ever changing, ever destroying; it means only that oft sought relics have been granted a slight reprieve from obliteration.
>
> To preserve a flag one does not hang it on a pole during a full gale: it is folded and packed away safely. One does not store precious china on an exposed mountain ridge where it is subject to rock falls, summer sun, and winter snow: it is kept in a glass case under controlled conditions. An artifact must be preserved *from* the elements of nature, not consigned to its capriciousness; the longer it is constrained to these wild forces the less likely it is to survive intact, to be found and appreciated by future generations.

Today the *San Diego* is almost unrecognizable as a warship. Much of the hull that used to be intact is now sagging dreadfully, and hull plates have fallen off the frames like leaves in autumn. This condition is what NOAA calls "in situ preservation."

In the Introduction to *Shipwrecks of New Jersey – North* (2000) I wrote:

> To wreck-divers it is evident that shipwrecks undergo a continual process

of collapse. Academics and archaeologists would make the public believe that sunken wrecks exist in a state of perpetual preservation, as if they were frozen in time like fossils in rock. But wiser heads accept that long-term immersion in a hostile and dynamic environment is destructive. From the moment a ship is built the process of deterioration begins. This process does not end until the wreck is no longer recognizable, until nothing of man's original handiwork remains.

The proof of the pudding is in the eating. Wrecks that were nearly intact when I first started diving on them are now dilapidated structures or skeletal steel frames.

Anyone who disbelieves these sentiments could compare the image of the *Robert J. Walker* on the bottom with the painting on the cover of this book. They do not look anything alike. The wreck has clearly disintegrated. The wreck will continue to disintegrate. That is what wrecks do. They age and die the same as people do. Anyone who cannot see the difference between these images, cannot comprehend the concept of decay, and cannot accept this logical scenario, is just plain stupid.

In this view of the future, the *Robert J. Walker* has no future other than the one it would have had anyway without NOAA's involvement – except that anything that is left on the wreck will eventually deteriorate and be lost forever, destroyed by the fickle forces of nature. The wreck will then be nothing more than a memory.

Commemoration

One positive result of the identification of the *Robert J. Walker* was a commemorative marker. Obviously such a marker was not placed on the wreck site, where few people would ever see it, and where it would soon be overgrown with marine fouling organisms such as barnacles, coral, sea anemones, and hydroids. Instead, it was placed in a prominent location so that non-divers could see it and be made aware of the tragedy of yesteryear.

According to NOAA, "The station is in Atlantic City, at the intersection of Pacific Ave and Rhode Island Ave, at the Absecon lighthouse historical site. It is a commemorative disk inscribed USCS Steamer *Robert J. Walker* 1847-1860, set in top of a 6-inch concrete pad, 8 ft in diameter, at the center of a compass rose. It is 68.2 ft (slope) northeast from the northeast corner of Keepers House, 33 ft north from the lighthouse and 32.5 ft south-southeast from the southeast corner of oil storage building."

If you have a GPS receiver, the coordinates are 39° 21' 59.21572" and 74° 24' 51.08623" (according to NOAA); 39-21.988 and 74-24.845 according to my GPS.

The stability of the marker is given thus: "Monuments of questionable or unknown reliability."

NOAA also hosted a widely publicized commemoration ceremony. Some fifty people attended. According to NOAA's write-up about this solemn occasion:

> Sunday, June 21, was World Hydrography Day, a day set aside to recognize the important work of hydrographers. Measuring and describing the physical features of ocean, seas, and coastal areas is essential not only to the safe navigation of the everyday mariner, but to our nation's economic development, security and defense, scientific research, and environmental protection.

This year's observation was particularly noteworthy for NOAA, as we honored the lost crew members of the U.S. Coast Survey Steamer *Robert J. Walker*, by dedicating a memorial at the Absecon Lighthouse in New Jersey.

On June 21, 1860, the *Robert J. Walker* was hit by a commercial schooner while transiting from Norfolk to New York after months of surveying in the Gulf of Mexico. The ship sank 12 miles offshore, as they were heading to the Absecon Lighthouse after they were hit. Coast Survey lost twenty crew members that night, and another man died from his injuries the next day, in the largest single loss of life in Coast Survey and NOAA history.

Dr. James Delgado, director of maritime heritage at NOAA's Office of National Marine Sanctuaries, described the events of that long-ago day, and spoke of the partnership between NOAA and the New Jersey diving community in identifying the previously unidentified wreck.

Steve Nagiewicz, co-director of the *Robert J. Walker* Mapping Project, recognized a dozen private citizens who assisted with the project, as he talked about the importance of collaborative efforts in conserving the nation's history.

As part of the ceremony, "A historic hydrographer's bell rang for every crew member that lost their life." A Coast Guard color guard presented the colors. Speeches were made.

Also, "We were very pleased that representatives from the National Geospatial-Intelligence Agency attended the NOAA event. In a show of solidarity, the hydrographic office of the U.S. Navy held their own simultaneous ceremony at their location in Stennis, Miss. [Mississippi]"

As a way to sell greeting cards, Hallmark Cards has created more celebratory "days" than all the government agencies in the world. Do not bother to look in your local card store. The company does not (yet) have a card for World Hydrography Day.

Certain Future

Like people, all shipwrecks including the *Robert J. Walker* have no future. You have seen how much the wreck has deteriorated in the past century and a half. That deterioration will continue until nature has reclaimed what man has wrought. Unless NOAA takes affirmative action to conserve the site, instead of merely monitoring its rate of collapse while NOAA control freaks rally in Hitler's shadow, eventually nothing will remain but a rust spot in the sand. That is the great demise of all shipwrecks that are left untended on the bottom of the ocean.

And that's all she wrote.

The pictures on the opposite page show the memorial at the Absecon lighthouse in Atlantic City. The plaque that stands left of the lighthouse is shown at the top of the page. The two bronze medallions are embedded in the compass rose in the center of the field of stones: the upper medallion in the center, the lower medallion near the perimeter. Notice that NOAA included its emblem on every item as a way to bathe in the light of a survey vessel that worked for the Department of Transportation, whereas NOAA works for the Department of Commerce.

THE VESSEL ~ NOMINATION AND FUTURE

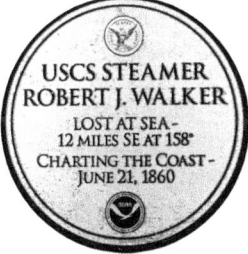

Robert J. Walker – the Vessel
National Register of Historic Places

The Janus Face of NOAA

What follows is the full version of the nomination form for the wreck of the *Robert J. Walker*. On the first page you will notice that the wreck is "address restricted."

As noted earlier, NOAA speak with forked tongue. From one side of its mouth NOAA proclaimed, in the words of James Delgado, "We want to enhance the dive experience and support the dive industry with enhanced access to this wreck."

From the other side of its mouth NOAA has restricted access to the wreck by issuing instructions to the NRHP to redact all information that relates to the location of the site whenever anyone requests a copy of the form. This means that only those few who already knew the location have access to the wreck, while all newcomers who obtain a copy of the nomination form for position information, will find that they have been effectively debarred from the site because Nerp, at NOAA's request, has redacted the essential numerical data. This hardly qualifies as "enhanced access to this wreck."

That is why I posted the GPS coordinates on the title page: so that my readers will be able to do what NOAA in reality wants to prevent them from doing: visiting the wreck and seeing it for themselves.

In this case you do not have to read between the lines to know that NOAA does not have your best interests at heart. You have only to read the lines – or rather, not be able to read the lines because they have been redacted – to reach that obvious conclusion.

I should mention too that nowhere on the NOAA website pages that are dedicated to the *Robert J. Walker* are the GPS coordinates given. Delgado's report goes into excruciating and irrelevant detail about how NOAA "found" the wreck by correlating multi-beam sonar data with side-scan sonar data and adjusting for magnetic field declination, to create search parameters that measured two square miles, when they already had the exact numbers courtesy of the recreational dive community, which willingly shared the location with NOAA.

(To avoid confusion, please note that the difference between true north and magnetic north is called "magnetic declination" on a topographic map, while it is called "compass variation" on a nautical chart. For elucidation, true north is based on the Earth's rotational axis. Magnetic north is based on the Earth's magnetic axis, which is constantly in motion; currently the north magnetic pole is located in Hudson Bay.)

Delgado's report subverted NOAA's scheme to hide the position from interested parties. It is the only place in NOAA's public records where the approximate position was given: on page 29, where the AWOIS listing is printed. The GPS numbers were converted from loran C numbers that Tony Vraim provided to NOAA before the advent of the Global Positioning System. Although the converted GPS numbers are not exact, they are close enough to the actual site that the wreck can be located with a little persistence.

Score one against NOAA!

I will make comments where necessary beneath the pages of the nomination form. Except for my appended explanations, what you see is what you get if you order a copy from Nerp. Here is page 1.

NATIONAL PARK SERVICE

NATIONAL REGISTER OF HISTORIC PLACES

WARNING

THE LOCATION OF THIS PROPERTY IS RESTRICTED INFORMATION. THIS DOCUMENTATION MAY BE REPRODUCED ONLY WITH THE CHIEF OF REGISTRATION'S PERMISSION.

* WHEN PHOTOCOPYING OR OTHERWISE REPRODUCING THIS DOCUMENT, BE CERTAIN TO COVER ALL LOCATION INFORMATION, INCLUDING THE ADDRESS BLOCKS, VERBAL BOUNDARY DESCRIPTION, UTM COORDINATES, MAPS OR ANY SECTIONS IN THE TEXT DESCRIBING LOCATION.

Property Name _____ ROBERT J. WALKER, Shipwreck and Remains

State _____ NEW JERSEY

County _____ Atlantic

Reference Number _____ 14000064

NPS Form 10-900
United States Department of the Interior
National Park Service

OMB No. 1024-0018

64

National Register of Historic Places Registration Form

RECEIVED 2280

This form is for use in nominating or requesting determinations for individual properties and districts. See instructions in National Register Bulletin, *How to Complete the National Register of Historic Places Registration Form*. If any item does not apply to the property being documented, enter "N/A" for "not applicable." For functions, architectural classification, materials, and areas of significance, enter only categories and subcategories from the instructions.

JAN 31 2014

JAN 31

1. Name of Property
Historic name: ROBERT J. WALKER, shipwreck and remains
Other names/site number: _____
Name of related multiple property listing:
    N/A
(Enter "N/A" if property is not part of a multiple property listing)

2. Location
Street & number: Offshore
City or town: Atlantic City   State: NJ   County: Atlantic
Not For Publication: [x]   Vicinity: [ ]

3. State/Federal Agency Certification

As the designated authority under the National Historic Preservation Act, as amended,

I hereby certify that this [X] nomination ___ request for determination of eligibility meets the documentation standards for registering properties in the National Register of Historic Places and meets the procedural and professional requirements set forth in 36 CFR Part 60.

In my opinion, the property [X] meets ___ does not meet the National Register Criteria. I recommend that this property be considered significant at the following level(s) of significance:

 [X] national   ___ statewide   ___ local
Applicable National Register Criteria:
 [X] A   ___ B   [X] C   [X] D

_____ - NOAA Federal Preservation Officer
Signature of certifying official/Title: Date: Jan. 29, 2014
NATIONAL OCEANIC AND ATMOSPHERIC ADMINISTRATION
State or Federal agency/bureau or Tribal Government

In my opinion, the property ___ meets ___ does not meet the National Register criteria.

Signature of commenting official: _____   Date

Title: _____   State or Federal agency/bureau or Tribal Government

---

Page 2 - The redactor either forgot or overlooked Nerp's warning that the address of this site was restricted. This was one of only two instances in the nomination form in which the location was given as "Atlantic City." In all other instances, the words "Atlantic City" have been redacted so as not to give away the starting point to interested parties such as recreational divers and charter boat skippers. Note that beneath "Atlantic City" the box is checked for "Not For Publication."

NATIONAL REGISTER OF HISTORIC PLACES 101

National Park Service / National Register of Historic Places Registration Form
NPS Form 10-900   OMB No. 1024-0018

ROBERT J. WALKER, shipwreck and remains
Name of Property

Offshore Atlantic, NJ
County and State

4. National Park Service Certification

I hereby certify that this property is:

✓ entered in the National Register
___ determined eligible for the National Register
___ determined not eligible for the National Register
___ removed from the National Register
___ other (explain:) _____

Signature of the Keeper   Date of Action: 3/19/14

5. Classification

Ownership of Property
(Check as many boxes as apply.)

Private: ☐
Public – Local: ☐
Public – State: ☐
Public – Federal: ☒

Category of Property
(Check only **one** box.)

Building(s): ☐
District: ☐
Site: ☒
Structure: ☐
Object: ☐

Page 3 - Note that only offshore Atlantic county was given as the site location.

United States Department of the Interior
National Park Service / National Register of Historic Places Registration Form
NPS Form 10-900   OMB No. 1024-0018

ROBERT J. WALKER, shipwreck and remains   Offshore Atlantic, NJ
Name of Property   County and State

Number of Resources within Property
(Do not include previously listed resources in the count)

Contributing	Noncontributing	
_____	_____	buildings
___1___	_____	sites
_____	_____	structures
_____	_____	objects
___1___	_____	Total

Number of contributing resources previously listed in the National Register ___0___

6. Function or Use
Historic Functions
(Enter categories from instructions.)
TRANSPORTATION – WATER RELATED
GOVERNMENT – WATER RELATED
_____
_____
_____
_____

Current Functions
(Enter categories from instructions.)
VACANT/NOT IN USE
_____
_____
_____
_____

Page 4 - Again only offshore Atlantic county was given for the site location.

NATIONAL REGISTER OF HISTORIC PLACES

United States Department of the Interior
National Park Service / National Register of Historic Places Registration Form
NPS Form 10-900 OMB No. 1024-0018

ROBERT J. WALKER, shipwreck and remains
Name of Property

Offshore Atlantic, NJ
County and State

7. Description

Architectural Classification
(Enter categories from instructions.)
N/A

Materials: (enter categories from instructions.)
Principal exterior materials of the property: ____N/A____

Narrative Description
(Describe the historic and current physical appearance and condition of the property. Describe contributing and noncontributing resources if applicable. Begin with **a summary paragraph** that briefly describes the general characteristics of the property, such as its location, type, style, method of construction, setting, size, and significant features. Indicate whether the property has historic integrity.)

Summary Paragraph

See Continuation Sheets

Narrative Description

See Continuation Sheets

Page 5 - And again the site location was given only as offshore Atlantic county. This approximate site location was repeated over and over.

United States Department of the Interior
National Park Service / National Register of Historic Places Registration Form
NPS Form 10-900 OMB No. 1024-0018

ROBERT J. WALKER, shipwreck and remains Offshore Atlantic, NJ
Name of Property County and State

8. Statement of Significance

Applicable National Register Criteria
(Mark "x" in one or more boxes for the criteria qualifying the property for National Register listing.)

[x] A. Property is associated with events that have made a significant contribution to the broad patterns of our history.

[ ] B. Property is associated with the lives of persons significant in our past.

[x] C. Property embodies the distinctive characteristics of a type, period, or method of construction or represents the work of a master, or possesses high artistic values, or represents a significant and distinguishable entity whose components lack individual distinction.

[x] D. Property has yielded, or is likely to yield, information important in prehistory or history.

Criteria Considerations
(Mark "x" in all the boxes that apply.)

[ ] A. Owned by a religious institution or used for religious purposes

[ ] B. Removed from its original location

[ ] C. A birthplace or grave

[ ] D. A cemetery

[ ] E. A reconstructed building, object, or structure

[ ] F. A commemorative property

[ ] G. Less than 50 years old or achieving significance within the past 50 years

---

Page 6 - Applicable criterion C accurately described the wreck of the *Robert J. Walker*, especially with regard to engine design and hull construction. My vote for engineering ingenuity goes to John Ericsson's *Goliath* (1846-1851) in Lake Huron. In his twin screw design, both propellers were counter-rotated by one single-piston engine, by means of a pair of offset shafts that were geared to vertical connecting rod assemblies. For pictures and more details, see *Great Lakes Shipwrecks: a Photographic Odyssey*.

United States Department of the Interior
National Park Service / National Register of Historic Places Registration Form
NPS Form 10-900   OMB No. 1024-0018

ROBERT J. WALKER, shipwreck and remains
Name of Property

Offshore Atlantic, NJ
County and State

Areas of Significance
(Enter categories from instructions.)
GOVERNMENT
MARITIME HISTORY
COMMERCE
ENGINEERING
EXPLORATION
ARCHITECTURE
TRANSPORTATION
ARCHAEOLOGY - HISTORIC

Period of Significance
1847-1860

Significant Dates
11/27/1847 (launch)
6/21/1860 (sinking)

Significant Person
(Complete only if Criterion B is marked above.)

Cultural Affiliation
N/A

Architect/Builder
Tomlinson and Company, Pittsburg, Pennsylvania (Builder)

Page 7 - To areas of significance I would add the person for whom the vessel was named. NOAA has played down Robert J. Walker (the man), perhaps because his actions were so fraudulent and unscrupulous, stating only that he was a Senator and a Secretary of the Treasury. NOAA wants to be associated with the wreck but not with its namesake, when in actuality NOAA's reputation is more akin to the person than to the wreck.

United States Department of the Interior
National Park Service / National Register of Historic Places Registration Form
NPS Form 10-900   OMB No. 1024-0018

ROBERT J. WALKER, shipwreck and remains   Offshore Atlantic, NJ
Name of Property   County and State

Statement of Significance Summary Paragraph (Provide a summary paragraph that includes level of significance, applicable criteria, justification for the period of significance, and any applicable criteria considerations.)

See Continuation Sheets

Narrative Statement of Significance (Provide at least **one** paragraph for each area of significance.)

See Continuation Sheets

NATIONAL REGISTER OF HISTORIC PLACES 107

United States Department of the Interior
National Park Service / National Register of Historic Places Registration Form
NPS Form 10-900   OMB No. 1024-0018

ROBERT J. WALKER, shipwreck and remains
Name of Property

Offshore Atlantic, NJ
County and State

9. Major Bibliographical References

Bibliography (Cite the books, articles, and other sources used in preparing this form.)

See Continuation Sheets

Previous documentation on file (NPS):

____ preliminary determination of individual listing (36 CFR 67) has been requested
____ previously listed in the National Register
____ previously determined eligible by the National Register
____ designated a National Historic Landmark
____ recorded by Historic American Buildings Survey #_____
____ recorded by Historic American Engineering Record #_____
____ recorded by Historic American Landscape Survey #_____

Primary location of additional data:
____ State Historic Preservation Office
____ Other State agency
____ Federal agency
____ Local government
____ University
_x_ Other
Name of repository: _National Oceanic and Atmospheric Administration's Office of National Marine Sanctuaries_

Historic Resources Survey Number (if assigned): _____

10. Geographical Data

Acreage of Property _2.471_

Use either the UTM system or latitude/longitude coordinates

Latitude/Longitude Coordinates

Datum if other than WGS84:_____
(enter coordinates to 6 decimal places)

Page 9 - Notice that NOAA established ownership of the wreck by claiming itself as the Name of repository. Notice, too, that NOAA left blank the place for the coordinates of the site.

108 NATIONAL REGISTER OF HISTORIC PLACES

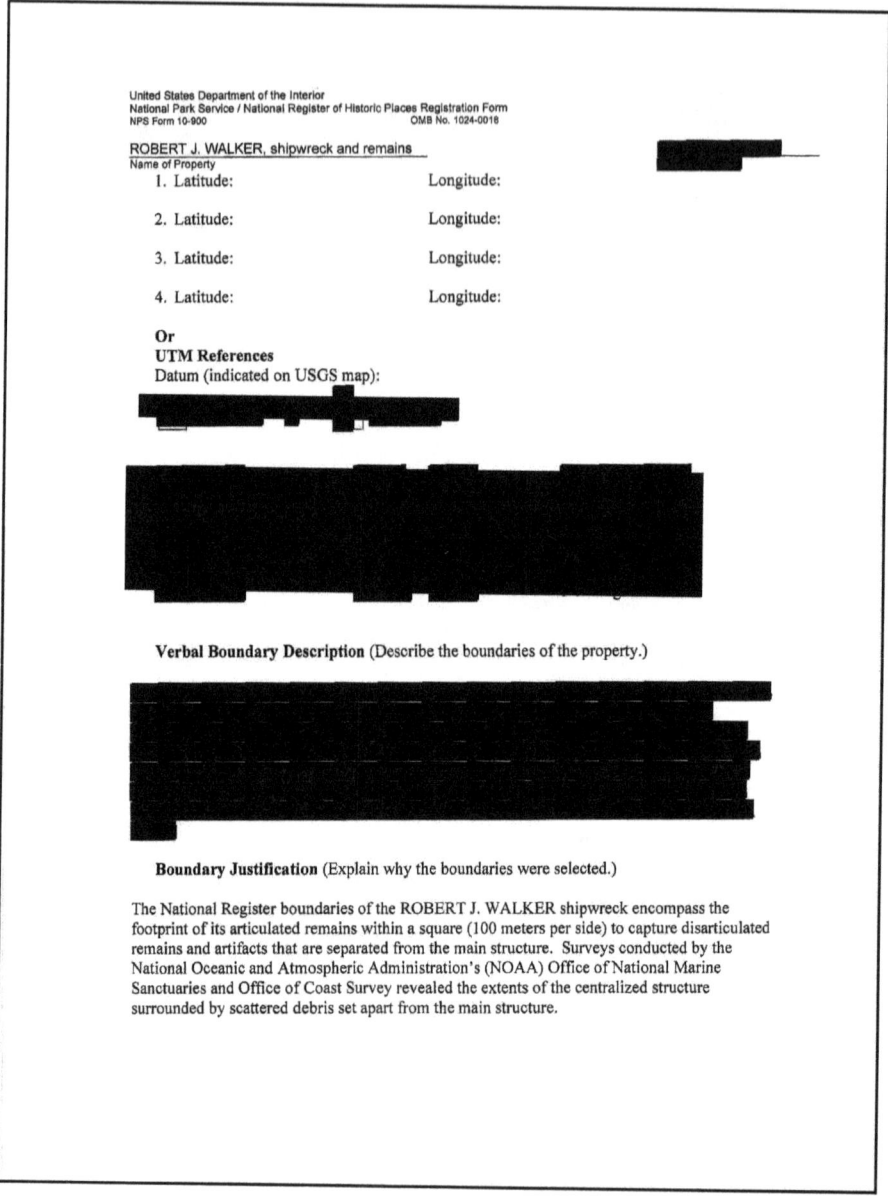

United States Department of the Interior
National Park Service / National Register of Historic Places Registration Form
NPS Form 10-900   OMB No. 1024-0018

ROBERT J. WALKER, shipwreck and remains
Name of Property

1. Latitude: Longitude:

2. Latitude: Longitude:

3. Latitude: Longitude:

4. Latitude: Longitude:

Or
UTM References
Datum (indicated on USGS map):

Verbal Boundary Description (Describe the boundaries of the property.)

Boundary Justification (Explain why the boundaries were selected.)

The National Register boundaries of the ROBERT J. WALKER shipwreck encompass the footprint of its articulated remains within a square (100 meters per side) to capture disarticulated remains and artifacts that are separated from the main structure. Surveys conducted by the National Oceanic and Atmospheric Administration's (NOAA) Office of National Marine Sanctuaries and Office of Coast Survey revealed the extents of the centralized structure surrounded by scattered debris set apart from the main structure.

Page 10 - On this heavily redacted page, not only did NOAA not provide the latitude and longitude as required by regulation, and then redacted the map and the boundary description, but also redacted Atlantic County and New Jersey in the upper right corner, whereas those latter approximate locations were printed on the previous and following pages. How stupid is that!

NATIONAL REGISTER OF HISTORIC PLACES 109

United States Department of the Interior
National Park Service / National Register of Historic Places Registration Form
NPS Form 10-900   OMB No. 1024-0018

ROBERT J. WALKER, shipwreck and remains
Name of Property

Offshore Atlantic, NJ
County and State

11. Form Prepared By

name/title: Deborah Marx, Maritime Archaeologist, Matthew Lawrence, Maritime Archaeologist, and James Delgado, Ph.D., Director of Maritime Heritage
organization: NOAA/Office of National Marine Sanctuaries
street & number: 1305 East West Hwy Building: SSMC4
city or town: Silver Spring   state: MD   zip code: 20910
e-mail Deborah.Marx@noaa.gov
telephone: 781-545-8026 ex 214
date: 1/23/14

Additional Documentation

Submit the following items with the completed form:

- **Maps:** A **USGS map** or equivalent (7.5 or 15 minute series) indicating the property's location. See page 46 Map 1 and Map 2.

- **Sketch map** for historic districts and properties having large acreage or numerous resources. Key all photographs to this map.

- **Additional items:** (Check with the SHPO, TPO, or FPO for any additional items.)

Page 11 - Note that James Delgado claimed, "We want to enhance the dive experience and support the dive industry with enhanced access to this wreck." Notwithstanding his statement, he helped to prepare the nomination form and to redact the very access information that he claimed he wanted to share. Go figure!

United States Department of the Interior
National Park Service / National Register of Historic Places Registration Form
NPS Form 10-900   OMB No. 1024-0018

ROBERT J. WALKER, shipwreck and remains   Offshore Atlantic, NJ
Name of Property   County and State

Photo Log/Index of Photos

Name of Property: ROBERT J. WALKER, shipwreck and remains
City or Vicinity: Offshore - Atlantic County
County: Offshore - Atlantic   State: Offshore - NJ
Photographer: W. Martin
Date Photographed: 1852
Description of Photograph(s) and number: 1852 painting of the ROBERT J. WALKER by W. Martin (courtesy of the Mariners' Museum, Newport News, VA). Photo 0001.
1 of 8.

Name of Property: ROBERT J. WALKER, shipwreck and remains
City or Vicinity: Offshore - Atlantic County
County: Offshore - Atlantic   State: Offshore - NJ
Photographer: W.A. Lighthall
Date Photographed: 23 October 1849
Description of Photograph(s) and number: Lighthall Patent Lever Half-Beam Engine (Patent 6811, U.S. Patent Office). Photo 0002.
2 of 8.

Name of Property: ROBERT J. WALKER, shipwreck and remains
City or Vicinity: Offshore - Atlantic County
County: Offshore - Atlantic   State: Offshore - NJ
Photographer: W.A. Lighthall
Date Photographed: 23 October 1849
Description of Photograph(s) and number: Lighthall Patent Lever Half-Beam Engine (side elevation) (Patent 6811, U.S. Patent Office). Photo 0003.
3 of 8.

Name of Property: ROBERT J. WALKER, shipwreck and remains
City or Vicinity: Offshore - Atlantic County
County: Offshore - Atlantic   State: Offshore - NJ
Photographer: Tane Casserley, NOAA's Office of National Marine Sanctuaries
Date Photographed: 23 June 2013
Description of Photograph(s) and number: ROBERT J. WALKER's starboard paddlewheel hubs including broken sections of the arms. Photo 0004.
4 of 8.

Page 12 - Note that the phrase "City or Vicinity" is given as "Offshore - Atlantic County."

United States Department of the Interior
National Park Service / National Register of Historic Places Registration Form
NPS Form 10-900   OMB No. 1024-0018

ROBERT J. WALKER, shipwreck and remains   Offshore Atlantic, NJ
Name of Property   County and State

Name of Property: ROBERT J. WALKER, shipwreck and remains
City or Vicinity: Offshore - Atlantic County
County: Offshore - Atlantic   State: Offshore - NJ
Photographer: Matthew Lawrence, NOAA's Office of National Marine Sanctuaries
Date Photographed: 23 June 2013
Description of Photograph(s) and number: One of ROBERT J. WALKER's anchors lies buried beneath the bow remains. Photo 0005.
5 of 8.

Name of Property: ROBERT J. WALKER, shipwreck and remains
City or Vicinity: Offshore - Atlantic County
County: Offshore - Atlantic   State: Offshore - NJ
Photographer: Matthew Lawrence, NOAA's Office of National Marine Sanctuaries
Date Photographed: 23 June 2013
Description of Photograph(s) and number: Possible blankets on the ROBERT J. WALKER site. Photo 0006.
6 of 8.

Name of Property: ROBERT J. WALKER, shipwreck and remains
City or Vicinity: Offshore - Atlantic County
County: Offshore - Atlantic   State: Offshore - NJ
Photographer: NOAA's Office of Coast Survey
Date Photographed: 2013
Description of Photograph(s) and number: Multibeam sonar image of the ROBERT W. WALKER wreck site in 2013. Photo 0007.
7 of 8.

Name of Property: ROBERT J. WALKER, shipwreck and remains
City or Vicinity: Offshore - Atlantic County
County: Offshore - Atlantic   State: Offshore - NJ
Photographer: NOAA's Office of Coast Survey
Date Photographed: 23 June 2013
Description of Photograph(s) and number: Side scan sonar image of the ROBERT W. WALKER wreck site in 2013. Photo 0008.
8 of 8.

Paperwork Reduction Act Statement: This information is being collected for applications to the National Register of Historic Places to nominate properties for listing or determine eligibility for listing, to list properties, and to amend existing listings. Response to this request is required to obtain a benefit in accordance with the National Historic Preservation Act, as amended (16 U.S.C.460 et seq.).
Estimated Burden Statement: Public reporting burden for this form is estimated to average 100 hours per response including time for reviewing instructions, gathering and maintaining data, and completing and reviewing the form. Direct comments regarding this burden estimate or any aspect of this form to the Office of Planning and Performance Management. U.S. Dept. of the Interior, 1849 C. Street, NW, Washington, DC.

Page 13 - Note the statements at the bottom of the page.

NPS Form 10-900-a
OMB No. 1024-0018
United States Department of the Interior
National Park Service

ROBERT J. WALKER, shipwreck and remains
Name of Property
Offshore Atlantic, NJ
County and State

National Register of Historic Places Continuation Sheet

Name of multiple listing (if applicable)

Section number __7__ Page __1__

Section 7 - Description

SUMMARY

The ROBERT J. WALKER site is the shipwrecked remains of an iron hulled side paddle wheel steamship owned and operated by the United States government, as part of the Coast Survey. The steamship sank on 21 June 1860 after colliding with a schooner off the New Jersey coast. Twenty men died in the incident, making it the single greatest loss of life suffered by the Department of Commerce's National Oceanic and Atmospheric Administration (NOAA) or any predecessor agency. ▇▇▇▇▇▇▇▇▇▇▇▇ ROBERT J. WALKER's extant remains are substantially embedded and buried in the sediment. Structural components consist of its upright, articulated iron hull, present largely from the turn of its bilge to its keel, along with more intact sections of hull at its bow and stern. Its bow points towards the northwest in the direction it was traveling during its final moments. ROBERT J. WALKER's steam engines, portions of the paddle wheels and boilers are present on the site as well as other features such as its anchors and smaller cultural artifacts. The steamship's engines represent the only known remains of this early type of American marine steam engine yet located and available for study.

ROBERT J. WALKER's remains represent the oldest known iron-hulled steamship wreck of a U.S. Government vessel yet located and available for study in the United States; it is the only known wreck of a U.S. Coast Survey vessel. The U.S. Coast Survey's work, from the early 19th century until modern times, has charted the coastal and offshore waters of the United States, making not only scientific contributions but also effectively marking the waterways as part of a national effort to open these waterways to maritime trade and commerce.

ROBERT J. WALKER 1847-1860

Shipbuilders Stackhouse and Tomlinson of Pittsburgh, Pennsylvania launched the iron hulled, side paddlewheel steamship ROBERT J. WALKER on 27 November 1847. The vessel's dimensions were 125 feet long by 26 feet wide. The 358-ton steamship had one deck and was built for the U. S. Revenue Service, but was transferred to the U. S. Coast Survey shortly after its launch (Trimble 1975:162). An 1852 painting of the steamship depicts the vessel with a black hull and paddle boxes accented with a red stripe painted encircling the hull and paddle boxes at main deck level (see Figure 1). The white painted aft deck house extended aft of the paddle wheels. Rectangular portholes in the vessel's iron outer hull provided light and ventilation. The ROBERT J. WALKER had two masts and was rigged as a hermaphrodite brig (Martin 1852). By combining its steam engine with sail power, the steamship was more stable and faster during long transits. Due to the unreliability and inefficiency of steam machinery at this time, wind

NPS Form 10-900-a
OMB No. 1024-0018

United States Department of the Interior
National Park Service

**National Register of Historic Places
Continuation Sheet**

ROBERT J. WALKER, shipwreck and remains
Name of Property
Offshore Atlantic, NJ
County and State
Name of multiple listing (if applicable)

Section number 7   Page 2

power often supplemented or replaced the use of engines to extend ROBERT J. WALKER's operating range.

Figure 1. 1852 painting of the ROBERT J. WALKER by W. Martin (courtesy of the Mariners' Museum, Newport News, VA).

Two horizontal, lever half beam, "Lighthall's patent" condensing steam engines powered ROBERT J. WALKER (see Figure 2 and 3). William A. Lighthall of Albany, New York patented his lever half-beam steam engine on October 23, 1849 (Patent 6811). The engines were placed side by side at amidships aft of the boilers. Each horizontal steam cylinder measured two feet nine inches in diameter. Two ascending single flue boilers provide steam for the engines while a single black smokestack sat between its masts exhausting heat and ashes from the boilers up and away from deck. In 1852, Messrs. Merrick and Son of Philadelphia replaced the steamship's boilers with two rectangular fifteen foot long single flue boilers (Isherwood 1852). The steamship carried two black longboats on its port side and an additional two on its starboard

Page 15 - Here as everywhere else in NOAA's writings and reports, NOAA called attention to an engine that William Lighthall patented in 1849, without mentioning that the *Robert J. Walker* was built two years earlier, in 1847.

I do not know what information was redacted on the previous page.

NPS Form 10-900-a
United States Department of the Interior
National Park Service

National Register of Historic Places Continuation Sheet

OMB No. 1024-0018

ROBERT J. WALKER, shipwreck and remains
Name of Property
Offshore Atlantic, NJ
County and State
Name of multiple listing (if applicable)

Section number _7_ Page _3_

side (Martin 1852). These boats were used for boarding other vessels, rowing to shore, surveying in shallow waters, or as a lifeboat in an emergency. Lastly, for defensive measures the steamship carried a 32-pounder gun and ammunition (Delgado 2013).

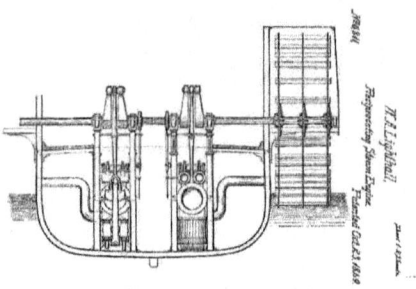

Figure 2. Lighthall Patent Lever Half-Beam Engine (Patent 6811, U.S. Patent Office).

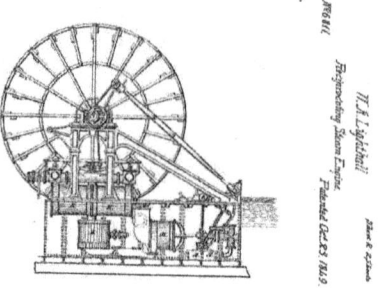

Figure 3. Lighthall Patent Lever Half-Beam Engine (side elevation) (Patent 6811, U.S. Patent Office).

Page 16 - This is the Lighthall engine that was patented two years after the *Robert J. Walker* was put into service.

NATIONAL REGISTER OF HISTORIC PLACES 115

NPS Form 10-900-a
OMB No. 1024-0018

United States Department of the Interior
National Park Service

**National Register of Historic Places
Continuation Sheet**

ROBERT J. WALKER, shipwreck and remains
Name of Property
Offshore Atlantic, NJ
County and State

Name of multiple listing (if applicable)

Section number __7__ Page __4__

SETTING

ROBERT J. WALKER lies partially buried on the muddy seafloor of the continental slope offshore of Atlantic City, New Jersey. The continental shelf offshore of New Jersey where the ROBERT J. WALKER sits is broad and gently sloping to the southeast known as the New Jersey Coastal Plain. Strong tidal currents are present on the site and create scours around portions of the steamship. The ROBERT J. WALKER has taken on an ecosystem role as hard substrate for encrusting invertebrates and shelters a diverse variety of fish species.

The water's off New Jersey extending from Cape May to New York have been active shipping routes for hundreds of years. Vessels transiting up and down the coast as well as those heading in and out of port crossed the waters where the ROBERT J. WALKER sank. The area is also a popular recreational and commercial fishing ground due to the abundant natural resources. Hundreds of shipwrecks sank along the coast and just off shore Atlantic City including the ROBERT J. WALKER due to storms, fire, collision, and other maritime calamities. As a result of the large number of shipwrecks there is an active dive community in and around New Jersey that has visited the ROBERT J. WALKER since the early 1970s.

ARCHAEOLOGICAL REMAINS OF ROBERT J. WALKER

The following description of the ROBERT J. WALKER's archaeological remains is based on multibeam sonar, side scan sonar, and diver surveys conducted by NOAA's Office of Coast Survey and Office of National Marine Sanctuaries in 2013 as well as recreational diver logs and reports. Recreational divers have visited the ROBERT J. WALKER for many years and their observations and images are published in popular dive guides and shipwreck books as well as on the World Wide Web, often with extensive research and detailed observations. This information supplements the archaeological data and provides details not captured by the NOAA surveys. The vessel's size, observed site characteristics, and location all indicate that the site is the U. S. Coast Survey Steamship ROBERT J. WALKER.

The ROBERT J. WALKER's overall site remains measure 133 feet long by 35 feet wide with 15 feet of vertical relief above the seafloor. This measurement reflects the hull's articulated length stretching from it bow to stern. The site's main feature is its machinery components, which lie partially intact listing slightly to port. Amidships, highly deteriorated boiler furnaces lie forward of the steam machinery indicative of the steamship's centered engineering spaces. Two smaller clusters of wreckage northwest and southeast of the main structure indicate the location of the bow and stern, respectively. The wreck's point of greatest relief above the seafloor is its bow, which has fallen on its port side.

Page 17 - Oops! The redactor forgot to redact "Atlantic City." Note that wreck site measurements usually differ from the vessel's measurements; this is due to the manner in which a wreck collapsed (inboard or outboard), and how much wreckage was covered by sand, silt, or mud.

NPS Form 10-900-a
OMB No. 1024-0018
United States Department of the Interior
National Park Service

**National Register of Historic Places
Continuation Sheet**

ROBERT J. WALKER, shipwreck and remains
Name of Property
Offshore Atlantic, NJ
County and State

Name of multiple listing (if applicable)

Section number 7   Page 5

The ROBERT J. WALKER's two Lighthall's patent horizontal, lever half beam, condensing engines are partially intact and in their original position inside the steamship's hull. The two engines are located side by side near amidships and aft of the boilers. The position and placement of the horizontal six-foot long steam cylinders match ROBERT J. WALKER's construction records. In addition to the steam cylinders, the steamship's paddlewheel components are present on the site. While all of the basic mechanical and structural elements of the engines and paddlewheel mechanisms appear to be on site, the propulsion machinery has suffered disarticulation. The most intact section consists of the starboard engine, condenser, air and water pumps, extending from the outboard lobe of the starboard paddle shaft crank outward towards the vessel's side. The crank has been split in two at the crank pin, freeing the half beam connecting rod. The paddleshaft is supported by its entablature and eccentrics are connected to the paddle shaft to properly actuate the machinery. The paddleshaft retains its perpendicular orientation to the vessel's hull. In contrast, the portside machinery is partially disarticulated beginning at the inboard side of the starboard paddle crank and extending outboard. While the steam cylinder and condenser retain their respective positions, the paddle shaft has been pulled off its supports, snapping the associated connecting rods and breaking the entablature.

Additional features associated with the starboard paddle wheel lie in the seafloor near the main starboard paddle wheel structure. Both the starboard and port paddlewheel hubs are secured to the paddle shaft. Measurement of the three hubs on the starboard side found them to be spaced three feet apart resulting in a paddle wheel width of six feet, which matches the historical dimensions of the ROBERT J. WALKER (see Figure 4). The three paddle wheel hubs retain the broken remnants of the iron paddle wheel arms. The wooden paddle wheel floats that attached to the arms have deteriorated after long exposure to the North Atlantic.

Page 18 - Note that the advanced state of collapse and disarticulation was the inevitable result of what NOAA calls in situ "preservation," which means no preservation at all.

NATIONAL REGISTER OF HISTORIC PLACES 117

NPS Form 10-900-a
United States Department of the Interior
National Park Service

OMB No. 1024-0018

**National Register of Historic Places
Continuation Sheet**

ROBERT J. WALKER, shipwreck and remains
Name of Property
Offshore Atlantic, NJ
County and State

Name of multiple listing (if applicable)

Section number 7   Page 6

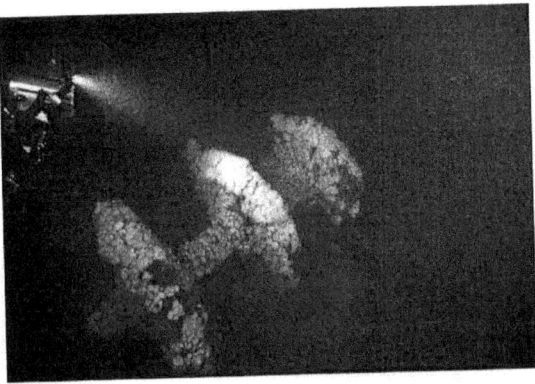

Figure 4. ROBERT J. WALKER's starboard paddlewheel hubs including broken sections of the arms (courtesy of Tane Casserley, NOAA's Office of National Marine Sanctuaries).

The remains of the steamship's two ascending single flue boilers lie forward of the engines. The boiler's iron plating has deteriorated, but retains some semblance of its original rectangular shape. The boilers' overall shape and size approximate historical drawings of the ROBERT J. WALKER's boilers.

ROBERT J. WALKER's bow lies at the northwest end of the site. The bow features has collapsed to port and includes portions of the iron stempost and associated structural components that extended from the gripe up to deck level. The steamship's starboard side flaring bow is the highest point of the feature. A single iron stock Admiralty Pattern anchor is located in the stowed or "catted" position at the northwest end partially buried beneath the bow remains. A second anchor of similar style lies aft of the first anchor further indicating that this end is the bow (see Figure 5).

Page 19 - If NOAA refuses to mark the site with a warning buoy, and neglects to publish the location in the Local Notice to Mariners, there is nothing to prevent trawlers and draggers from damaging the wreck by snagging it with their heavy-duty gear. That happened to the *Monitor* when a fishing boat hooked the propeller and, in the process of weighing anchor, tore the shaft from its mount and broke the A-frame and the skeg. NOAA *still* kept the *Monitor's* location secret: a clear case of administrative stupidity.

NPS Form 10-900-a
United States Department of the Interior
National Park Service

National Register of Historic Places
Continuation Sheet

Section number 7   Page 7

OMB No. 1024-0018

ROBERT J. WALKER, shipwreck and remains
Name of Property
Offshore Atlantic, NJ
County and State
Name of multiple listing (if applicable)

Figure 5. One of ROBERT J. WALKER's anchors lies buried beneath the bow remains (courtesy of Matthew Lawrence, NOAA's Office of National Marine Sanctuaries).

Evidence of ROBERT J. WALKER's iron riveted hull is extant throughout the site. Preservation varies based upon how much structure protrudes from the sediment. Sediment levels are greater on the starboard side resulting in frame ends above the turn of the bilge projecting from the sediment. Overall, hull material protrudes from the sediment to the breadth of the turn of the bilge forward of the machinery. Aft of the engineering spaces, the hull is largely buried beneath sediment except for stern post structures. Hull plating is comprised of 8-foot long iron plates $5/16^{th}$ of an inch thick attached to (10 pound) T-bar frames with rivets. Double and single $10/16^{th}$ of an inch rivets were used. Additionally there are riveted bulkheads secured to T-bar frames inside the hull matching historical reports that the ROBERT J. WALKER was built with thicker watertight bulkheads and separate coal bunkers.

Recreational divers have recovered artifacts over the last forty years from the ROBERT J. WALKER including several rectangular brass or bronze portholes, "Mason's" ironstone china, a glass ink well, bottles, a single cannonball, and a steam vent with a thermometer. The NOAA survey observed several artifacts related to the crew in the ship's bilge, including a bottle neck and a piece of blue fabric. The fabric was believed to be woolen blankets (see Figure 6). It was located on the portside in the vicinity of the collision point with the schooner. A possible

Page 20 - This glass inkwell was recovered from the wreck of the *Robert J. Walker.*

NPS Form 10-900-a
OMB No. 1024-0018

United States Department of the Interior
National Park Service

ROBERT J. WALKER, shipwreck and remains
Name of Property
Offshore Atlantic, NJ
County and State
Name of multiple listing (if applicable)

**National Register of Historic Places
Continuation Sheet**

Section number 7   Page 8

explanation for the blanket's location can be found in a contemporary account of the sinking that includes the crew's attempt to plug the collision hole near the coal bunker with blankets:

> Some of the men were sent down into the coal-bunker, where they found the water rushing in. They tried to stop the leak with beds and blankets, but found it impossible, as the hole was so large that they no sooner put a bed into it than it was carried through. In this way, one bed after another was lost in the effort (Vincent 1860:558).

Figure 6. Possible blankets on the ROBERT J. WALKER site (courtesy of NOAA's Office of National Marine Sanctuaries).

The steamship's geographic orientation matches the reports of its last moments as its crew turned the vessel ▮▮▮▮▮ in an attempt to reach shallow water before sinking. Furthermore, the wreck's geographic location coincides closely with historical accounts of ROBERT J. WALKER's loss, ▮▮ While the disarticulation of the portside machinery components and some hull degradation is likely due to commercial fishing gear, some of which was found entangled on the vessel's portside hull plating, the steamship has considerable integrity. Overall, the site is characterized as a small

Page 21 - This bottleneck of a different kind was recovered from the *Robert J. Walker*. The exposed fabric that is pictured above will deteriorate quickly if it is not rescued from the ravages of the sea. The redacted text appears to refer to location information that NOAA wants to hide from the public, so that divers and anglers who are not already in the know will not be able to find the wreck.

NPS Form 10-900-a
OMB No. 1024-0018
United States Department of the Interior
National Park Service

**National Register of Historic Places
Continuation Sheet**

ROBERT J. WALKER, shipwreck and remains
Name of Property
Offshore Atlantic, NJ
County and State

Name of multiple listing (if applicable)

Section number 7   Page 9

paddlewheel steamship with an iron hull with two highly unusual horizontal, half beam condensing engines. Additionally the shipwreck's size, machinery, and visual construction features all clearly correspond to ROBERT J. WALKER's historically reported characteristics.

SITE INVESTIGATIONS

While the general location of ROBERT J. WALKER's loss was known based on survivor accounts, the wreck was not relocated or salvaged, and an 1864 chart of the area does not indicate its location. The site has been "known" since World War II as an obstruction and it was also marked as a fisherman's hang site, but had never been charted officially as a wreck. The Office of Coast Survey's Automated Wreck and Obstruction Information System (AWOIS) record for the site states it is an unknown wreck/obstruction and notes: 178 ANTHONY VRAIM, DIVERS; OBSERVED SUNKEN WWI FREIGHTER; LORAN-C 9960-X-26929.10, 9960-Y-42939.30 (ASF CORRECTED) POS.39-13-28.5N, 74-17-17.25W.

Local divers started visiting the steamship in the early 1970s, when it became known as the "$25 Dollar Wreck." The New Jersey Wreck Divers website describes the wreck site as follows:

> In the early seventies the wreck was discovered by a local fisherman and the loran co-ordinate was sold for $25 dollars to a local party boat. Hence its original name, the $25 Dollar Wreck. Captain Ed Boyle of the original Atlantic City dive boat Gypsy began taking charters to the wreck, discovering barrels, square portholes, a large toppled engine (sic) with an upright bow and two paddlewheels in the debris. The starboard paddle was standing vertical and the port lays on its side in the sand. Visibility was often limited at that time, because a sewage outfall pipe north of the wreck was still in operation, and the wreck remained infrequently visited. The untreated outfall was capped in the mid-eighties and soon visibility greatly improved. On a dive in the late eighties Atlantic Divers discovered a barrel of white china with the markings labeled Mason on the bottom. Because of the previous names bad reputation, Atlantic Divers rechristen [sic] the wreck Mason's Paddle Wheeler to stimulate more exploration of the site. Soon it became a popular dive and much discovery continued. Dave Keller recovered a large brass steam vent with a thermometer enclosed. Several bottles, and more pieces of china have been uncovered since that time and numerous copper pipe lay ambiguously in the debris. Today the water is clear over the wreck with a healthy abundance of marine life. More needs to be uncovered to verify its identity (NJwreckdivers 2013).

Page 22 - The unofficial name of the paddlewheeler was the $25 Wreck, or the sometimes the 25 Dollar Wreck, but not the $25 Dollar Wreck, in which the symbol "$" and the word "Dollar" are redundant. The reader might recall from a previous chapter that Gene Peterson (Atlantic Divers) expressly forbid NOAA to credit him with providing crucial information that led to identifying the wreck.

NPS Form 10-900-a
OMB No. 1024-0018
United States Department of the Interior
National Park Service

**National Register of Historic Places
Continuation Sheet**

ROBERT J. WALKER, shipwreck and remains
Name of Property
Offshore Atlantic, NJ
County and State

Name of multiple listing (if applicable)

Section number 7   Page 10

Investigations by highly skilled wreck divers have provided a large amount of information about the ROBERT J. WALKER shipwreck prior to the first archaeological survey of the site by NOAA in 2013. New Jersey has an active corps of wreck divers, many of whom invest considerable personal sums to outfit dive expeditions to locate and identify the many wrecks off the shore. Some collect artifacts, others do not. Many divers donate their artifacts to the New Jersey Maritime Museum, a non-profit educational institution located in Beach Haven, New Jersey. Others retain their finds in personal collections. Without the attention paid to this wreck by New Jersey divers, its presence and ultimate identification as ROBERT J. WALKER would not have occurred.

In 2004, NOAA's Office of Coast Survey surveyed the ROBERT J. WALKER with multibeam sonar as part of a larger survey of the area as required to update nautical charts. The imagery provided information about the wreck's basic characteristics and orientation. It determined that the wreck was approximately 40 meters or 134 feet in length with three main points of relief. The wreck's identity was not known at that time, but it was charted as an obstruction and marked on nautical charts.

In 2013, NOAA's Office of Coast Survey and Office of National Marine Sanctuaries conducted a joint mission to survey the site with multibeam sonar, side scan sonar, and divers to conclusively identify the ROBERT J. WALKER. On 21 June 2013, the 153rd anniversary of ROBERT J. WALKER's loss, the NOAA ship *Thomas Jefferson* surveyed the wreck site with multibeam sonar and side scan sonar in conjunction with larger surveys as a result of hurricane Sandy conducted by the Office of Coast Survey (see Figures 5 and 6). On 22-23 June 2013, archaeologists from NOAA's Office of National Marine Sanctuary and an Office of Coast Survey hydrographer conducted a close-order side scan sonar survey of the site in addition to completing several dives on the site from the NOAA ship *SRVx*. The fieldwork sought to answer research questions about the site's characteristics and record the site's extant remains to augment earlier remote sensing work. The survey gathered sufficient information to determine the level of structural integrity and assess its remains to determine if it was potentially eligible for nomination to the National Register of Historic Places. Additional surveys of ROBERT J. WALKER are planned to continue the site assessment and archaeological analysis.

Page 23 - I suspect that James Delgado was responsible for seeing that recreational divers received credit for helping to identify the wreck. He might be the only NOAA employee who does not hate recreational divers with a passion. Although NOAA claimed that additional surveys were planned "to continue the site assessment and archaeological analysis," NOAA never conducted any such additional surveys. After wringing as much media attention as possible from identifying the wreck, NOAA has since ignored it and moved on to other ways to garner media attention.

NPS Form 10-900-a
OMB No. 1024-0018
United States Department of the Interior
National Park Service

ROBERT J. WALKER, shipwreck and remains
Name of Property
Offshore Atlantic, NJ
County and State

National Register of Historic Places Continuation Sheet

Name of multiple listing (if applicable)

Section number 7   Page 11

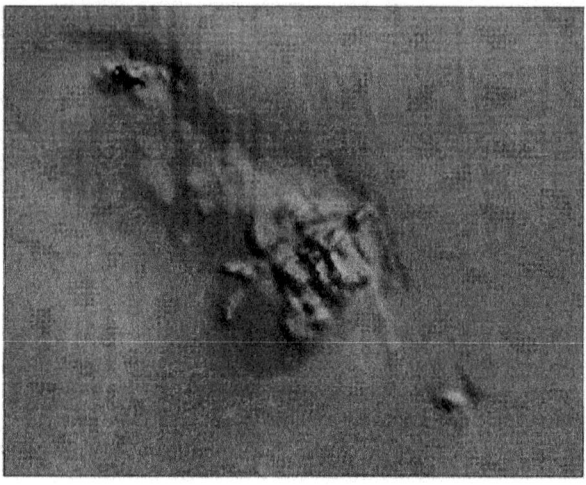

Figure 7. Multibeam sonar image of the ROBERT W. WALKER wreck site in 2013 (courtesy of NOAA's Office of Coast Survey). The steamship's bow is at the top left and the stern is located at the bottom right.

NPS Form 10-900-a
OMB No. 1024-0018
United States Department of the Interior
National Park Service

**National Register of Historic Places
Continuation Sheet**

ROBERT J. WALKER, shipwreck and remains
Name of Property
Offshore Atlantic, NJ
County and State

Name of multiple listing (if applicable)

Section number __7__ Page __12__

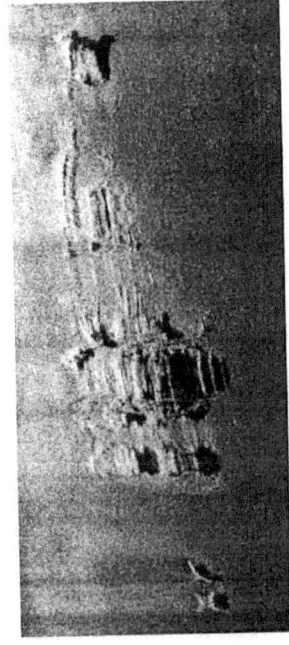

Figure 8. Side scan sonar image of the ROBERT W. WALKER wreck site in 2013 (courtesy of NOAA's Office of Coast Survey). The steamship's bow is at the top of the image and the stern is at the bottom of the image.

NPS Form 10-900-a
OMB No. 1024-0018

United States Department of the Interior
National Park Service

**National Register of Historic Places
Continuation Sheet**

ROBERT J. WALKER, shipwreck and remains
Name of Property
Offshore Atlantic, NJ
County and State

Name of multiple listing (if applicable)

Section number 8   Page 13

Section 8 – Statement of Significance

SUMMARY

ROBERT J. WALKER was built in the first half of the nineteenth century as the United States Government began to expand its role in the surveying, marking, and control of its coastal waters. At the same time, government entities and commercial business world-wide were adopting steam technology and iron hulls into their vessel fleets. The intact archaeological remains of the steamship ROBERT J. WALKER are significant at the national level under National Register of Historic Places Criteria A, C, and D.

ROBERT J. WALKER qualifies for listing under National Register of Historic Places Criteria A based upon the vessel's association with the development and growth of the United States' Coast Survey. The Coast Survey, established in 1807 by Thomas Jefferson, is America's oldest scientific government agency. The ROBERT J. WALKER was a small ship that accomplished a large job. Over the course of its twelve year career with the Coast Survey, its crew acquired over 700,000 hand lead-line soundings, charted the Gulf Coast from Mobile Bay to the Mississippi Passes, and made a substantial contribution to opening up many of the Gulf ports to increased commerce. ROBERT J. WALKER provided survey data that was a key step in establishing the parameters for safe navigation in support of commerce and industry of the United States during a period of national expansion. In addition, its mapping work would also prove invaluable in that it ultimately supported the Union Navy's planning efforts for actions on the Gulf Coast during the American Civil War. Hydrographic charts produced from the ROBERT J. WALKERs soundings proved vital to naval commanders. Surveys undertaken by the ROBERT J. WALKER's crew generated charts that informed the attack on New Orleans, the blockade of a number of ports, the establishment of Ship Island as a major base of operations, and the Battle of Mobile Bay. It also contributed to the scientific knowledge base of the Gulf of Mexico region by helping: 1) detail changes in bottom configuration of various areas with the passage of storms; 2) document the changing nature of the marshes of the Mississippi Delta region; 3) understand the tides of the Gulf of Mexico; and 4) understand the bottom configuration of the deep Gulf of Mexico by obtaining some of the first deep sea soundings in that area. The ROBERT J. WALKER made contributions far out of proportion to its physical stature as a small steamer with relatively small crews to the commercial, military, and scientific history of the Gulf Coast region.

ROBERT J. WALKER qualifies for listing under National Register of Historic Places Criteria C based upon the vessel's distinctive characteristics that embody a time of transition in iron steamship construction and use by the United States government. ROBERT J. WALKER was one of the first iron revenue cutters built for federal service and is the earliest known shipwreck of a U.S. Government iron-hulled steamship yet located and available for study. It was

Page 26 - The value of the *Robert J. Walker's* depth soundings cannot be over-emphasized.

NPS Form 10-900-a   OMB No. 1024-0018

United States Department of the Interior
National Park Service

ROBERT J. WALKER, shipwreck and remains
Name of Property
Offshore Atlantic, NJ
County and State

**National Register of Historic Places
Continuation Sheet**

Name of multiple listing (if applicable)

Section number __8__   Page __14__

specifically designed and constructed in a time when marine steam technology combined with iron steamship design was at its infancy. Its intact steam engine and associated machinery comprise the only known example of their type in existence today. Prior to the construction of the ROBERT J. WALKER and 7 other *Legare*-class steamships ordered by the Revenue Marine Service, only a single iron steamship had been built for the U. S. government. As noted above, the highly unusual Lighthall Patent horizontal half beam engines, of which there are no other examples in existence, installed in the steamship represents the government's attempts to identify the best technology for its vessels. ROBERT J. WALKER's engines and associated machinery represent the only known remains of this early type of American marine steam engine yet located and available for study. While it did not ultimately serve under the Revenue Marine, ROBERT J. WALKER successfully operated for the Coast Survey for twelve years proving that iron steamship technology was both feasibly, safe, reliable, and economical. ROBERT J. WALKER served the people of the United States by charting the coast's harbors and waterways that allowed the country to expand its commercial trade pathways and military networks on the eve of the Civil War.

ROBERT J. WALKER qualifies for listing under the National Register Criteria D based upon the archaeological site's likelihood to yield information import to history. ROBERT J. WALKER is the only one of the eight *Legare*-class iron steamships built by the Revenue Marine Service to be located and archaeologically documented. These steamships were the first steamships built for the Revenue Marine Service and laid the groundwork for the widespread use of iron steamship by the United States government. ROBERT J. WALKER's remains will provide information on early iron steamship construction. Only a few early American iron-hulled vessels have been located are accessible for study. Details about hull and machinery construction will add primary source data on a vessel type, whose builder's plans along with machinery blueprints, have been lost to history. Archaeological survey will also indicate if ROBERT J. WALKER was modified to meet the needs of the Coast Survey. For twelve years it surveyed mainly in the Gulf of Mexico and its remains might include alterations to more effectively operate in that specific area. Documentation of ROBERT J. WALKER's material culture will yield information about its crew and answer questions about ethnicity, social class, and shipboard life. ROBERT J. WALKER's crew was forced to quickly flee the sinking vessel, leaving their personal effects behind. Archaeological investigation of the shipwreck's hull, machinery, cargo, and cultural artifacts may provide information that will confirm or contradict historical records as recorded from the vessel's crew or otherwise not available due to a paucity of historical documentation.

Page 27 - It is true that archaeological investigations will likely provide information about contemporary life at sea, but so far NOAA has not bothered to conduct any such investigations. So what is the point?

NPS Form 10-900-a
United States Department of the Interior
National Park Service

OMB No. 1024-0018

ROBERT J. WALKER, shipwreck and remains
Name of Property
Offshore Atlantic, NJ
County and State
Name of multiple listing (if applicable)

National Register of Historic Places
Continuation Sheet

Section number 8   Page 15

UNITED STATES REVENUE MARINE SERVICE

Following the Revolutionary War, the fledgling United States was in significant debt to the creditors that financed the conflict. The nation needed a supply of income to fund the U. S. Federal government; import tariffs were seen as the solution to this problem. Widespread smuggling and illegal activities hampered the effectiveness of the tariff laws and prevented the government from raising the funds it needed to operate. To combat this problem an agency was needed to enforce tariff and general maritime law. "At first, the United States depended completely on revenue from merchant shipping to survive. No other federal taxes were collected during the nation's first five years under the Constitution" (King 1989:29). Establishment of a Federal maritime service was essential to manage American commerce and ensure that revenue flowed into Federal coffers.

The United States established the Revenue Marine Service (later renamed the Revenue Cutter Service in 1894), a predecessor of today's U. S. Coast Guard, to provide assistance to the government in the protection of its resources and uphold the revenue laws. Alexander Hamilton, the first Secretary of the Treasury, called for the construction and operation of revenue cutters that would patrol the coastal waters to ensure compliance with customs and revenue laws while protecting against smuggling and illegal activities. On 4 August 1790, Congress passed Hamilton's bill which authorized the creation of a revenue service to, "regulate the collection of the duties imposed by law on the tonnage of ships or vessels, and on goods, wares, and merchandise, imported into the United States" (Smith 1932: 1). The act called for the construction and outfitting of a fleet of ten vessels at a cost $1,000.00, each manned by two officers and six marines (see Table 1). Armament onboard consisted of swivel guns, muskets, bayonets, and pistols.

The fleet was to be distributed along the United States coast as follows: two for Massachusetts and New Hampshire, one for Long Island Sound, one for New York, one for Delaware Bay, two for the Chesapeake, one for North Carolina, one for South Carolina, and one for Georgia (King 1989:5). The first ten commissioned revenue cutters, *Vigilant, Active, General Green, Massachusetts, Scammel, Argus, Virginia, Diligence, South Carolina,* and *Eagle,* were small sailing vessels with shallow drafts (4 to 7 feet). Each was rigged as a schooner or sloop, measured from 40-60 feet in length with beams from 15-17 feet and a tonnage of 35-50. By 1793, all ten had been launched and were in active service (King 1989:13-14).

NPS Form 10-900-a
OMB No. 1024-0018
United States Department of the Interior
National Park Service

National Register of Historic Places
Continuation Sheet

Name of Property: ROBERT J. WALKER, shipwreck and remains
County and State: Offshore Atlantic, NJ
Name of multiple listing (if applicable):

Section number 8   Page 16

Name	Builder	Launched	Dimensions (L x B)	Rig	Fate
Massachusetts	Searle and Tyler (MA)	7/23/1791	60' x 17'8"	schooner	sold Oct. 1792
Argus	unknown (CT)	1791	47'9" x 16'3"	schooner, altered to sloop	sold 1804
General Green	unknown (PA)	8/5/1791		schooner	sold Dec 1797
Scammel	unknown (NH)	8/24/1791	57'10" x 15'8"	schooner	sold Aug 1798
Vigilant	unknown (NY)	1791	48' x 15'	schooner, altered to sloop	sold Sept 1798
Virginia	unknown (VA)	1791	40' x 17'	schooner	sold 1798
Active	David Stodder (MD)	4/9/1791		schooner	sold 1800
Diligence	unknown (NC)	June 1792		schooner	sold Nov 1798
South Carolina	unknown (SC)	1793		schooner	sold 1798
Eagle	unknown (GA)	1793		schooner	sold 1799

Table 1. First ten cutters of the U.S. Revenue Marine Service (Canney 1995:2-4).

The Revenue Marine Service's original duties included boarding incoming and outgoing vessels to check registration and manifest documentation to insure cargoes were correctly documented, sealing cargo holds of incoming vessels, and seizing vessels in violation of the law. Due to the limited ability of the United States government to have an on water presence, as there was no Navy, the revenue cutters expanded their responsibilities to include actions not related to protecting revenue. They included enforcing quarantine restrictions, charting the coast, and enforcing neutrality and embargo acts (King 1989:30-31). Despite the various responsibilities placed on the new revenue cutters service, their primary job was protecting the country's revenue and deterring smuggling. The cutters were the nation's first line of defense and the only maritime law enforcement force until the Naval Act of 1794 created the first Navy of the United States of America (Coast Guard 2013:slide 7).

The revenue cutters immediately proved to be a crucial arm of the government, but their small size limited their effectiveness. Soon a new group of cutters comprised of faster brigs and schooners with a larger tonnage and more heavily armed joined the service. The cutters were pulled from their duties during the Quasi-War with France between 1798 and 1801 to aid the U.S. Navy by patrolling the French waters off the West Indies for privateers. A total of 45 U.S. vessels served in the conflict including eight revenue cutters, even capturing several armed prizes (King 1989:20, 24). The cutter's effectiveness for law enforcement led Congress in 1799 to authorize the President to maintain as many revenue cutters as needed to provide the appropriate collection of import and tonnage duties. The Revenue Marine Service continued to expand not

NPS Form 10-900-a
OMB No. 1024-0018
United States Department of the Interior
National Park Service

**National Register of Historic Places
Continuation Sheet**

ROBERT J. WALKER, shipwreck and remains
Name of Property
Offshore Atlantic, NJ
County and State
Name of multiple listing (if applicable)

Section number 8   Page 17

only in numbers of vessels, but in its responsibilities. Peacetime operations were put on hold again during the War of 1812, the Mexican-American War, the Seminole Wars, and also during the fight against the slave trade and piracy off Florida and in the Caribbean. "In many instances, revenue cutters formed integral parts of joint naval (and, at times Army) operations in these campaigns" (Canney 1995:1).

In 1832, Secretary of the Treasury Louis McLane issued orders for the revenue cutters to conduct winter cruises to aid mariners in need. By 1837 Congress officially sanctioned these efforts. This was the start of government lifesaving missions that later led to the formation of the U.S. Life Saving Service and eventually the U.S. Coast Guard (Canney 1995:1).

> These diversified missions resulted in some marked variations in cutter design through the years. The first revenue vessels built from 1791 to 1792 were relatively small – 50 to 75 tons – and, as mentioned earlier, not fitted for ordnance. The onset of the war with France resulted in a class obviously built for war purposes; over 100 tons and rated at fourteen guns. . . . By the 1830s the size of cutters was again at the 100 ton range, particularly those serving in the heavier weather off New England (Canney 1995:1).

Up until the late 1830s and early 1840s, the United States Revenue Marine Service focused on contracts to build wooden sailing revenue cutters. Vessel design was dictated by the economics of construction, operation, and speed. Wooden vessels were economical and designs well-tested so those became the vessel of choice for many decades. In addition, to building its own vessels, the service also chartered or purchased additional vessels to supplement their construction efforts. Between 1791 and 1843, 125 vessels, mainly sloops, schooners, and topsails schooners had served in the Revenue Marine Service (see Table 2).

Time Period	Vessel Class	Number (built, purchased, or chartered)	Type	Tons
1791-1793		11	schooners	35-70
1793		3	2 sloops and 1 schooner	50-98
1797-1798	*Diligence* class	7	3 brigs, 3 schooner, 1 unknown	131-143
1798-1814		42	25 unknown, 8 schooners, 3 brigs, 4 sloops, 2 galleys	65-195
1815	*Surprise* class	2	2 topsail schooners	51
1815	*Search* class	2	2 topsail schooners	65

NPS Form 10-900-a
OMB No. 1024-0018

United States Department of the Interior
National Park Service

**National Register of Historic Places
Continuation Sheet**

ROBERT J. WALKER, shipwreck and remains
Name of Property
Offshore Atlantic, NJ
County and State

Name of multiple listing (if applicable)

Section number 8   Page 18

Date	Class	Count	Types	Range
1815-1819		7	6 unknown, 1 schooner	38-79
1819	*Alabama* class	2	2 topsail schooners	56
1819-1825		5	2 unknown, 2 schooners, 2 topsail schooners	73-75
1825	*Marion* class	2	2 schooners	115
1825		1	1 schooner	110
1825	*Wasp* class	2	2 schooners	62
1825-1830		6	4 unknown, 2 schooners	18-74
1830-1833	*Morris-Taney* class	13	13 topsail schooners	112
1830-1843		20	8 unknown, 7 schooners, 3 topsail schooners, 1 brig, 1 sloop	40-190

Table 2. U.S. Revenue Marine Service vessels prior to the construction of ROBERT J. WALKER and the seven other *Legare* class iron steamships (Canney 1995:2-19).

While United States and British naval architects had experimented with steam power and iron hulls since the 1820s, the Revenue Marine Service did not consider building a iron steamship until the 1840s. Instead, the Revenue Marine Service closely followed the trials and tribulations the American and British navies faced adopting iron steamship technology.

DEVELOPMENT OF IRON NAVAL STEAMSHIPS

Naval commanders immediately grasped the tactical advantage offered by steam propulsion. No longer dependent on the wind, the fight could be carried to the enemy at the most opportune time. However, the unreliability of early steam machinery prevented the immediate adoption of the technology. Following the advent of commercial steam navigation in the first decade of the nineteenth century, steam propulsion technology achieved sufficient reliability for naval consideration. In 1814, the United States Navy took the very first step with the *Demologos*. Designed by Robert Fulton, the floating gun battery used a single, central paddle wheel. Slated to protect New York Harbor during the War of 1812, the craft was delivered to the U. S. Navy in 1816, long after the conflict ended. It ultimately served a single day in active service before being reduced to a barge in 1821 (Gardiner 1993:14).

The next American naval steamer to appear on the scene was the wooden-hulled *Seagull* hired by the U.S. Navy in 1822 to serve as an unarmed dispatch and transport steamer to suppress piracy in the shallow waters around the West Indies. Laid up in 1825 and ultimately sold in 1840, the *Sea Gull* failed to impress the U.S. Navy (Bennett 1896:16). More significantly, steam pioneers

NPS Form 10-900-a　　　　　　　　　　　　　　　　　　　　　　　　　　　　　OMB No. 1024-0018
United States Department of the Interior
National Park Service

ROBERT J. WALKER, shipwreck and remains
Name of Property
Offshore Atlantic, NJ
County and State
Name of multiple listing (if applicable)

**National Register of Historic Places
Continuation Sheet**

Section number 8   Page 19

Charles Napier and Aaron Manby built the first seagoing iron-hulled steamship, the British merchant steamer *Aaron Manby*, in 1821(Gardiner 1993:60).

Following the experiment with the *Sea Gull*, the U.S. Navy abandoned the technology for another decade during which time significant advances in steamship technology were made in commercial vessels. In 1821, Britain launched its first paddle wheel vessel for the navy, the steam tug *Comet* (Brown 1993:11). This was followed by a spate of smaller paddle wheel steamers, twenty in number, through the 1830s. In 1831, the Royal Navy had fourteen steamships, eight of them in commission (Brown 1993:16). Small, and fitted with oscillating or side-lever steam engines ranging from 80 to 200 nominal horsepower, these vessels were ultimately armed and many served through the 1860s (Brown 1933:13-16). Nearly, two decades after the *Demologos*, America's second naval steamer, the wooden-hulled *Fulton II*, was launched in 1837. A failure as an seagoing vessel *Fulton II* was found to be much better suited for harbor defense (Gardiner 1993:17, 19). The 1830s and 1840s were a period of continued adoption of steam mainly in Great Britain, and experiments in design of the hulls, machinery and propulsion, or, as Brown (1993) termed it, "a time of change." American shipyards launched the wooden hulled paddle wheel steamships *Missouri* and *Mississippi* in 1841. The two paddle frigates served successfully along the coast and in rivers with their conventional ship hulls and side lever engines (Gardiner 1993:27).

The switch to iron hulls for steamships in the United States and in Great Britain occurred within a few years of each other. In 1841/1842 plans were drawn up for the paddle wheel steamer *USS Michigan*, American first iron-hulled naval steamship. The *Michigan* was subsequently launched in December 1843 (Bennett 1896:44). Britain followed suit and ordered its first iron-hulled steamship in January 1843. Launched by Ditchburn & Mare in 1846, the 850-ton, 180-foot long, 31 foot, 6-inch beam steamer *Trident* was classified as third-class sloop fitted with a Boulton & Watt oscillating engine rated at 350 nominal horsepower and armed with two 10-inch guns on pivot mounts and two 32-pound carronades (Brown 1993:42). Within two years of *Trident*'s completion, Great Britain laid down its last paddlewheel-driven warship, *Barracouta*, in 1848, transitioning away from the limitations of imposed by paddlewheel technology (Brown 1993:42).

While the switch to iron hulls for naval and steamships was gradual it was soon realized their benefits were substantial. Iron hulls did not weigh as much as a comparable wooden hull (about 20 percent less) and with smaller frames and bulkheads possessing about 20 percent more internal space, and being a rigid structure were "better able to resist vibration" from steam machinery than wood. While not always favored because of the brittle nature of wrought iron, improvements in metallurgy and steam machinery in the 1850s and 1860s and the battle success of ironclads in the Civil War ultimately led to the abandonment of wooden-hulled warships.

NPS Form 10-900-a   OMB No. 1024-0018

United States Department of the Interior
National Park Service

ROBERT J. WALKER, shipwreck and remains
Name of Property
Offshore Atlantic, NJ
County and State

National Register of Historic Places Continuation Sheet

Name of multiple listing (if applicable)

Section number 8   Page 20

EXPERIMENTATION WITH IRON REVENUE CUTTERS

In February 1837, Secretary of the Treasury Andrew Jackson presented the House of Representatives with a cost estimate for the construction of an iron revenue cutter, taking the first step towards building of a Federal iron steamship fleet. Justification for the use of iron hulls came from the belief that the iron vessels would be more effective than traditional wooden sailing vessels, especially in the winter, for assisting vessels in distress. In 1839, the Boston *Journal* wrote that, "We learn that a petition to Congress to establish a steam cutter in this service, has been prepared, and is now awaiting signatures. Every merchant, indeed every man interested in navigation, (and who is not) should sign it" (Smith 1932:46). In January 1844, a Revenue Marine Service report provided additional rationale for the use of iron steamships. The report recommended iron steamships to interdict smuggling by steamboats on the Great Lakes. Furthermore, steamships could patrol the approaches to ports where strong currents and variable winds made it difficult for a sailing vessel to perform the job of enforcing revenue laws in all weather conditions.

Built for the United States Revenue Service for the enforcement of customs, ROBERT J. WALKER was one of eight transitional iron-hulled steamships constructed in the 1840s by the United States Government to "naval designs." The steamships were to test, through practical application, various theories of construction and propulsion – in the latter, different types of paddlewheels as well as propellers. Enthusiasm in the ranks of the Revenue Marine for iron hulls was captured by Captain William A. Howard who asserted that not only would iron-hulled steamers be stronger than wood, but that they would also not rot, be damaged by marine borers, and would cost 50 percent less to repair over a 20-year time period than a comparable wooden ship (Browning 1992:26). "He [Commandant of the Revenue Marine, Captain Alexander V. Fraser] figured a 350-ton iron steamer would cost $50,000, a wooden sail boat of the same size, $62,500" (King 1989:117). Fraser went onto write in the 1843 annual report of the United States Revenue Marine that:

> The principle advantages arising from the use of iron are; economy in the original construction; durability, lightness of material, and consequently, increased buoyancy; increased strength, particularly in the ability to withstand shocks sustained by taking the ground when passing shoal water bars; and the value when worn out, of the old materials (Smith 1932:59).

The U.S. Navy was at the same time also building its first iron steamer; the gunboat USS *Michigan*, expressly for service on the Great Lakes in 1843 (Rodgers 1996). Built by

NPS Form 10-900-a
OMB No. 1024-0018
United States Department of the Interior
National Park Service

**National Register of Historic Places
Continuation Sheet**

Name of Property: ROBERT J. WALKER, shipwreck and remains
County and State: Offshore Atlantic, NJ
Name of multiple listing (if applicable):

Section number 8   Page 21

Stackhouse and Tomlinson of Pittsburg, Penn. the side paddle wheel steamship measured 177 feet long. Its wrought iron hull proved to be incredibly long-lived, it served in the American Civil War and remained on the U.S. Navy's rolls until 1927. While this was a period of steady adoption of iron in shipbuilding, it remained highly individualistic as various yards and builders experimented. A few decades into the process, the major marine insurance company in the world, Lloyds of London, had not adopted standards for iron ships as the technology was "still in its infancy" without any "well-understood general rules" (Lloyds 1884:77).

For some time the United States government marine services had been interested in finding alternatives not only to wooden hulls, but to the side paddle wheel design for warships. Traditional side mounted paddle wheels positioned outside the hull at amidships made them vulnerable to damage either while in port, at sea, or by an enemy action. Furthermore, the paddle wheels limited the armament carried broadside. Naval architects designed alternatives to the standard side paddle wheel design, many of which were eventually tried by the Revenue Marine Service.

> John Ericsson and Richard Loper had patented screw propellers, and Navy Lieutenant William Hunter proposed horizontally mounted paddle wheels, which rotated merry-go-round style within the hull, below the waterline. Apertures in the hull sides allowed the paddles wheels to act on the surrounding waters. Hunter had succeed in interesting the Navy in his idea, and the Revenue Service followed suit (Canney 195:20).

By the 1840s, the Revenue Marine Service needed to update and increase its fleet to expand the reach of its patrols. Several important ports such as New Bedford, Portsmouth, Lake Ontario, and the area off Florida's coast between Pensacola and the Tortugas were unguarded. New vessels were requested by the service to provide service at these stations (Smith 1932:58). At that time, the existing Revenue Marine Service fleet consisted solely of wooden schooners so the government decided to experiment with using iron steamships to determine if this new vessel type would be appropriate for future widespread use. The plan was not considered lightly, it took the endorsement of the idea by "prominent personages, voluminous petitions, signed by wealthy corporations and leading merchants" who believed that iron steamships would, "prove of inestimable benefit to commerce, while trebling the efficiency, and enhancing tenfold, the usefulness of the Revenue Marine." The introduction of steam, as a motive power, into the Revenue Marine Service, forms an eventful and suggestive chapter in its history (Smith 1932:62).

While Captain Fraser advocated for the construction of iron steamships for the service, "he failed to anticipate the enormous difficulties that would confront the service during the transition away

NPS Form 10-900-a
United States Department of the Interior
National Park Service

**National Register of Historic Places
Continuation Sheet**

OMB No. 1024-0018

ROBERT J. WALKER, shipwreck and remains
Name of Property
Offshore Atlantic, NJ
County and State
Name of multiple listing (if applicable)

Section number __8__ Page __22__

from wood and sail. Nor did he take into account the primitive state of marine engineering, the difficulty of combining sail and steam, or the problem of selecting a proper propulsion system" (King 1989:117). The Revenue Marine Service proceeded with an initial request for bids to construct six iron steamers in April 1843, and soon had contracts in place to build the steamers *Spencer*, *Bibb*, *Dallas*, and *McLane*, with Hunter's experimental paddlewheel, and two steamers, *Legare* and *Jefferson*, with Ericsson's helicoidal propellers (Browning 1992:27). The contracts for the six steamers were followed by contracts for two side-wheel steamships; *Polk* and ROBERT J. WALKER, in December 1844 and January 1845 (see Table 3).

> The steamers now in the course of construction are of such models as will insure their performance under canvas alone, equally if not better than those built of wood, while steam is intended to be used as an auxiliary motive power in case of necessity, in chase or entering and departing from harbors during the prevalence of adverse winds and tide; the expenditure of fuel, and the necessity of its use, to be strictly accounted for by the commanders (Smith 1932:59).

While work on the last two steamers slowly progressed, the Hunter wheel propelled vessels proved to be immediate failures. They were leaky, slow and inefficient in their consumption of coal and had excessive wear and tear on their machinery necessitating expensive repairs and cost overruns. Ultimately, the Hunter's wheel steamers were refitted with new propulsion systems. The Hunter's wheels on the *Bibb*, *Dallas*, and *McLean* were replaced with traditional side paddle wheels and the Hunter's wheel on the *Spencer* was replaced in 1845 with two propellers. The *Spencer* thus became the first twin screw steamship in U. S. government service.

Name	Dimensions (L x W in feet)	Launch	Builder	Propulsion	Revenue Marine Service Duty	Fate
Legare	160 x 24	1843 or 1844	R. and G.L. Schuyler (NY)	Ericson's propeller	1844-47	To Coast Survey 1847, converted to lightship
Spencer	160 x 24	1844	West Point Foundry Co (NY)	Hunter's wheels, changed to propellers 1845		Converted to lightship
Jefferson	160 x 24	1845	Freeman, Knapp, and Totten (PA)	Ericson's propeller	1845-49	To Coast Survey 1849
Bibb	160 x 24	10 April 1845	Freeman, Knapp, and Totten (PA)	Hunter's wheels, changed to side	1845-47	To Coast Survey 1847,

NPS Form 10-900-a
United States Department of the Interior
National Park Service

**National Register of Historic Places
Continuation Sheet**

OMB No. 1024-0018

ROBERT J. WALKER, shipwreck and remains
Name of Property
Offshore Atlantic, NJ
County and State
Name of multiple listing (if applicable)

Section number 8   Page 23

				paddle wheel		decommissioned 1879
Dallas	160 x 24	4 April 1846	Stilliman, Statton and Co (NY)	Hunter's wheels, changed to side paddle wheel	1846-48	To Coast Survey 1849, sold 1851
McLane	160 x 24	Between Feb and Nov 1846	Cyrus Alger (MA)	Hunter's wheels, , changed to side paddle wheel	1845-47	Sold 1847, Converted to floating light
Polk	160 x 24	1846 or 1847	Anderson (VA)	Side paddle wheels, altered to bark (1848)	1845-54	Sold 1854
Robert J. Walker	160 x 24	Nov/Dec 1847	Thomlinson (PA)	Side paddle wheels	1847-48	To Coast Survey 1847, Sank of NJ in 1860

Table 3. *Legare*-Class Iron Steamships (Canney 1995: 20).

The first six revenue cutters assumed their duties shortly after launch and trials. The *Legare* took up station on the Florida coast where it served until transferred to the Gulf of Mexico in 1846 to support the U.S. Navy during the Mexican-American War. After that service it was transferred to the U.S. Coast Survey and eventually turned into a lightship. The *Spencer* was first stationed in New York until being retrofitted with propellers in 1845. It was also sent south to support the navy's efforts, supplying the U. S. forces in Texas throughout 1846 when it took up station in Virginia. The *Spencer* was transformed into a lightship in 1848. The *Jefferson* worked on Lake Ontario until being transferred to the U.S. Coast Survey in 1849. After its initial sea trials, the *Bibb* almost immediately had its Hunter's wheels converted to traditional side paddle wheels. It then worked off New Orleans before being involved with blockade duty off the Mexican coast during the Mexican-American War in 1846. In 1847, the U.S. Coast Survey took command of the *Bibb*. The *Dallas* had its Hunter's wheel removed after its launch and replaced with side paddle wheels. It was transferred to the U.S. Coast Survey in 1848, but was never put into service and later sold in 1851. The *McLane* also had its Hunter's wheel removed after launched and replaced with side paddle wheels. It supported the American involvement in the Mexican American War during 1846 by transporting troops and supplies and sold in 1847 and later turned into a floating light (U.S. Coast Guard 1989:105-111, 389, 394).

Weather and labor problems significantly delayed the *Polk*'s construction; it was eventually completed at Richmond, Virginia in March 1847. It joined the fleet and was ordered to support the U.S. Navy in the Gulf of Mexico. After it was found to leak badly, the steamship was returned to the Treasury Department where it patrolled off New York for a year before being converted to a bark in 1848. It continued to serve with the Revenue Marine Service until 1854

NPS Form 10-900-a
OMB No. 1024-0018

United States Department of the Interior
National Park Service

**National Register of Historic Places
Continuation Sheet**

ROBERT J. WALKER, shipwreck and remains
Name of Property
Offshore Atlantic, NJ
County and State

Name of multiple listing (if applicable)

Section number 8   Page 24

when it was moved to California and sold. The *Polk* served the Revenue Marine Service longer than any of the other seven sister steamships (U.S. Coast Guard 1989:128).

CONSTRUCTION OF ROBERT J. WALKER

Despite problems with the other seven iron steamers, the Revenue Marine Service continued its plans to build one last steamship, named ROBERT J. WALKER. The steamship was slated for station on Mobile Bay, one of the Revenue Marine Services key coastal ports. The contract to build ROBERT J. WALKER was issued in 1846, but work did not commence until March 1847. The contract for the steamer was issued to Pittsburgh shipyard of Joseph Tomlinson. Poor weather and material supply problems delayed the start of work. Disputes between the Revenue Marine and Joseph Tomlinson, its builder, as well as poor quality construction drawings led to an order to defer the launch of the steamer for a few months (Browning 1992:34). On 30 March 1847 the *Richmond Enquirer* reported that work on the ROBERT J. WALKER was arrested due to the failure of the *Polk*. On 21 May 1847 the *Times-Picayune* falsely reported that ROBERT J. WALKER's construction had been cancelled in consequence of the *Polk*'s failure. Ultimately, Tomlinson completed the steamship and finally launched it on 27 November 1847. Named for United States Senator Robert John Walker of Mississippi (1801-1869), who served as Secretary of the Treasury in the cabinet of President James K. Polk from 1845 to 1849, ROBERT J. WALKER cost $104,825.53 (Department of the Treasury 1847:68). Richard Evans, the Commandant of the Revenue Marine and initial master called the steamer "the finest iron vessel ever built in this country" (Browning 1992:34).

Joseph Tomlinson and his business partner Samuel Stackhouse were ship and engine-builders of considerable reputation. Tomlinson, a Philadelphia native, moved to Pittsburgh in 1816 with his parents. He went on to establish an iron foundry and machine shop. During the War of 1812 the foundry he purchased had provided Oliver Hazard Perry's ships with anchors. Under Tomlinson, it was said to have built more "boats" than any other shipbuilder in the western country including the *Michigan*, the Navy's first iron warship (Rodgers 1996:11). Tomlinson, in addition to ships and engines later built rail cars and constructed two ironclad river monitors for the U.S. Navy at the end of the Civil War.

After being rigged and being fitted with its 32-pounder guns and ammunition, the ROBERT J. WALKER left Pittsburgh on 14 December 1847 for New Orleans (Pittsburgh *Daily Gazette*, May 4, November 29, December 15, 1847). On that date, the *Semi-Weekly Natchez Courier* noted that the "new iron steamer 'Robert J. Walker', lately built at Pittsburgh, has been launched, and may soon be expected down the Mississippi River, on her way to the Gulf of Mexico (Natchez, Mississippi *Semi-Weekly Natchez Courier*, December 14, 1847).

NPS Form 10-900-a
United States Department of the Interior
National Park Service

National Register of Historic Places
Continuation Sheet

ROBERT J. WALKER, shipwreck and remains
Name of Property
Offshore Atlantic, NJ
County and State
Name of multiple listing (if applicable)

Section number 8   Page 25

Instead of heading to Mobile as planned, ROBERT J. WALKER was transferred by the Revenue Marine Service to the United States Coast Survey at New Orleans on 11 February 1848. The reason for the quick transfer was explained in 1852 by Benjamin Isherwood, Chief Engineer of the United States Navy:

> The experiment tried by the Treasury, of substituting steam for sailing cutters, having signally failed from the too large size of the steamers, the expense of maintaining them, and the abortive character of their machinery and propelling instruments, they were either turned over to the Coast Survey, or otherwise disposed of. Of the eight, only three now remain in the Government service, viz: the *Legarè*, the *Bibb*, and the *Walker*, and they are employed as Surveying Steamers" (Isherwood 1852:49-50).

"In all, the experience was a disaster. The service built eight steamers at a total cost of $620,000.00 and not one proved adequate as a cutter" (King 1989:120). Providentially, the ROBERT J. WALKER became available to the U.S. Coast Survey at a time when the agency was growing to chart the coastal waters to provide safe navigational routes to mariners around the United States. The Coast Survey would be the only ones to profit from the failure of the iron revenue cutters. Five of them, including ROBERT J. WALKER, were transferred to the Coast Survey between 1847 and 1849 (Canney 1995:20).

GROWTH OF THE UNITED STATES COAST SURVEY

The United States Coast Survey, established in 1807, was expanding its coastal surveys under an energetic new Superintendent, Alexander Dallas Bache. Appointed in 1843, Bach succeed the first Superintendent Ferdinand Hassler, who had initially led the Survey from 1816-1818, and then resumed his post when the Survey was reauthorized and commenced duties again in 1832. Coincidentally, A. D. Bache's brother-in-law was Treasury Secretary Robert J. Walker. The 1807 legislation that started the U. S. Coast Survey authorized the President to begin a survey of the coast of the United States including the islands and shoals, with roads or places of anchorage, within twenty leagues of the shore along with determining the distances between principle capes or head lands (Shalowitz 1964b: 4). Congress did not provide appropriations for the agency until 1843 and at the same time extended the survey limits seaward to include soundings to 120 fathoms deep (Shalowitz 1964b: 9).

The Coast Survey was the first major scientific agency of the U.S. government, formed initially as a geodetic survey network, but it expanded its reach taking on both topographic surveys and hydrographic surveys in coastal waters. Surveys mapped the land and water simultaneously

NPS Form 10-900-a
United States Department of the Interior
National Park Service

OMB No. 1024-0018

**National Register of Historic Places
Continuation Sheet**

ROBERT J. WALKER, shipwreck and remains
Name of Property
Offshore Atlantic, NJ
County and State

Name of multiple listing (if applicable)

Section number 8   Page 26

using the same coastal triangulation stations to produce views of coastal features such as lighthouses and entrances to harbors combined on charts showing underwater features (Cloud 2011:6). The first survey work called for by Hassler focused on New York, but when Bache took control in 1843 he, "divided the Atlantic coast, and later the Gulf and Pacific coasts, into numbered sections of the coast. He insisted that survey work proceed in every section, every year" (Cloud 2011:7).

While the Coast Survey was officially a civilian agency, its officers and men mainly came from the Navy and Army and frequently Navy ships were employed for survey work. The officers had watched the arrival of steam with considerable interest and advocated for the use of steamers in survey work because of the "independence of steam against wind and tide":

> Having the means of going in any direction, the surveyor is able to make a comprehensive and careful project of his work, and to carry it out with certainty; while, with sails only, he is obliged to accommodate his traverse to the direction of the wind and the course of the tide, and generally much time is lost in retracing his steps to windward to obtain a suitable position…the most favorable days for sounding are those on which the sea is calm, and then the steamer will accomplish the best work, both in amount and quality; but the sailing vessel lies idle for want of motive power. When sounding in deep water, it is often necessary to lessen the speed in order to get the depth accurately, and to ascertain the character of the bottom. The steam-vessel docs this easily, without diverging from her track; the sail vessel must change her course and lie to. By this, time is lost, labor is increased, and the continuity of the lines is broken (Coast Survey 1847:85).

Therefore, while the Revenue Marine Service was unhappy with their new steamers' performance, speed was not a requirement for a survey steamship, and as the poorest part of the government's sea services, the Coast Survey was willing to accept the Revenue Marine's cast-offs. The United States Coast Survey was also a sister agency of the Revenue Service, and both operated under the auspices of the United States Treasury Department. The Revenue Service temporarily reverted to sailing vessels while the Coast Survey embraced steam technology, particularly for offshore operations. The first of these vessels was *Bibb*, followed by ROBERT J. WALKER, *Legare*, *Dallas*, and *Jefferson*. An additional steam vessel, *Hetzel*, was transferred from the Army quartermaster department while a small steamer, *Active*, was procured on the Pacific coast, following the loss of *Jefferson* on the coast of Patagonia while in transit to San Francisco.

NPS Form 10-900-a
United States Department of the Interior
National Park Service

**National Register of Historic Places
Continuation Sheet**

OMB No. 1024-0018

ROBERT J. WALKER, shipwreck and remains
Name of Property
Offshore Atlantic, NJ
County and State
Name of multiple listing (if applicable)

Section number 8   Page 27

As Historian Albert Theberge notes, ROBERT J. WALKER joined the Coast Survey at a time when, under Bache, the agency

> .... experienced a remarkable expansion in its operations and responsibilities. Geographically, the coasts of Texas, Washington, Oregon, and California were added to the United States. New projects were begun and old functions expanded. The coastal triangulation network was continued north into Maine and south to Cape Hatteras, while beginnings of survey work were made in South Carolina, Georgia, Florida, Alabama, Mississippi, Louisiana, and Texas. Survey crews were sent to the western coast, although work did not begin there in earnest until 1850. Studies of the Gulf Stream were commenced in 1845 by the Coast Survey in a project that heralded the beginnings of modern oceanography. Many improvements were introduced in instrumentation and methodology that greatly improved the efficiency and accuracy of the work. The project to determine the differences of longitude between prominent points on the eastern seaboard of the United States and European observatories continued. The major hydrographic accomplishment of this half decade was the survey of Nantucket Shoals. These few years marked the period when Bache placed his indelible stamp upon the Coast Survey and were halcyon days with discoveries, inventions, and increased responsibilities coming one after the other (Theberge 1998:144).

In a mutually beneficial arrangement, naval officers were assigned to the Coast Survey. This afforded early command opportunities for these officers as well as training them in aspects of navigation, charting, inshore piloting, and other naval skills. With the addition of steam vessels, the Coast Survey became even more desirable as a training ground. For many naval officers attached to the Survey at this time, this was their first experience with steam vessels, preparing them for the upcoming conflict. The commanding officers of these vessels read like a "Who's Who" of Civil War fame as David Dixon Porter, John Rodgers, Samuel Philips Lee, C.R.P. Rodgers, Thornton Jenkins, Daniel Ammen, C. H. McBlair and Alban Stimers among others all served in the Coast Survey's steamships. These ships became an intrinsic part of great national endeavors driven by remarkable changes in transportation technology, new insights in science, and the unprecedented expansion of United States Coast line in the first half of the 19th Century.

ROBERT J. WALKER'S CAREER WITH COAST SURVEY

By the time ROBERT J. WALKER joined the Coast Survey in February 1848, the U. S. Coast Survey was active in every state along the Atlantic and Gulf coasts including Florida. Field

Page 40 - Note that Alban Stimers was not a commanding officer; he was a chief engineer. His greatest and most deserved claim to fame occurred when he served in his official capacity as chief engineer aboard the Civil War ironclad *Monitor* when she fought against the Confederate ironclad *Virginia* in the Battle of Hampton Roads. See *Ironclad Legacy* for more details.

NPS Form 10-900-a
OMB No. 1024-0018

United States Department of the Interior
National Park Service

National Register of Historic Places Continuation Sheet

ROBERT J. WALKER, shipwreck and remains
Name of Property
Offshore Atlantic, NJ
County and State
Name of multiple listing (if applicable)

Section number 8   Page 28

parties were deployed to work in different parts of the country at the same time and during the winter months operations moved south so year-round work could be accomplished (Slotten 1994:80). ROBERT J. WALKER was assigned to the portion of the United States coastline designated Section VIII by the Coast Survey. This section extended from Dauphin Island to Vermillion Bay including the coasts of Alabama, Mississippi, and Louisiana. The primary working area of ROBERT J. WALKER remained Section VIII for the next twelve years.

Since 1834, hydrographic surveys, or charting of the seafloor, had been in progress in U. S. waters to document the navigable waters around the country. Hydrographers recorded the water depth or soundings, bottom characteristics (rocks, mud, sand, etc.), and hazards. Soundings were then analyzed to determine the contours of the submerged land. Measurements were taken to determine the boats geographic location (latitude and longitude) based on known control stations ashore. Until the invention of echo sounders in World War I, surveys were made with hand thrown lead and line or with a graduated sounding pole (Shalowitz 1964b: 53).

> Measuring depth for navigational purposes was a relatively straight-forward operation. A sailor, standing in the bow or working from a small boat, cast a lead attached to a line over the side and let it run through his hands. He counted the markings on the line that indicated how many fathoms had run out until he felt it hit the bottom. . . . surveyors not only carried out lines of sounding within a harbor or port, but also ran longer lines out to sea to record the approach to shore. Increasingly higher standards of surveying prompted hydrographers to carry lines of soundings farther and farther out to sea (Rozwadowski 2005:70-71).

Data was then turned into nautical charts for mariners. Additional features on the nautical charts might be locations of aids to navigation, tide and current information, and magnetic variations affecting compasses. Charts were essential to promote commerce and develop trade around the world. The movement of goods between harbors, fishing, shipbuilding, and defense all depended on safe navigable water. The first published Coast Survey nautical chart is from 1835 of Bridgeport Harbor, Connecticut (Shalowitz 1964b: 89).

> In the early years of the Bureau's history, when the Nation's commerce was carried in comparatively small, shallow-draft, sailing ships, it was unnecessary to extend surveys offshore into deep water. With the advent of the steamer, however, and its subsequent increase in size, draft, and speed, the early requirements were radically modified, and the emphasis gradually shifted from shoal to deep water (Shalowitz 1964b: 231).

NPS Form 10-900-a   OMB No. 1024-0018
United States Department of the Interior
National Park Service   ROBERT J. WALKER, shipwreck and
                                                              remains
                                                              Name of Property
National Register of Historic Places   Offshore Atlantic, NJ
Continuation Sheet   County and State
                                                              Name of multiple listing (if applicable)
Section number 8   Page 29

Time Period	Commander	Survey Area(s)
11 February 1848 – 1849	Carlile P. Patterson	Mobile Bay
1849-1851	James Alden	Mobile Bay, Florida
1851	Samuel Phillips Lee	Virginia Capes and Maryland
March 1851 – 1857	Benjamin Franklin Sands	Mobile Bay, Pensacola to mouth of Mississippi, Gulf of Mexico, Gulf Stream from Florida to Cape Hatteras
1859-1860	Thomas Bee Huger	Florida
1860	John Julius Guthrie	Florida, Gulf of Mexico

Table 4.   ROBERT J. WALKER's commanders and survey areas (Coast Survey Annual Reports 1848-1861).

The Revenue Marine Service turned over ROBERT J. WALKER to the Coast Survey on 11 February 1848. The Coast Survey placed it under the command of Lieutenant Carlile P. Patterson. Patterson was a promising officer destined to become the fifth superintendent of the Coast Survey in 1874. Patterson served with the Coast Survey with distinction as a naval officer on detached service, and commanded the Survey's first vessel in the Gulf of Mexico, the schooner *Phoenix*, in 1845. Just prior to assuming the command of ROBERT J. WALKER, Patterson had surveyed the vicinity of Mobile Bay's entrance with the schooner *Forward*. He continued work in that area with the ROBERT J. WALKER and was able to develop a direct comparison of the cost of sail versus steam for surveying purposes. Patterson reported that for a given unit of hydrographic surveying production in offshore waters where the steamship was the primary surveying platform, it was 40% less costly to operate than a sailing vessel. Patterson also felt that the most economical use for steamers was for offshore or sea work or where small boat (or launch) work was a small portion of the steamer's duties. This report helped assure the growth of the steam vessel fleet in the Coast Survey (Coast Survey 1848 Annual Report 1849: 50-51).

In its first year, ROBERT J. WALKER finished surveying the offshore approaches to Mobile Bay and the approaches to Cat and Ship Islands. The work accomplished by the vessel also helped to determine the somewhat unique nature of tides in the Gulf of Mexico. Because of the small range of tides in the Gulf of Mexico coupled with the great influence of winds on the tidal levels, it was a triumph of perseverance and analysis to discern that the tides in this area were composed of only one high and one low per day as opposed to the twice daily tides of both the Atlantic and Pacific coasts. Studies of shifting channels, accreting and eroding barrier islands, and appearing and disappearing islands, all issues in the Gulf of Mexico today were first noted in the 1848 report (Coast Survey 1848 Annual Report 1849:10, 48, 50).

NPS Form 10-900-a
OMB No. 1024-0018

United States Department of the Interior
National Park Service

**National Register of Historic Places
Continuation Sheet**

ROBERT J. WALKER, shipwreck and remains
Name of Property
Offshore Atlantic, NJ
County and State

Name of multiple listing (if applicable)

Section number __8__ Page __30__

In addition, the commercial significance of the survey of Mobile Bay and entrance was not lost on the Mayor of Mobile: "… We trust sir, that the labors you are about to bestow upon Mobile Bay will fully confirm our present anticipations, and establish beyond controversy, the fact that our bay and harbor are capable of affording at least equal facilities with any other southern port to shipping of any description" (Coast Survey 1848 Annual Report 1849:107). Although plans were in the making for a Mobile and Ohio Railroad, it was necessary to assure that Mobile Bay would be able to handle deep draft vessels if the railroad was to be successful. 24 June 1848 marked the end of ROBERT J. WALKER's first season, and it returned to New York on 29 July 1848. The Coast Survey's annual report gave no statistics for the cruise other than the vessel and crew had acquired 2,000 lineal miles of hydrographic data.

ROBERT J. WALKER's second survey season began in Mobile Bay on 26 February 1849. During this season, the ship surveyed 145 square miles in Mobile Bay, obtained 71,745 soundings, and ran 1,160 lineal miles. When work ended on 3 July 1849 Patterson recommended the placement of numerous buoys and fixed aids to navigation in Mobile Bay, Cat Island Harbor, and Ship Island Harbor (Coast Survey 1849 Annual Report 1850:51-52). Notable on this cruise was the death of Passed Assistant Surgeon Silas Holmes and five men who were with him in a small boat that capsized in a squall off Mobile on 21 May 1849. Only one man in the boat's complement lived, "sustaining himself on an oar" (Baltimore *Sun* 29 May 1849). After the 1849 survey season the ROBERT J. WALKER was hauled out at the Pensacola Navy Yard and repaired (*Daily Picayune* 22 August 1849).

Patterson was followed as captain of ROBERT J. WALKER in quick progression by Lieutenant James Alden, a promising naval officer who had served in the Wilkes Expedition, on board USS *Constitution*, and in the Mexican-American War, where he served with the Home Squadron off Mexico. Detached for Coast Survey duty, from the summer of 1849 through the late winter of 1851, Alden first commanded the steamer *John Y. Mason* and then ROBERT J. WALKER. In 1850 he started his command of the ROBERT J. WALKER stationed in the Gulf of Mexico, probably at the naval base at Pensacola. Prior to Alden assuming command, the steamer had been used by another government agency (an unauthorized use according to Bache which "deranged" plans for work in Section VIII).

An article on 19 January 1850 in the *Pensacola Gazette* explained the use of the ROBERT J. WALKER by the unnamed agency. The steamer, under the command of Captain Roberts, sailed from Mobile, Alabama on 16 January 1850 for Vera Cruz, Mexico to transport the U.S. Minister to Mexico, Honorable R. P. Letcher, back home. Onboard were also Letcher's servants and attachés as well as the U.S. Counsel to Mazatlan, John Parratt, and his servant. An additional sixteen other passengers made the voyage to Mexico on the steamer including both U.S. and Mexican citizens.

NPS Form 10-900-a   OMB No. 1024-0018
United States Department of the Interior
National Park Service

**National Register of Historic Places
Continuation Sheet**

ROBERT J. WALKER, shipwreck and remains
Name of Property
Offshore Atlantic, NJ
County and State
Name of multiple listing (if applicable)

Section number 8   Page 31

ROBERT J. WALKER's trip to Mexico caused a delay in its readiness for use by the Coast Survey until March that was further exacerbated by difficulties in finding a crew. However, Alden did manage a reconnaissance of Cedar Keys, Florida, and reported the existence of a shoal extending out eight or ten miles from Sea Horse Key. He then recommended establishing a light at the end of the shoal. Alden also completed a survey of the Mobile Delta and almost completed the survey of Mobile Bay. In all, the ship and crew gathered 25,096 soundings in a shortened season with a 536 mile run in the bay (Coast Survey 1850 Annual Report 1851:43-47).

After closing work in the section, ROBERT J. WALKER proceeded to Key West and then Norfolk, where the ship was turned over to its third commander Samuel Phillips Lee for work offshore of the Virginia Capes and Maryland in mid-1850. This was one of the few occasions when ROBERT J. WALKER conducted work anywhere but in Section VIII. Under Lee, the steamship obtained 22,029 soundings in the offshore areas and 31,117 soundings by boat in bay areas. ROBERT J. WALKER traversed 1,115 sounding miles offshore and small boat crews surveyed 518 miles in the bay (Coast Survey 1850 Annual Report 1851:28). On 14 July 1850 two crewmembers, Henry Cavennor and John Patrick, drowned in the surf off Maryland or Virginia. It is likely that they were in the small survey boat at the time, but no further details are given in the newspapers about the incident (*The Sun* 10 September 1850).

In 1851, Benjamin Franklin Sands became ROBERT J. WALKER's fourth commanding officer and the longest serving master of the steamer. Sands' autobiography notes that he took command in March in Mobile, and commenced surveys from Pensacola to the mouth of the Mississippi. Sands' work included 28,244 soundings and 688 miles of sounding (Coast Survey 1851 Annual Report 1852:77-78). The ROBERT J. WALKER then sailed to Hampton Roads, and thence to Baltimore, where Alden laid up the steamer. He and the crew continued working local waters in two smaller coastal schooners (Sands 1899:213). ROBERT J. WALKER was relegated to a repair facility at the end of the season where it received new boilers. According to Benjamin Isherwood, "During the present year, the *Walker* has been refitted with new boilers at the works of Messrs. Merrick & Son, Philadelphia" (Isherwood 1852:50). This machinery remained in place for the remainder of ROBERT J. WALKER's life.

Reactivating ROBERT J. WALKER in December 1852, Sands took the steamer back into the Gulf, where he commanded it through 1857. During his time on board, he wrote:

> I was engaged upon this interesting hydrographic work in the Gulf of Mexico, the fields of my especial surveys being the Florida Keys and the west coast of that state, including Cedar Keys, Tampa Bay and Pensacola Harbor, thence west, taking in the Bay of Biloxi, Chaudeleur Sound, the

NPS Form 10-900-a
United States Department of the Interior
National Park Service

National Register of Historic Places
Continuation Sheet

OMB No. 1024-0018

ROBERT J. WALKER, shipwreck and remains
Name of Property
Offshore Atlantic, NJ
County and State

Name of multiple listing (if applicable)

Section number 8   Page 32

Deltas of the Mississippi, and the westward thereof, including Atchafalaya Bay and Sabine Pass on the Texas Coast (Sands 1899:213).

Following the boilers repairs, ROBERT J. WALKER continued surveying in Mississippi Sound from Dauphine Island to the longitude of Round Island including Horn Island Passage, made outside soundings (ten miles to sea) from the middle of Petit Bois Island to the middle of Horn Island, conducted a reconnaissance to the South and Southwest Passes of the Mississippi Delta, and made a survey of Naso Roads at the north end of Chandeleur Island. 65,362 soundings were taken over 1,486 miles of sounding line (Coast Survey 1852 Annual Report 1853:44-46). After this season's work it was hauled out at the Brooklyn Navy Yard for repairs (*Daily Picayune* 17 February 1853).

In 1853, ROBERT J. WALKER, under Sands' command, engaged in checking for changes to hydrography in the vicinity of Ship Shoal, Horn Island Pass, and Chandeleur Islands at the beginning of the season in response to the Great Mobile Hurricane of 1852 (a precursor of modern work in clearing channels and checking for obstructions in the wake of every great coastal storm). The ship then began work in Mississippi Sound. The crew made 69,079 soundings over 1,430 sounding miles (Coast Survey 1853 Annual Report 1854:69-70). The ship was laid up in Pensacola following the 1853 season, probably sometime in June. While there, the steamer's crew was stricken during a Yellow Fever outbreak. The New Orleans *Daily Picayune* reported on 17 September 1853 that "the surveying steamer Walker was laid up for the summer with an officer and a crew of eight men to take care of her. The officer (Engineer Nones) and six men have died, so that only two remain."

In 1854, the ROBERT J. WALKER's field season did not commence until mid-March due to difficulties procuring crew. The season's survey work began with searching for a shoal at 27° N 89° W south of the "Belize," (the east pass of the Mississippi River). Deep sea soundings and temperature measurements were made as far south as 26° 40'. "What is not a little curious is, that the bottle thrown overboard in latitude 28° 58', in the longitude of Mobile, where the surface temperature was 69 degrees, was found near Jupiter Inlet, on the eastern coast of Florida, having found its way to, probably by wind and counter-currents, into the comparatively warm current of the Gulf Stream." This observation is perhaps the first indication of the Gulf of Mexico Loop Current. The bottle was thrown over on 8 April, 78 miles south of the west end of Dauphin Island and found two months later on 6 June by a Mr. Douglas Dummet near Mosquito Inlet. The bottle had traveled over 750 miles if it had taken a straight course over the 59 days. Total survey statistics for 1854 included 11,943 soundings obtained over 1,167 miles. 11,602 of those soundings were made outside of Horn and Ship Islands (Coast Survey 1854 Annual Report 1855:71-73).

NPS Form 10-900-a
United States Department of the Interior
National Park Service

National Register of Historic Places Continuation Sheet

OMB No. 1024-0018

ROBERT J. WALKER, shipwreck and remains
Name of Property
Offshore Atlantic, NJ
County and State
Name of multiple listing (if applicable)

Section number 8   Page 33

Captain Sands closed the Gulf survey season on 1 June 1854 taking the steamer to Philadelphia for repairs before he reported to Washington for office work. While heading back south in the winter for the next survey season the ROBERT J. WALKER, was fired upon off Jacksonville after departing Savannah, Georgia.

> As the U.S. Steamer *Walker*, bound from this port to Jacksonville, Florida, was nearing that place five cannon were fired at her from the shore. A ball from one of the guns passed through the cabin injuring a waiter. The reason for this singular performance is stated to be the fact that she came from an infected city, and the citizens used this method to prevent her from landing (*Daily Cleveland Herald* 23 September 1854).

Yellow fever was rampant throughout the United States in 1854, especially around Philadelphia, Baltimore, New York, and along the Mississippi River steamboat route. The infection had already claimed the lives of seven of ROBERT J. WALKER's crew the previous year. In 1854, 1,000 people died from yellow fever in Savannah causing the citizens of Jacksonville to be highly suspicious of any vessel that had recently called on that port. However, a shot across the steamer's bow would have been a much more reasonable response.

January 1855 ended up with a succession of gales followed by foggy and hazy weather in February. Weather finally cleared and work continued on the Mississippi coast and offshore islands. Ultimately, 1855 proved to be highly productive for the surveyors on ROBERT J. WALKER. In total, 105,591 soundings were acquired over 2,319 miles of sounding line. During the season, Captain Sands invented a bottom sampling device that worked on all seafloor varieties except a hard rocky bottom. Sands even had his crew take soundings in the Gulf Stream while running north at the end of the season. In October, the steamer surveyed portions of the section south from Nantucket, one of the more difficult sections run in the past because of its length (Coast Survey 1855 Annual Report 1856:88-90).

In 1856, ROBERT J. WALKER attempted to leave Philadelphia early in the year, but ice on the Delaware River detained the steamer. ROBERT J. WALKER set out again in the middle of March, but the ice damaged its paddlewheels necessitating further delay at New Castle for repair. A stormy passage south prevented the collection of deep sea soundings until reaching the latitude of Cape Fear, where the surveyors began sounding until reaching Cape Canaveral. From Key West surveyors collected deep sea soundings north to the Mississippi Delta. ROBERT J. WALKER reached Pass Christian on May 1, but proceeded to Pensacola for provisions as the weather was too inclement for surveying. On 5 May, surveyors commenced operations off Pass Christian and continued till closing the season on 11 June. The steamer's crew collected 62,434

NPS Form 10-900-a	OMB No. 1024-0018
United States Department of the Interior National Park Service	ROBERT J. WALKER, shipwreck and remains Name of Property Offshore Atlantic, NJ County and State
National Register of Historic Places Continuation Sheet	Name of multiple listing (if applicable)

Section number __8__ Page __34__

soundings during the short season and traversed 1,716 miles of sounding line (Coast Survey 1856 Annual Report 1857:75-76).

ROBERT J. WALKER left Philadelphia on 19 November 1856 for the 1857 season. On its way south the crew attempted deep sea soundings but poor weather in vicinity of Cape Hatteras stopped their efforts. Gales and boiler repairs at Key West delayed the steamer's arrival down south and it eventually arrived in Pensacola on 1 February. Despite the delays, ROBERT J. WALKER had a successful season working as far west as Bay St. Louis and then Chandeleur Sound. The ship and crew ran a line of deep sea soundings from Pass a l'Outre to Key West. The deepest sounding measured was 1511 fathoms and brought up blue mud. Surveyors obtained 75,529 soundings over 1,832 miles of sounding line in 1857. The steamship then returned to Philadelphia for winter layup (Coast Survey 1857 Annual Report 1858:101-102).

The ROBERT J. WALKER left Delaware Bay on 4 January 1858, having been detained due to a shortage of officers (Coast Survey 1858 Annual Report 1859:106). As the steamer headed south, its crew, as well as the seamen on Coast Survey steamer *Varina* responded to help combat a major fire ashore at Fort Pickens, Pensacola on 10 January. The Annual Report of the Coast Survey noted:

> While detained at Pensacola, assistance was rendered by Commander Sands, with the men and boats of the steamer WALKER, on the occasion of a fire which happened at Fort Pickens on the night of the 20th of January. On the day following the accident, a communication was addressed to him by Captain John Newton, corps of U.S. engineers, commanding the harbor of Pensacola, in acknowledgment of the obligation to the officers and crew, who, in conjunction with the hydrographic party in the C.S. schooner VARINA, had promptly repaired to the scene of the disaster (Coast Survey 1857 Annual Report 1858:102)

ROBERT J. WALKER's survey party commenced work in Atchafalaya Bay on 6 February 1858. In March, the steamer's surveyors conducted a hydrographic examination of the western end of Lake Borgne, collecting 2,152 soundings over 37 miles of sounding lines. While proceeding back to Philadelphia at the end of the Gulf season, the steamer's crew collected deep sea soundings on a line from the Mississippi River's Southwest Pass to the Tortugas. While on this transit, the deepest sounding hydrographers collected measured 1710 fathoms. The season ended on 3 May, by which time the crew had made 75,951 soundings over 1,117 sounding miles. ROBERT J. WALKER arrived in Philadelphia in early June and afterwards went into the Philadelphia Navy Yard for routine repairs (*New York Daily Tribune* 16 August 1858). Once in

NPS Form 10-900-a
United States Department of the Interior
National Park Service

**National Register of Historic Places
Continuation Sheet**

Section number __8__   Page __35__

OMB No. 1024-0018

ROBERT J. WALKER, shipwreck and remains
Name of Property
Offshore Atlantic, NJ
County and State
Name of multiple listing (if applicable)

---

port, Commander B. F. Sands detached from the steamer and Lieut. Cmdg. Thomas B. Huger became the next commanding officer in September, 1858 (Coast Survey 1858 Annual Report 1859:106).

Thomas Bee Huger, ROBERT J. WALKER's fifth commanding officer, joined the U.S. Navy as a Midshipman in 1835 and served in the Mediterranean and Home Squadrons. He was promoted to Lieutenant in 1848. Under Huger's command, the steamer arrived on the west coast of Florida in early January 1859 and conducted an investigation of the channel into Cedar Key, Florida, with the crew making 15,102 soundings over a 166 mile run. The steamer then proceeded to Pensacola for provisioning and departed for Atchafalaya Bay on 15 January. On that run, 69,447 soundings were observed over 743 sounding miles. During that season's survey work, ROBERT J. WALKER served as a hotel ship for small boat survey teams because of the working area's shallow waters. The ship did conducted deep sea soundings on the trip south to Key West and then ran a section of Gulf Stream from the Tortugas to Havana while on the way north (Coast Survey 1859 Annual Report 1860:80, 85).

On the eve of the Civil War, the issue of slavery was at the forefront of the nation's social and political discourse. ROBERT J. WALKER's crews were diverse and included naval and merchant marine veterans, immigrants, foreign nationals, and a racially diverse crew that often included African-Americans. The steamer figured in an incident involving one of its black sailors while in Charleston sometime in late 1858. The sailor, G. E. Stevens, explained in a letter to J. C. White from Pensacola on early January 8, 1859 that:

> My duty on board this ship required that I should go ashore. The laws of South Carolina forbade my doing so. The day after I arrived I was ordered ashore and obeyed. When walking up King Street I was seized and arraigned before the Mayor. Fortunately for me, a young gentleman, a friend of Captain Huger (the Capt. of the Walker) saw the arrest and informed him immediately. The Captain rendered securities and I was released (Sterling 1973).

On 23 April 1859, the *Daily Picayune* newspaper published an article about the protection of the southern coast against slavers (slave ships). The article mentioned the ROBERT J. WALKER as a possible intercept vessel while on survey duty in the Gulf of Mexico.

> The Apalachicola Advertiser, alluding to the report that our Government, in view of the recent events, had taken measures to prevent the landing of negroes on that coast, says that there is no vessel of light draught enough in the home squadron to

NPS Form 10-900-a	OMB No. 1024-0018
United States Department of the Interior National Park Service	ROBERT J. WALKER, shipwreck and remains Name of Property Offshore Atlantic, NJ County and State
National Register of Historic Places **Continuation Sheet**	Name of multiple listing (if applicable)

Section number 8   Page 36

accomplish the object. The only United States vessel in the Gulf suited for the purpose of intercepting slavers, are those belonging to the coast survey, the steamer Walker, in Mississippi Sound, and the Vixen, ordered to Matagorda Bay.

All of the U. S. Navy's shallow draught steamers were tied up with the Paraguay expedition; as a result there were no other government vessels besides ROBERT J. WALKER and *Vixen* to prevent slaves from being landed in the southern states. There is no historical evidence to support whether or not the ROBERT J. WALKER ever participated in these activities.

In Philadelphia, Lieutenant Cmdg. John Julius Guthrie was assigned as ROBERT J. WALKER's sixth and final commanding officer on 10 October 1859. He had served in the Navy continuously since 1834. Just before heading south the steamship was hauled out at the Brooklyn Navy yard for repairs including the painting of its hull red (*New York Herald* 12 November 1859). The 1860 season began on 20 January with a thorough examination of the Cedar Key area on its way to the Gulf Coast. These first efforts generated 41,811 soundings along 467 miles of sounding run. Once it arrived in Chandeleur Sound, ROBERT J. WALKER's hydrographers collected 13,072 soundings along 244 miles. Moving on, the steamer collected 34,916 soundings along 612 miles of sounding run on the Mississippi Passes. Upon leaving the Gulf, ROBERT J. WALKER reached Norfolk in mid-June. Continuing north, the steamer intended to stop in New York City. On the approaches to New York Harbor off Absecon Light, New Jersey, the ROBERT J. WALKER collided with the schooner *Fanny* on the night of 21 June 1860 (Coast Survey 1860 Annual Report 1861:81-84, 89).

Year	Number of Soundings by ROBERT J. WALKER	Total Number of Soundings Made by Coast Survey	Percentage of All Soundings Completed by ROBERT J. WALKER	Linear Miles Surveyed by ROBERT J. WALKER	Total Linear Miles Surveyed by Coast Survey	Percentage of All Linear Miles Run by ROBERT J. WALKER	Number of Coast Survey Vessels
1848	unknown	255,003	unknown	2,000	8,047	24	unknown
1849	71,745	265,824	26	1,160	4,299	27	unknown
1850	47,125	264,718	17	1,651	5,995	27	unknown
1851	28,244	371,660	7	688	10,590	6	5-8 schooners, 1 brig, 4-6 steamers
1852	65,362	288,375	22	1,486	9,534	15	4-8 schooners, 3-5 steamers
1853	69,079	305,377	22	1,430	9,056	15	6-9 schooners, 3-5 steamers
1854	11,943	162,454	7	1,167	9,141	12	6 schooners, 4 steamers

NPS Form 10-900-a   OMB No. 1024-0018
United States Department of the Interior
National Park Service

National Register of Historic Places
Continuation Sheet

ROBERT J. WALKER, shipwreck and remains
Name of Property
Offshore Atlantic, NJ
County and State
Name of multiple listing (if applicable)

Section number 8   Page 37

1855	105,591	526,875	20	2,319	13,115	17	6-7 schooners, 3-5 steamers
1856	62,434	439,614	14	1,716	15,305	11	4-7 schooners, 3-5 steamers
1857	75,529	506,043	14	1,832	12,377	14	5-7 schooners, 5-6 steamers
1858	75,951	513,607	14	1,117	8,884	12	2 schooners, 5 steamers
1859	85,529	398,053	21	909	9,103	9	2 schooners, 5-6 steamers
1860	41,811	372,251	11	467	9,438	4	3 schooners, 5 steamers
TOTAL	740,343	4,669,854	15	17,942	124,884	14	

Table 5.   Soundings and Linear Miles run by ROBERT J. WALKER and all Coast Survey vessels between 1848 and 1860 (Coast Survey Annual Reports 1848-1861).

In ROBERT J. WALKER's twelve year career, its hydrographers made 704,343 soundings and surveyed 17, 942 linear miles. This accounted for a total of 15% of all the soundings and 14% of all the linear miles run by Coast Survey vessels during those 12 years. The Coast Survey fleet during that time ranged in number from 2-9 schooners and 2-5 other steamships during any given year conducting hydrographic work around the United States. ROBERT J. WALKER's main operating area was Section 8, the coast of Alabama, Mississippi, parts of Louisiana, and Florida. It completed surveys in other areas as warranted and conducted soundings along the Gulf Stream during passages north and south between seasons. Its operations schedule began in January with passage to southern waters and then survey work in the Gulf of Mexico until early summer, at which time it would return north for survey work off the Eastern Seaboard followed by a lay-up period and repairs in the late summer and fall. ROBERT J. WALKER successfully charted new areas of the United States and re-charted known areas to indicate changes and new navigational recommendations. The steamer allowed vessels to safely enter and transit strategic ports in the Gulf of Mexico to support commercial growth and military defense of the growing nation on the eve of the Civil War.

ROBERT J. WALKER'S CREW

As an early steamer in the service of the United States Government, ROBERT J. WALKER served as a training platform for a number of officers eager to learn the operation of steamships at a time when there were not enough of the vessels to provide an opportunity for all who had the interest or desire to learn. In addition to its six commanding officers, among those assigned to ROBERT J. WALKER from the U.S. Navy was Alban C. Stimers, a 25-year old second engineer attached to the ship on November 18, 1852. Stimers rose rapidly in naval ranks and during the

NPS Form 10-900-a
OMB No. 1024-0018

United States Department of the Interior
National Park Service

**National Register of Historic Places
Continuation Sheet**

ROBERT J. WALKER, shipwreck and remains
Name of Property
Offshore Atlantic, NJ
County and State

Name of multiple listing (if applicable)

Section number __8__   Page __38__

Civil War served as the Chief Engineer of the United States Navy. He played a major role in working with John Ericsson on the construction of USS *Monitor*, and sailed with the ironclad, although not a member of the crew, on its voyage south from New York in 1862 to Hampton Roads, where it engaged in battle with CSS *Virginia*, the former USS *Merrimac*.

ROBERT J. WALKER's executive officer in 1855, William Gamble, went on to command the ironclad USS *Osage* in 1865 and retired as a commander. Another noted ROBERT J. WALKER crew member was a young officer, Joseph Fry, who served aboard in 1850-1851. Fry left the U. S. Navy at the start of the Civil War and served the Confederacy with distinction as a blockade runner. "On the beach" after the war, Fry accepted the position of master of the steamer *Virginius*, chartered by Cuban nationalists to run guns into Cuba to support an uprising against the island's Spanish rulers. *Virginius* was captured off Cuba by a Spanish warship on October 30, 1874. The "*Virginius*" Affair" was one of the more prominent diplomatic crises faced by the United States in the late nineteenth century. Fry and his crew were imprisoned, tried as pirates and most were executed within days despite diplomatic protests. This notorious case inflamed passions on both sides of the Atlantic and nearly brought Spain and the United States to blows. Undoubtedly, the incident encouraged hostilities that led to the Spanish-American War a few decades later.

ROBERT J. WALKER's DEMISE

After the completion of the 1860 survey season in the Gulf of Mexico the ROBERT W. WALKER headed back north to New York for repairs, after a brief stop in Norfolk, under the command of Lieutenant Guthrie (*New York Times* 23 June 1860). On 21 June 1860, the steamer, with a possible crew of 78 and the wife of executive officer Joseph Seawell, sank off ▇▇▇, New Jersey following a collision with the 250-ton schooner *Fanny*, bound from Philadelphia to Boston with 240 tons of coal and running close-reefed before a gale (Vincent 1860:560-561).

The executive officer, Joseph A. Seawell, was the ROBERT J. WALKER's officer on watch at the time of the collision. Seawell was a naval veteran, but had been dismissed from the U. S. Navy on the recommendation of the Efficiency Board in 1855. At a quarter past two in the morning the weather was cloudy with a northeast wind, when the lookouts spotted the *Fanny* sailing south before the wind. As the schooner approached, Seawell ordered the steamer's wheel hard to port, turning the steamer to starboard to clear the schooner. At the same time, the *Fanny* turned to port making a collision inevitable. ROBERT J. WALKER's quartermaster Charles Clifford recounted the next moments.

NPS Form 10-900-a
United States Department of the Interior
National Park Service

**National Register of Historic Places
Continuation Sheet**

Section number __8__   Page __39__

OMB No. 1024-0018

ROBERT J. WALKER, shipwreck and remains
Name of Property
Offshore Atlantic, NJ
County and State
Name of multiple listing (if applicable)

> She struck the steamer forward of the port guard and wheelhouse, cutting her down to the water's edge, and carried away her own head booms. The schooner hung for a moment, then swung alongside, and carried away the forward and quarter boats of the steamer. Getting clear of the schooner, we worked ahead, but found the Walker was sinking; cut away her mainmast, booms, and got everything movable on deck, to make a raft for the men. Everybody cool, and the officers behaving with great presence of mind, lowered both starboard boats and dropped them astern for use when the vessel went down. By this time every soul was on deck except those who may have been killed or injured by the collision, and a sick man on board, nearly seventy years of age, almost helpless, had been carefully lifted out and put in one of the boats. All was orderly (*New York Herald* 23 June 1860).

Captain Mayhew of the *Fanny* indicated that his vessel's bow had struck the ROBERT J. WALKER's port bow with considerable force, and that it was his opinion that his bow anchor, catted forward, had opened up the plates of ROBERT J. WALKER's hull. With considerable damage done to his vessel and thinking the steamer was in no danger, Mayhew proceeded on to ▬▬▬▬▬▬▬▬▬▬▬▬ ROBERT J. WALKER's crew mustered and went below decks to try and stop the incoming water with pumps, filling the holes with mattresses and canvasses to no avail. With steam pressure still up in its boilers, the steamer's bow was pointed towards shore and its remaining starboard boats launched into the water and towed astern. The crew stayed with the sinking vessel until rising water extinguished the boilers and there was no hope of saving it. "... the crew lined up without pushing or panic [and] commenced loading the boats. Probably they were unaware that there was insufficient room for all of them on the boats" (Theberge 1998). As the boats rowed away 20 to 30 men were left on deck and many of them drowned as they hung onto portions of the vessel as it sank. Captain Guthrie stayed onboard until the steamer went down and just before it slipped totally beneath the waves he jumped into the water where he was picked up by one of the boats. Quartermaster Charles Clifford described the final moments.

> Lieutenant Sewall was drawn down in the vortex, and, after remaining for a considerable time floating on a portion of the wreck, was also rescued by one of the boats. A heavy sea was running, and many of the men were doubtless washed off the spars and drowned from the mere exhaustion of holding on, while others were killed or stunned on rising to the surface by concussion with spars and other parts of the wreck. The steamer had entirely sunk from sight in thirty minutes after the collision. Many of the crew

NPS Form 10-900-a
United States Department of the Interior
National Park Service

National Register of Historic Places Continuation Sheet

OMB No. 1024-0018

ROBERT J. WALKER, shipwreck and remains
Name of Property
Offshore Atlantic, NJ
County and State
Name of multiple listing (if applicable)

Section number __8__   Page __40__

were rescued by the boats, in which were about forty-four persons, and they were in turn picked up by the schooner *R.G. Porter*, Captain S.S. Hudson. He did nobly, keeping his vessel about the spot where the wreck went down until two o'clock in the day, and using every endeavor to render us comfortable and afford the desired assistance. Finding that it was useless to remain longer in searching for the missing, Captain Hudson stood into ▮▮▮▮▮ where he arrived about four o'clock on Thursday afternoon (*New York Herald* 23 June 1860).

Having suffered terribly from the collision and subsequent sinking, ROBERT J. WALKER's crew arrived in port having lost all their effects and many of their comrades. One of the survivors, Essex D. Cochran, later died on 24 June at the Baltimore Naval Hospital. ROBERT J. WALKER sinking took the lives of twenty crewmen, making it the worst single disaster to strike the Coast Survey. Superintendent Bache referred to this tragedy in only three widely separated paragraphs in his 1860 Annual Report; perhaps he found it too painful to deal with, or maybe the events overtaking the country overwhelmed all else in 1860 and 1861. With the approaching Civil War, there was never an inquiry concerning the causes of this accident and the assignment of responsibility for its consequences. Surprisingly, Superintendent Bache never printed a listing of names of the surviving or deceased crewmen.

First	Middle	Last	Position
Michael		Allman	Seaman
Robert		Bell	Quartermaster
William		Boyes	
Michael		Boyle	Coal Passengers
John		Brien or Bryan	Quartermaster
John		Brown	
John		Burton	Master at Arms
Burnett		Canah	Ordinary Seaman
Bernard		Carrah	
John		Cazmer	
Joseph		Clark	Quartermaster
James		Clark	
Charles		Clifford	Quartermaster
Jefferson		Cravens	
James		De Courcey	
Peter		Decker	boy

NPS Form 10-900-a
United States Department of the Interior
National Park Service

**National Register of Historic Places
Continuation Sheet**

Section number __8__ Page __41__

OMB No. 1024-0018

ROBERT J. WALKER, shipwreck and remains
Name of Property
Offshore Atlantic, NJ
County and State

Name of multiple listing (if applicable)

James		Delorse		
John		Desmond		Quartermaster
Henry		Dick		
Frederick or Patrick		Dougherty		
Daniel		Evans		
James	A	Golden or Golding		Seamen
B	W	Guthrie		Fourth Officer
John	J	Guthrie		Lieut. Commanding
John	R	Hall		
John		Harrison		
Jas.		Hellum		Surgeon
George		Henn		
Alonzo		Hood		
Henry		Hotten		
Henry		Hunter		
John	C	Johnson		Boatman's Mate
William	J	Jones		Quartermaster
William		Logan		Quartermaster
Edward		Lynch		Arm's Mate
Michael		Lyons		
William	H	Mapes		
Charles		Marriott		Assistant Surgeon
John		McCaffrey		
John		McMullen or McMillan		Captain Main Top
Joseph		Meary		Quartermaster
John	A	Miner		
Jos		Morg.		
George		Penn		Quartermaster
Joseph		Peterson		Quartermaster
C T	Thomas	Rixley or Riley		
John		Rowe		Quartermaster
Joseph	A	Seawell or Sewell		Executive Officer
Jas.		Shankland		
John		Smith		Quartermaster
R	B	Swift		Engineer
John		Taylor		Firemen

NPS Form 10-900-a   OMB No. 1024-0018

United States Department of the Interior
National Park Service

**National Register of Historic Places
Continuation Sheet**

ROBERT J. WALKER, shipwreck and remains
Name of Property
Offshore Atlantic, NJ
County and State

Name of multiple listing (if applicable)

Section number 8   Page 42

First	Middle	Last	Position
John	C	Thompson	
John	W	Walsh	
John		Welch	
Joseph or James		Wilson	Sailmaker
Andrew		Young	Quartermaster
James		Young	Gunner's Mate

Table 6. List of ROBERT J. WALKER's possible crewmen that survived its loss. Sources have conflicting lists of who survived so the names above are a compilation of all potential crewmen that could have been onboard (*New York Times* 23 June 1860; Coast Survey 2013; Theberge 1998).

First	Middle	Last	Position
Joseph		Bates	Second Class Fireman
Marquis		Bonevento or Buoneventa	Ward Room Steward
John or James	M	Brown	Captain of the Guard or Quartermaster
Essex	D	Cochran	(died in hospital 24 June 1860)
Jeremiah		Coffee	Cooper
Timothy		Conner	Quarter Gunner
Peter		Conway	First Class Fireman
Cornelius		Crowe	Landsman or Ordinary Seaman
John		Driscoll	Seaman
John		Farren	Second Class Fireman
James		Farren	Second Class Fireman
George	W	Johnson	Landsman
Michael	M	Lee	Cook (African-American)
Charles		Miller	Ordinary Seaman
James		Patterson	Ward Room Cook (African American)
George		Price	Second Class Fireman
Henry	H	Reed	Second Mate
Samuel		Sizer	First Class Fireman
Daniel		Smith	First Class Fireman
Robert		Wilson	Seaman

Table 7. List of ROBERT J. WALKER's crew that perished as a result of its loss

NPS Form 10-900-a
United States Department of the Interior
National Park Service

**National Register of Historic Places
Continuation Sheet**

Section number __8__ Page __43__

OMB No. 1024-0018

ROBERT J. WALKER, shipwreck and remains
Name of Property
Offshore Atlantic, NJ
County and State
Name of multiple listing (if applicable)

(*New York Times* 23 June 1860; National Archives RG 217 Department of Treasury).

The contemporary newspapers carried accounts of the sinking and the names of the crew, but the Annual Report of the Coast Survey did not focus on the human loss. Instead, Superintendent A. D. Bache focused on the impact of ROBERT J. WALKER's loss on the Coast Survey itself, and included these observations, appearing at different places in the report (Coast Survey 1860 Annual Report 1861:16).

> The progress of the work has been, taking all its branches together, greater than during the year before, but the loss of one of our best steamers by collision at sea has been a sad drawback to the general prosperity of the work. As my estimates for the time of completion of the survey must be materially affected by this loss, I earnestly recommend a special appropriation to replace the steamer at the earliest practicable period. (Coast Survey 1860 Annual Report 1861:1).

> The loss of the steamer *Walker*, by collision at sea, requires an appropriation to replace her. As the government acts as its own insurer, this is an indispensable item of estimate. The loss of a considerable part of the records of last season's work, and the loss of time from having no steamer to take the *Walker*'s place in the Gulf of Mexico, will be sensibly felt in our progress, and I would respectfully urge that another steamer be supplied at the earliest practicable period, so as to enable us to work up again as soon as possible to the former efficiency (Coast Survey 1860 Annual Report 1861:10).

> I have elsewhere referred to the wreck of the steamer *Walker*, on the 21st of June of the present year. This disaster, which involved loss of life to twenty of her crew, with the total loss of the vessel and all the records on board, was occasioned by collision with a schooner laden with coal, and occurred about three o'clock in the morning, while the *Walker* was off ▓▓▓▓▓▓ New Jersey, in command of Lieutenant J. J. Guthrie, U. S. N., and on her passage from Norfolk to New York. The officers of the *Walker* and survivors of her crew were rescued from imminent peril by Captain L. J. Hudson, [referred to as Captain S. S. Hudson in most accounts] of the schooner *R. G. Porter*, and safely conveyed to May's Landing, on the coast of New Jersey. The steamer sunk in less than half an

Page 56 - The redacted text must be "Absecom," as I used the same quote on my page 54.

NPS Form 10-900-a
OMB No. 1024-0018

United States Department of the Interior
National Park Service

**National Register of Historic Places
Continuation Sheet**

ROBERT J. WALKER, shipwreck and remains
Name of Property
Offshore Atlantic, NJ
County and State

Name of multiple listing (if applicable)

Section number 8   Page 44

hour after the collision, ▮▮▮▮▮▮▮▮▮▮
(Coast Survey 1860 Annual Report 1861:44)

Other contemporary reports indicated that after Superintendent Bache received a telegram on June 21, notifying him that the ROBERT J. WALKER had sunk and twenty of the crew were missing, he immediately wrote to Guthrie, asking him to report the circumstances of the disaster. Guthrie wrote Superintendent Bache on June 23 with the following information.

> It becomes my painful duty to report to you the loss of the U.S. Coast Survey Steamer "Walker" which was sunk at sea in five fathoms of water about ▮▮▮▮▮▮▮▮▮▮ on the coast of New Jersey, in consequence of being run into by a schooner - supposed to be the "Fanny" on the morning of the 21st of this month about 2:20 A.M..... Two of the boats were stove in and rendered useless by the collision, the two remaining ones were lowered, and many of the crew saved by this means, and the timely assistance of the "R. G. Porter," of Mays Landing, N. J., Capt. S. S. Hudson, who came to our assistance in this hour of need... I cannot withhold ... profound regret for the melancholy fate of that portion of the crew who are still missing and who it is to be feared have found a watery grave. During this sad catastrophe the sea was running high and the wind very fresh... I need not add that the loss of my own professional reputation, necessarily incident to such an accident occasioned very slight regrets compared to the depths of sorrow I endure for the missing - and heartfelt sympathy entertained for the anxious and bereaved families and friends - I am sure you understand the workings of the heart sufficiently to render it unnecessary for me to essay to unfold mine in written terms...
> (National Archives RG 23 1860).

Lieutenant Guthrie finished his letter with a request for Superintendent Bache to notify the Secretary of the Navy and "obtain for me a court of inquiry and investigation." Bache replied to this letter on June 25: "I have telegraphed to request a detailed report of the circumstances of the disaster to the "Walker" as the one now made gives no idea of the facts of the case..." Guthrie responded with additional detail:

> "... On the night of the 21st about 2:20 A.M., I was awakened by an unusual noise on deck, and my first thought was that the 1st officer was getting a cast of the lead, but soon after heard the Executive Officer tell someone to call the Captain - an officer came down and reported to me that the vessel was sinking - I went on deck and directed her to be headed

Page 57 - The first redaction is "which took place about twelve miles from land." I used the same quote on my page 54. The second redaction is "six miles SE of 'Absecum light'." I used the same quote on my page 43.

NPS Form 10-900-a
OMB No. 1024-0018
United States Department of the Interior
National Park Service

National Register of Historic Places
Continuation Sheet

ROBERT J. WALKER, shipwreck and remains
Name of Property
Offshore Atlantic, NJ
County and State
Name of multiple listing (if applicable)

Section number __8__   Page __45__

inshore, and to give her all the steam speed possible, seeing ▇ distinctly - being about West - Nor. West - ▇ were sinking - soon after this the engineer reported the fires extinguished - and the water gaining very rapidly on us - I had previously sent men down in the coal bunkers to see if the leak could be stopped in any possible way – it was found to be impracticable - finding she must inevitably go down soon - I directed the mainmast to be cut away - the boats to be lowered and some of the ladders to be towed astern for buoys - and also directed the quartermaster to get a cast of the lead - he reported ▇ water - Soon after she sunk. It was found two of the boats had been crushed .... the two remaining ones picked up what portion of the crew they thought they could carry in safety; Nothing was saved, except what was on and about the persons of those who were rescued - all the Note Books, Instruments, charts of the vessel etc. went down with her and as all the records are gone - I have to depend upon memory for the facts - all of which it is impossible to remember distinctly...." (National Archives RG 23 1860).

Lieutenant Guthrie thought that the ROBERT J. WALKER might be raised or that the engines and machinery could be recovered. Guthrie was mistaken. The steamer had sunk in approximately ▇ fathoms that Guthrie initially thought, and was now thought to be about ▇ . If there is any criticism of Guthrie, it is that he had no idea where his ship was when it was struck and also that he was not awake and on deck as his vessel had just passed the busy entrance to Delaware Bay and would be approaching progressively more congested waters as it approached New York City.

By July, the ROBERT J. WALKER's location was known and a steamer from New York placed a buoy on the site to prevent vessels from colliding with its mast that was sticking a few feet out of the water. On 18 July 1860 the Baltimore *Sun* newspaper printed a request for proposals to salvage the ROBERT J. WALKER. Proposals were requested to raise and deliver the steamer to New York and were to be addressed to Samuel Hein, Coast Survey's General Dispersing Agent. It is unclear if any attempts were actually made to recover the wreck, but a newspaper article did state that, "An attempt will be made to raise her, and should it fail, the wreck will be blown up" (*The Sun* 4 July 1860).

Lieutenant Guthrie's second letter seemed to appease Superintendent Bache. Bache wrote back on July 6, "If your desk could be procured containing the papers of the survey, it would be worth $2,500 and if the engines or parts of it can be had it would help us materially." Bache also

NPS Form 10-900-a
United States Department of the Interior
National Park Service

OMB No. 1024-0018

ROBERT J. WALKER, shipwreck and remains
Name of Property
Offshore Atlantic, NJ
County and State
Name of multiple listing (if applicable)

National Register of Historic Places Continuation Sheet

Section number 8   Page 46

advised Guthrie "to consult the District Attorney, for which I will pay, as to the propriety of libeling the Sch. Fanny, making in conjunction with Mr. Seawell's statement of facts to him upon which he will ground his opinion" (National Archives RG 23 1860). After Superintendent Bache's allusion to "libeling" the *Fanny*, there seemed to be little additional effort to conduct an investigation into the causes of the accident or the placing of blame. Bache lost interest in the disaster except from the view that there was lost data and future lost productivity. The U. S. Navy did not also express much concern or desire to conduct a formal hearing. The advent of the Civil War pushed the affair out of the way and out of the spotlight.

WRECKSITE MANAGEMENT

ROBERT J. WALKER was not abandoned after its sinking in 1860 and is therefore still owned by the U.S. Government consistent with the laws and policies that apply to sovereign immune public vessels. For example, the President's Statement on the United States Policy for the Protection of Sunken State Craft explains how the U.S. Government retains title to all of its sunken vessels, "unless title has been abandoned or transferred in the manner Congress authorized or directed," regardless of the passage of time.

As the U.S. Government owns ROBERT J. WALKER, laws regarding the protection and management of Government property apply, including, but not limited to: the National Historic Preservation Act (NHPA) (16 U.S.C. § 470); and laws regarding the destruction or theft of U.S. Government property (18 U.S.C. § 641 et seq.). Under the maritime law of salvage, public and private owners have the right to deny salvage. In addition, U.S. sovereign wrecks are immune from arrest under the law of salvage without the consent of the U.S. Government, and in this instance the Department of Commerce's (DOC) National Oceanic and Atmospheric Administration (NOAA) as the management agency. As such, the law of salvage and authority of Federal Admiralty courts may also provide protection of ROBERT J. WALKER from looting and unauthorized salvage.

ROBERT J. WALKER was managed by the U.S. Coast Survey when it sank. Since then, the wreck has neither been abandoned nor been designated surplus property by the United States. As the Coast Survey is now part of NOAA, DOC/NOAA is the federal agency that manages the ROBERT J. WALKER on behalf of the U.S. Government. The steamer is a historic shipwreck, therefore DOC/NOAA, through the Office of National Marine Sanctuaries, also has a responsibility under the NHPA to consider it for listing as a "historic property" on the National Register of Historic Places and to develop a plan for its management and preservation. Plans include a memorandum of agreement between NOAA, the US Coast Guard, the Bureau of Ocean Energy Management, the New Jersey Historic Preservation Office, and the local diving community through an appropriate non-profit partner. The shipwreck will be prominently

---

Page 59 - The issues surrounding ownership of title and the President's statement are demolished in Part 2. Note that NOAA has asserted itself as the managing agency, despite the fact that NOAA is part of the Commerce Department, whereas the *Robert J. Walker* was part of the Transportation Department. So far NOAA has done nothing toward developing a plan for preservation of the wreck. By that I mean real preservation from the destructive forces of nature, not the political figment that NOAA pronounces in place of affirmative action.

NPS Form 10-900-a
United States Department of the Interior
National Park Service

**National Register of Historic Places
Continuation Sheet**

OMB No. 1024-0018

Name of Property: ROBERT J. WALKER, shipwreck and remains
County and State: Offshore Atlantic, NJ
Name of multiple listing (if applicable):

Section number 8   Page 47

marked on official U.S. nautical charts and other notices. NOAA will ask the fishing community to avoid trawling or dredging near it; NOAA will also work with others to avoid any activities that might harm the site and therefore make it less of a diving attraction as well as an historic site.

CONCLUSIONS

The story of ROBERT J. WALKER is an important one in the development of the United States and, in particular, ensuring safe navigation for those who work on the nation's waters, and for the facilitated and safe flow of commerce by water. It is a story of innovation, of science at sea, and of long hours of service to the nation. It is also a story of those who paid the ultimate price for that service and devotion to duty. The intact archaeological remains of the steamship ROBERT J. WALKER are significant at the national level and it qualifies for listing on the National Register of Historic Places based on Criteria A, C, and D.

Page 60 - This promise can be viewed as a political statement that is designed to satisfy Nerp reviewers. So far NOAA has not marked the site in any way, shape, or form: prominently or otherwise. Instead, it has done just the opposite, which the redacted text proves. This begs the question: How can NOAA ask the fishing community to avoid trawling and dredging near the wreck when NOAA has refused to reveal and disseminate its location? NOAA's definition of working with others is an oxymoron.

NPS Form 10-900-a
United States Department of the Interior
National Park Service

OMB No. 1024-0018

National Register of Historic Places Continuation Sheet

Name of Property: ROBERT J. WALKER, shipwreck and remains
County and State: Offshore Atlantic, NJ
Name of multiple listing (if applicable):

Section number 9   Page 48

Section 9 – Bibliography

Bennett, Frank M.
1896   *The Steam Navy of the United States*. Press of W.T. Nicholson, Pittsburgh, PA.

Brown, Alexander Crosby
1951   Notes on the Origins of Iron Shipbuilding in the United States: 1825-1861. MA thesis, The College of William and Mary, Williamsburg, VA.

Brown, Allen H.
1881   The Character and Employments of the Early Settlers of the Sea-Coasts of New Jersey. *Proceedings of the New Jersey Historical Society, Second Series*, Vol. VII:27-64.

Brown, David K.
1993   *Paddle Warships: The Earliest Steam Powered Fighting Ships: 1815-1850*. Conway Maritime Press, London.

Browning, Robert
1992   The Lasting Injury: The Revenue Marine's First Steam Cutters. *American Neptune* 52(1):25-37.

Canney, Donald L.
1995   *U.S. Coast Guard and Revenue Cutters, 1790-1935*. Naval Institute Press, Annapolis, MD.

Cloud, John
2011   The U.S. Coast Survey in the Civil War. Publication of the Office of Coast Survey's "Charting a More Perfect Union" Preserve America Initiative project.

Coast Guard
1989   *Records of Movements, Vessels of the United States Coast Guard 1790 – December 31, 1933*. United States Coast Guard, Washington, D.C.

Coast Guard
2013   United States Revenue Cutter Service 1790-1912. Powerpoint Presentation. <www.uscg.mil/history/uscghist/USCGCombatHistory2010.ppt> Accessed 21 August 2013.

NPS Form 10-900-a
United States Department of the Interior
National Park Service

**National Register of Historic Places
Continuation Sheet**

Section number 9   Page 49

OMB No. 1024-0018

ROBERT J. WALKER, shipwreck and remains
Name of Property
Offshore Atlantic, NJ
County and State
Name of multiple listing (if applicable)

Coast Survey
1847   Letter from the Acting Secretary of the Treasury (1847) *Report of the Superintendent of the Coast Survey...December 15, 1847.* Senate Executive Doc. 6, 309th Cong. 1st Sess.

Coast Survey
1849-1861 Annual Reports of the Superintendent of the Coast Survey, Showing the Progress of the Survey During the Year 1848-1860. Washington D.C. Digital copies available through the NOAA Central Library.

Coast Survey
2013   "The Story of the Coast Survey Steamer ROBERT J. WALKER" Office of Coast Survey digital publication. Silver Spring, MD.
<http://www.nauticalcharts.noaa.gov/RobertJWalker/The%20Story%20of%20the%20Robert%20J.%20Walker.pdf>

Delgado, James P.
2013   Identification of the Wreck of the U.S.C.S.S. *Robert J. Walker* off Atlantic City, New Jersey. Report by NOAA's Office of National Marine Sanctuaries. September 2013. Silver Spring, MD.

Department of the Treasury
1847   *An Account of the Receipts and Expenditures of the United States, For the Year 1847.* Ritchie & Hiess, Washington D.C.

Gardiner, Robert (editor)
1993   *Steam, Steel, and Shellfire.* Naval Institute Press, Annapolis, MD.

Isherwood, Benjamin
1852   "Notes on the U.S. Surveying Steam *Walker*," *Journal of the Franklin Institute*, Vol. XXIV, Third Series(1), 49-55.

King, Irving H.
1989   *The Coast Guard Under Sail, The U.S. Revenue Cutter Service 1789-1865.* Naval Institute Press. Annapolis, MD.

Letter from the Acting Secretary of the Treasury
1847   *Report of the Superintendent of the Coast Survey...December 15, 1847.* Senate Executive Doc. 6, 309th Cong. 1st Sess.

NPS Form 10-900-a
OMB No. 1024-0018

United States Department of the Interior
National Park Service

**National Register of Historic Places
Continuation Sheet**

ROBERT J. WALKER, shipwreck and remains
Name of Property
Offshore Atlantic, NJ
County and State

Name of multiple listing (if applicable)

Section number 9   Page 50

Martin, W.E.
1852 Painting of the *Robert W. Walker*. Mariners Museum, Newport News, VA.

National Archives
1860 Correspondence between Lieutenant John J. Guthrie, Superintendent Bache, and executive officer Joseph A. Seawell. Records of Coast and Geodetic Survey (RG 23). MF642, roll 220, volume IX, pp. 207-261. National Archives, Washington, D.C.

National Archives
1820-1898 Accounting Offices of the Department of Treasury. Muster roll and pay receipts for ships and shore units 11/1/1820 – 8/31/1898. Volume 1268. A1. Entry 818. Box 114. National Archives, Washington, D.C.

New Jersey Wreck Divers
2013 Atlantic Divers, Inc. <http://www.njwreckdivers.com/p/shipwreck-info.html>. Accessed 28 August 2013.

Rodgers, Bradley A.
1996 *Guardian of the Great Lakes: The U.S. Paddle Frigate Michigan*. University of Michigan Press, Ann Arbor MI.

Rozwadowski, Helen M.
2005 *Fathoming the Ocean: The Discovery and Exploration of the Deep Sea*. Harvard University Press. Cambridge, MA.

Sands, Benjamin Franklin
1899 *From Reefer to Rear-Admiral: Reminiscences and Journal Jottings of Nearly Half a Century of Naval Life, 1827 to 1874*. Frederick A. Stokes Company, New York, NY.

Shalowitz, Aaron L.
1964a *Shore and Sea Boundaries, with Special Reference to the Interpretation and Use of Coast and Geodetic Survey Data*. Publication 10-1. Volume 1. Department of Commerce, Washington, D.C.

Shalowitz, Aaron L.
1964b *Shore and Sea Boundaries, with Special Reference to the Interpretation and Use of Coast and Geodetic Survey Data*. Publication 10-1. Volume 2. Department of Commerce, Washington, D.C.

Page 63 - Once again Atlantic Divers (Gene Peterson) was credited despite his firm opposition to having his website quoted. The reader will see in Part 2 that NOAA quoted me in another context without asking my permission. NOAA's SOP is to take what it wants yet refuse to divulge public information to the public (as redactions demonstrate).

NPS Form 10-900-a   OMB No. 1024-0018
United States Department of the Interior
National Park Service

	ROBERT J. WALKER, shipwreck and remains
	Name of Property
National Register of Historic Places	Offshore Atlantic, NJ
Continuation Sheet	County and State
	Name of multiple listing (if applicable)

Section number __9__ Page __51__

Slotten, Hugh Richard
1994 *Patronage, Practice, and the Culture of American Science: Alexander Dallas Bache and the U.S. Coast Survey.* Cambridge University Press, New York, NY.

Smith, Horatio Davis
1989 *Early History of the United States Revenue Marine Service or (United States Revenue Cutter Service) 1789-1849.* Reprint of 1932 Naval Historical Foundation Publication. U.S. Coast Guard Bicentennial Publication, Washington, D.C.

Sterling, Dorothy, ed.
1973 *Speak Out in Thunder Tones: Letters and Other Writings by Black Northerners, 1787-1865.* Doubleday, Garden City, N.J.

Stevens, Dorothy
1973 *Speak Out in Thunder Tones: Letters and Other Writings by Black Northerners, 1787-1865.* Doubleday, Garden City, NY.

Theberge, Captain Albert E.
1998 *The Coast Survey: 1807-1867.* National Oceanic and Atmospheric Administration, Silver Spring, MD.

Trimble, William F.
1975 From Sail to Steam: Shipbuilding in the Pittsburgh Area, 1790-1865. *The Western Pennsylvania Historical Magazine.* April 1975, volume 58, number 2: 147-167.

Vincent, Francis, ed.
1860 *Vincent's Semi-Annual United States Register.* Francis Vincent, Philadelphia, PA.

NPS Form 10-900-a
OMB No. 1024-0018
United States Department of the Interior
National Park Service

**National Register of Historic Places
Continuation Sheet**

ROBERT J. WALKER, shipwreck and remains
Name of Property
Offshore Atlantic, NJ
County and State

Name of multiple listing (if applicable)

Section number Additional Documentation   Page   52

Page 65 - If an entire page is redacted, what purpose is served by creating the page? This is a complete waste of paper. This is NOAA laughing at the person who requests a copy of this form in the hope of obtaining useful information that NOAA has excluded from its website. *Public* information, I should add.

NPS Form 10-900-a
United States Department of the Interior
National Park Service

National Register of Historic Places
Continuation Sheet

OMB No. 1024-0018

ROBERT J. WALKER, shipwreck and remains
Name of Property
Offshore Atlantic, NJ
County and State
Name of multiple listing (if applicable)

Section number Additional Documentation Page 53

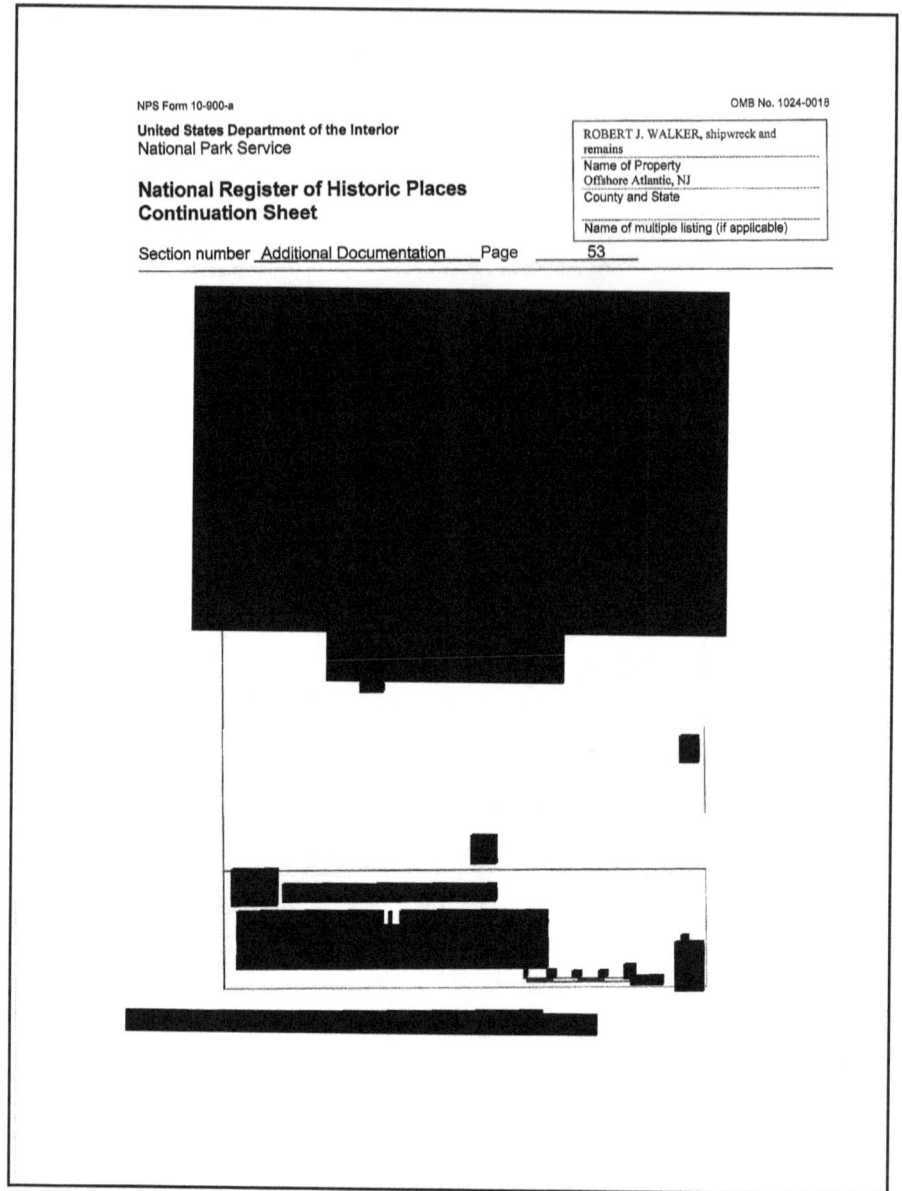

Page 66 - Another wasted page that is totally redacted. My guess is that either or both of these pages depict nautical charts on which the location of the wreck was shown and the GPS coordinates were given: knowledge that NOAA wanted to hide from recreational divers, commercial fishing and charter vessels, lobster boats, draggers, and trawlers - despite NOAA's avowal to want to work with these people.

The Hunting of NOAA's Snark
More Territorial Demands

NOAA's Bay Watch

When writing about NOAA's duplicities, it is difficult to know where to start. There are hundreds of trailheads that lead to lies, deceptions, and administrative abuse. And those trails lead to forks where other trails lead farther astray and form a tangled skein of additional perfidies.

NOAA is so crooked that it could hide behind a corkscrew.

I have already recounted the treacheries that related directly to the *Robert J. Walker*. There is no need to repeat them here. Instead, I will use the *Robert J. Walker* as a springboard to delve into other nefarious NOAA affairs that lie farther afield.

The issue that is the most directly related to the *Robert J. Walker* is the initiative to create a National Marine Sanctuary in New Jersey waters. The proposal is called the Sandy Hook Bay National Marine Sanctuary. The plan is to encompass all the waters of the bay, from the tip of Sandy Hook to the mainland along a line drawn approximately southwest from the tip.

The fancy language that was employed to advocate the need for such a sanctuary was typical bureaucratic gobbledygook: supposedly the sanctuary "would help provide sustainable resource management in the region."

Whatever *that* means.

The *Robert J. Walker* was the foot in the door. The newly proposed sanctuary is a foot in the face (or a kick in the family jewels).

This sanctuary would include not only Sandy Hook Bay, but would flow upstream on the Navesink River, the Shrewsbury River, and the tributaries to those rivers. These creeping watery fingers would put a stranglehold on the entire area by restricting access and fishing – how much is anyone's guess because no one in authority will put the restrictions in writing. Promises have been made orally, but NOAA has a history of breaking its promises in other sanctuaries.

Supposedly, the Sandy Hook Bay sanctuary "would aid improvements including fisheries, recreation and habitation."

Whatever *that* means.

The sanctuary would "provide a setting for exploration and education with regard to man/nature interactions and best combined land based and water based practices."

Whatever *that* means.

It seems to me that the local citizens and daily visitors already have a man/nature interaction that has been working for them for decades, or centuries. Who needs NOAA to tell them what to do? The quintessential problem with NOAA sanctuaries is that, once they are embedded, public input is totally ignored. NOAA does whatever it wants, whenever it wants, the public be damned.

In California, NOAA promised to close only 2% of sanctuary bottomlands to fishing. After NOAA took power, it closed 23% – and might close more in the future if it feels like it.

In Florida, NOAA wields absolute authority over two and a half *million* acres of water and land holdings. Since the creation of the sanctuary, numerous restrictions on both fishing and diving have been implemented. New seasonal and locational closures are applied all the time. "No take zones" now predominate in the sanctuary, with no checks-and-balances process in sight. The latest proposal advocates closure of 30% of the sanctuary.

According to Carl Liederman, president of Capt. Harry's Fishing Supply in Miami, "No members of the fishing community participated on the working group and no fishery related issues were identified during the process that would justify a need for any closures."

I explained working groups and Sanctuary Advisory Councils in *NOAA's Ark*, but in order for the readers of this book to understand the process, I must give a brief explanation here.

NOAA *appoints* volunteers to serve on SAC. Volunteers must go through a vetting process. Only those who approve of NOAA's goals are chosen to take a seat on the council. Those who oppose are excluded. When SAC members are sworn in, they must sign an oath to "assist to the best of my ability in achieving the Sanctuary goals."

The selection process and the swearing-in ceremony defeat the appointment of an unbiased council. SAC is nothing more than a NOAA sockpuppet: a fabricated and incestuous NOAA identity whose purpose is to lend legitimacy to NOAA's iniquitous goals of expansion and exclusive control. In other words, NOAA informs SAC what schemes it wants SAC to "study," then SAC advocates those schemes and "advises" NOAA of its acceptance.

Take this for instance. One of the SAC members of the Monitor NMS owns a dive shop in North Carolina. Her husband runs a charter business. Whenever NOAA needs to charter a boat, it charters her husband's boat. This is how NOAA repays its SAC members for their loyalty: a clear case of feeding at the NOAA trough.

So when NOAA promises for the Sandy Hook Bay NMS that "the management and enforcement style within the sanctuary is [sic] carried out in consultation with a Sanctuary Advisory Council," it is stating in effect that NOAA will manage and enforce whatever regulations it wants – again, the public be damned.

This vicious circular method of support also applies to so-called "working groups." Working group members are selected from volunteers who support NOAA's devious plots, while volunteers who object are excluded from membership. The working group then advises SAC to support NOAA's schemes – for expansion of sanctuary borders, for restrictions that give NOAA more control of the territory, and so on.

This instance of circles within circles confirms the adage that government agencies are run by big wheels. Thus NOAA has everything rigged from the get-go. The voice of the public is silenced.

Because the advisory council and its working groups are sockpuppets, when NOAA wrote that its goals for expansion were "approved by the advisory council and recommended for public review," I reiterate, it is essentially declaring, "We at NOAA approved our own goals for expansion." Citing the advisory council and working groups serves to legitimize NOAA's goals, as if NOAA did not want to expand the sanctuary, but it was advised to do so by "unbiased" advisors. Pure turkey turds.

The pronounced goals of the Sandy Hook Bay NMS suffer from other highfalutin lingo that intentionally muddles rather than clarifies the situation. Supposedly the sanctuary will "serve as a laboratory and thought leader for integrated man/nature interaction in a rich, complex, diverse and culturally developed environmental setting."

Whatever *that* means.

This obfuscatory language approach is standard operating procedure for NOAA. Multisyllabic ostentation is a confusing and concealing methodology that makes NOAA sound academic while actually saying nothing at all.

Consider this nonsensical diatribe: the sanctuary will "provide the citizens living along the sanctuary with a common resource to benefit all, and to serve as a focal point in their ability to co-exist with nature." Seems to me that the quoted citizens already have what NOAA professes to provide, except for the restrictions that NOAA intends to propose and enforce.

This proviso begs the question: Why would anyone willingly give up freedoms that he currently enjoys?

NOAA's sockpuppet for this latest upset of the status quo, so that NOAA can have greater control of the populace, is the Navesink Maritime Heritage Association. The Association claims that the sanctuary "would aid improvements including fisheries, recreation and habitation; provide a setting that integrates the water with adjoining land-based parks and public access points; and provide a setting for exploration and education."

Sound familiar?

I have heard a lot of promises, but I have not heard a word about how any of these so-called "benefits" will be brought about. It is NOAA's time-worn "blank check" routine: "Just give NOAA autonomous authority, and we will worry about the details later." Right.

There are seventeen towns within the borders of the proposed Sandy Hook Bay NMS. All of them will be adversely affected because control over waterfront and riverine activities will be taken away from them, and regulated by the whims of NOAA. Anglers will not be allowed to fish from the shores, clammers will not be allowed to dig for clams, duck hunters will not be allowed to stalk their game.

NMHA admitted that it "received answers to questions related to the marine environment" from NOAA, but has not admitted any further complicity.

In case you do not have a dictionary handy, please note that "marine" is defined as "of or pertaining to the sea." It goes without saying that rivers and streams and other freshwater waterways do not constitute a "marine environment," so that NOAA is out of its depth with regard to the instant sanctuary. But so was Hitler when he invaded Poland.

Local citizens were furious about the proposed invasion. When a meeting was held in a local library to discuss the issues at stake, in March of 2016, so many stakeholders arrived to protest the initiative and to vent their anger at the unsolicited proposal, that they could not all fit inside the assigned room.

More than a hundred people were turned away at the front door because the room was filled to capacity: 85 early birds inside and dozens of people standing on the stairs and the landing. And these were not just individuals who were representing themselves, but leaders of organizations who promised to fight the initiative at every step of the way.

Anglers cited how NOAA had severely restricted fishing access in Key Biscayne and the Dry Tortugas in Florida, and nearly the entire California coast.

Jim Donofrio, executive director of the Recreational Fishing Alliance, spoke for everyone when he declared, "We've been dealing with these scoundrels for twenty years. You're really stirring a hornet's nest with this idea. We have enough bureaucracy; we're not going to have it. We've said all there is to say; it's not going to happen."

Ever the activist, when Donofrio contacted Kim Guadagno, the Lieutenant General of New Jersey, she was unaware that such an initiative was afoot. She expressed disbelief when she responded that she was "rather surprised that something like this was moving forward without input from the state."

That is the way NOAA operates. NOAA has found it more expedient to use sniper tactics to keep the local citizenry unaware of its encroachment, than to don padded boxing gloves and ring a bell to announce its presence and willingness to listen patiently to aggrieved stakeholders. That way NOAA can catch the local yokels off guard and launch a less bloody invasion. Like Hitler did with Poland. It is more effective for an invader to win a war by not announcing its intentions; to trounce the enemy with a destructive military force before the locals have time to arm themselves.

I hate to say I told you so, but in *NOAA's Ark* I warned the country that this was going to happen if NOAA remained unchecked and was left to its own devices. I warned Californians about NOAA's hidden agenda. Shortly after the book was published, NOAA expanded the borders of three disarticulated sanctuaries so that they formed one massive mega-sanctuary that covered most of the stateside ocean.

Donofrio was not fooled by NOAA's sneak attack and empty promises. "What we've found is the marine sanctuary regulations are more restrictive than those outside the sanctuary. And then there will be some activities that will be deemed completely off-limits."

In essence, as always, NOAA wants to create a marine sanctuary despite contrary popular opinion, then write the rules and regulations after it acquires totalitarian authority.

New Jersey citizens beware. This is happening now.

The Balloon Hoax

Mega-sanctuaries are the way for NOAA to go. It is already trying to expand two East Coast sanctuaries: the Stellwagen Bank NMS off Massachusetts, and the Monitor NMS off North Carolina. In each case, NOAA wants to expand the borders of an offshore sanctuary all the way to the three-mile territorial limit. So far the Stellwagen Bank NMS expansion is in abeyance, but the Monitor NMS expansion has been revived, despite the opposition that NOAA received from the public meetings that were held in May 2012 – which I covered in excruciating detail in *NOAA's Ark*.

I let the public know about NOAA's latest machinations in my free online newsletter in January 2016. Read it and weep:

NOAA's Latest Antics

The government cancer known as NOAA has gone from remission to another spurt of malignant growth.

This will come as no surprise to those of you who read my book, *NOAA's*

Ark: the Rise of the Fourth Reich. Despite overwhelming opposition to expansion of the Monitor National Marine Sanctuary, NOAA has renewed its territorial demand. In this round, the anti-freedom agency has taken a new tack by offering choices to opponents about how much territory NOAA should be allowed to claim for itself: from every wreck off the coast of North Carolina to discreet concentrations of wrecks and handpicked wreck sites.

This is like Hitler giving an ultimatum to Poland in which he expressed a demand to occupy either the entire country, or only the rich cities and industrial areas, promising to leave the worthless land alone.

Why the need for expansion? There is no need; there is only NOAA's creeping jurisdiction in an attempt to dominate the underwater world. From a different perspective, there is the need of a cancer to keep spreading until it kills its host.

In the book noted above, I warned California residents that unless they took action, NOAA would expand and consolidate three existing sanctuaries into a single gargantuan sanctuary by stretching the borders of all three sanctuaries until their boundaries met, thereby tripling the total territory into one mega-sanctuary that would encompass nearly all the waters off the coast of the State. Residents did not heed my warning, so NOAA proceeded with its invasion . . . and won.

With regard to North Carolina, in a series of public hearings that were held in 2012, attendees from the fishing and diving communities registered unanimous disapproval of any attempt by NOAA to take control of the waters off the instant State, after which NOAA lied to Congress by stating that both residents and non-resident visitors were allied with NOAA's goal for expansion.

Both then and now again, NOAA claimed that its Advisory Council voted to expand the sanctuary in accordance with NOAA's demands. But the Advisory Council is nothing more than a NOAA sockpuppet: a handful of individuals who were given seats on the council by dint of their favorable attitude with respect to NOAA's goals. Volunteers who opposed NOAA's territorial encroachment were denied a seat in the selection process. In other words, NOAA created the Advisory Council as a disguise: it consists of handpicked individuals who were sworn to advise NOAA precisely the way NOAA wanted to be advised, so that NOAA could then state publicly that it was doing only what it had been advised to do.

Interested parties should know that NOAA has stated categorically that no changes will be made to Sanctuary regulations. Current regulations require that divers obtain a permit in order to dive within the boundaries of the Monitor sanctuary, and that fishing is prohibited. These restrictions will therefore apply to the proposed expanded sanctuary.

Recall that it took me eight years, four federal lawsuits, and tens of thousands of dollars to obtain the first permit to dive on the *Monitor*. Few people are willing to go that far in the cause of freedom. Thus fishing will be prohibited everywhere off the coast of North Carolina, and divers will have to fight individually for the right to dive on wrecks that lie within the boundaries of the newly expanded sanctuary.

NOAA has scheduled a series of public hearings to be held in early February. Dates and locations can be found at http://monitor.noaa.gov/management/expansion.html.

NOAA is also accepting written comments. But don't bother to write; NOAA discards unfavorable comments, and submits to Congress only those comments that are in agreement with its demands, in order to make it seem as if everyone wants expansion. In order to be heard, you must write to your Congressional representatives, both federal and State, as well as to the governor of North Carolina.

This is not NOAA's last territorial demand. It is only another in a long line of invasions.

That expresses the situation in a nutshell. I also wrote the following to my Congressional representatives and the governor of North Carolina:

I am opposed to expansion of any kind of the Monitor National Marine Sanctuary.

The issue of expansion was settled four years ago – in 2012 – when hundreds of people who attended NOAA's scoping meetings voiced unanimous opinions *against* any form of expansion.

As I pointed out in my book, *NOAA's Ark: the Rise of the Fourth Reich*, NOAA lied to Congress about this fact in its "Monitor National Marine Sanctuary Management Plan and Environmental Assessment," when it stated just the opposite.

To further defraud Congress, the MNMSMPEA included written letters from half a dozen sockpuppets who favored expansion, but did *not* include the *hundreds* of letters from those who expressed opposition to expansion. By not telling the truth, NOAA rigged the document to make it appear as if the majority of stakeholders favored expansion, when in reality no one but NOAA's pretenders favored expansion.

These pretenders were paid for their favoritism. For example, Debbie Boyce is on the Sanctuary Advisory Council that supposedly advised NOAA to expand the sanctuary. Yet NOAA charters her husband's boat for trips to and around the sanctuary.

SAC members are chosen on the basis of their allegiance to NOAA. Volunteers who objected to NOAA's goal for expansion were excluded from SAC.

Expansion of the sanctuary in any form would be an economic disaster for North Carolina.

According to sanctuary regulations, fishing is prohibited within the sanctuary. This means that commercial fishing will come to a grinding halt in the expanded sanctuary. Commercial boats must then move to adjacent States in order to continue their occupation to feed the public.

Tourism will mostly die because a large percentage of out-of-state visitors will not be allowed to charter sport-fishing boats, which must then leave the State and find patronage elsewhere.

Recreational diving in the sanctuary requires a permit from NOAA. Considering that it took me eight years, four federal lawsuits, and tens of thousands of dollars of my own money to obtain the first permit to dive within the sanctuary, all diving in the expanded sanctuary will cease to exist.

NOAA claims that it wanted expand the sanctuary in order to "preserve" surrounding shipwrecks. Yet NOAA has never done anything to preserve shipwrecks in any of its other sanctuaries. It has never installed cathodic protection on metal-hulled wrecks. It has never coated wooden hulls with anti-fouling paint. It has not stabilized collapsing hulls by installing support structures. It has not built cofferdams around fragile wrecks as a way to protect them from the violent marine environment.

Instead, NOAA simply lets shipwrecks rust and rot away. This does not constitute preservation. NOAA is using the word "preservation" as a façade to trick Congress into believing that NOAA will take a proactive stance toward saving shipwrecks from the forces of nature.

Everyone knows that a house or historic building cannot be preserved by never, *never* doing any kind of maintenance, such as mending a leaky roof, or repainting a peeling exterior, or repairing leaking pipes in the walls, or replacing cracked cement, or replacing worn and broken shingles.

Teredos eat shipwreck wood the way termites house wood. Yet NOAA has never done anything to stop these wood-boring mollusks from consuming wooden hulls.

I say NO to NOAA
2016 March 17

Once again, I pulled no punches when I told the truth about NOAA and its fraudulent methods for obtaining Congressional consent to expand sanctuaries that no one but NOAA wanted to have expanded.

This cachet was designed to advertise and promote NOAA, the *Monitor* Center, and The Mariners' Museum.

Dare County Consensus

Lest my readers think that I am the only one who stood against NOAA's invasionary tactics, you should know that letters of opposition numbered in the hundreds. Some were only a few sentences or paragraphs in length, others stretched on for pages and pages. One letter of opposition was written by a NOAA employee (whose job I must protect by not calling attention to the name).

Perhaps the opposition letter that had the most clout was submitted by the Dare County Commissioners. Dare County in North Carolina encompasses the entire Outer Banks, from Duck through Kill Devil Hills (the location of the Wright Brothers Memorial) to Hatteras Inlet. This stretch of sand comprises more than 80 miles of beachfront property. It goes without saying that county revenues will be severely curtailed by any form of sanctuary expansion and accompanying restrictions against . . . well . . . everything. Here is how the commissioners told it like it is (capitals and boldface are in the original document, but I have reduced the type size and deleted spaces between lines). As a political body, they were more diplomatic than I was.

COMMENTS BY THE COUNTY OF DARE ON THE PROPOSAL TO EXPAND THE BOUNDARIES OF THE MONITOR NATIONAL MARINE SANCTUARY (MNMS)
BACKGROUND

The Dare County Board of Commissioners appreciates the historical heritage of the Monitor National Marine Sanctuary (MNMS). Dare County has the utmost respect for the service and sacrifice of all U.S. military personnel and has demonstrated strong support for the recovery and identification of all U.S. Sailors whose lives were lost on December 31, 1862 off the coast of Hatteras Island.

Uniquely positioned on the Outer Banks of North Carolina, Dare County includes Hatteras Island and is home to the Graveyard of the Atlantic Museum. Our rich maritime tradition includes generations of heroic lifesaving and rescue operations assisting ships in distress off the Dare County coast.

POSITION OF THE DARE COUNTY BOARD OF COMMISSIONERS

The people of Dare County, through their elected officials, have enthusiastically supported many components of the MNMS mission including resource protection, education and outreach, and efforts to provide dignified care for recovered USS *Monitor* Sailors. However, **the Dare County Board of Commissioners strongly objects to any expansion of the sanctuary or the creation of additional Marine Sanctuaries.**

Although Dare County supports MNMS in protecting artifacts, educating the public, and preserving recovered remains, it cannot for the reasons stated in these comments, support any expansion of the MNMS. Neither does it support the creation of other Marine Sanctuaries off Dare County's shoreline. **The Board of Commissioners strongly objects to any expansion of the Sanctuary and to any effort that would limit or restrict recreational or commercial fishing activities now or in the future.**

Dare County believes that any concerns that MNMS may have about long-term site preservation can best be addressed through enhanced public education and by enforcing current regulations. Although enforcing regulations is challenging at the sanctuary due to its distance from the shore, the existing rules have proven adequate.

Any and all violators should be penalized as already provided in the current law, rather than expanding the number of regulations or extending the boundaries of the Sanctuary. This better serves the public interest rather than further infringement on responsible recreational and commercial fishing activities.

We respectfully request that officials of the MNMS work closely with elected leaders in coastal communities along with local fishermen, charter boat operators, and the scuba diving industry to promote an ongoing program of enhanced public education to assure long-term preservation of the site.

Dare County endorses MNMS efforts to raise public awareness about the sanctuary. The Dare County Board of Commissioners believes the cornerstone of these activities should center on the Graveyard of the Atlantic Museum. We believe this respected Hatteras Island museum should be given a prominent role in the display of artifacts, resource preservation, and expansion of educational programs.

As NOAA investigates Sanctuary expansion, we advocate a public process that fairly considers peer-reviewed science, citizen comments, and stakeholder input. As elected leaders who are geographically the closest to the Monitor National Marine Sanctuary, we believe the remarks made on behalf of Dare County's citizens should be given the greatest weight in decisions that are made about Sanctuary expansion.

The current Superintendent, David Alberg, has stated publically that he does not want expansion that excludes public access. Superintendent Alberg is a dedicated public servant and we take him at his word and believe his statement to be genuine and sincere. However, Dare County has witnessed firsthand, how promises made by other well-intended federal superintendents have later been set aside by those who follow after they have retired or are reassigned.

If, in spite of our objection, NOAA considers Sanctuary expansion, ironclad verbiage is needed to make sure that promises made today guarantee public access tomorrow for responsible SCUBA divers, and for recreational and commercial fishing. Expansion of the Sanctuary could result in the entire body of ocean waters off the Dare County seashore becoming a gigantic Marine Sanctuary in the future, which would result in highly restricted access that would devastate recreational and commercial fishing and seriously harm the economic stability of all of Dare County.

CONCLUSION

The Dare County Board of Commissioners supports the use of peer-reviewed science to protect resources, preserve archaeology and pursue ongoing research, monitoring, and conservation. We encourage MNMS in its education and outreach efforts and call upon NOAA to expand its utilization of the Graveyard of the Atlantic Museum.

We strongly object to any expansion of the MNMS or the creation of other Marine Sanctuaries off the Dare County coast. We call upon NOAA to use existing enforcement resources rather than expanding the regulations that now govern public access and fishing related activities.

We encourage NOAA to work closely with local and state officials, the general public, the fishing and dive communities, and other stakeholders on all aspects of the Monitor National Marine Sanctuary.

We further call upon the MNMS to involve the Dare County Board of Commissioners in any and all studies, advisory councils, and meetings concerning the Monitor National Marine Sanctuary now and in the future.

Respectfully submitted
Robert L. "Bob" Woodard, Sr. Chairman
Dare County Board of Commissioners

'Nuff said on that score.

In agreement, "The Outer Banks Association of REALTORS Board of Directors stands with the Dare County Board of Commissioners regarding their opposition to the expansion of the Monitor National Marine Sanctuary or the creation of other Marine Sanctuaries off Dare County's shoreline. We strongly feel that these actions would reduce the economic viability of our community."

The Ocracoke Civic & Business Association wholeheartedly concurred with the sentiments above.

Out-of-Staters must understand that tourism is a multi-*billion*-dollar industry in North Carolina. NOAA's proposed restrictions in any version of expansion would eliminate bottom fishing and severely restrict trolling: a catastrophe for the State's economy.

Also understand that the present size of the Monitor NMS is one square mile that is centered on the wreck. The proposed expansion would be *thousands* of times the size of the present sanctuary.

To counteract oppositional comments, two organizations favored expansion: The *Monitor* Center and Foundation, and The Mariners' Museum. But that is because NOAA provides funding for them, creates jobs for the people who work there, and pays their salaries. Not satisfied with selling their votes, these organizations submitted letters of approval multiple times, under different names, as a way to increase the number of supporters against the landslide number of non-supporters.

Andy Radford, of the American Oil Institute, seconded my comments (in *NOAA's Ark* as well as above) about the capriciousness of SAC and its working groups:

> Our review of the information provided on the models [by the working groups] showed that there was extremely limited information provided on the models and how they were derived. While SAC meetings and their minutes are available to the public, working group deliberations are generally not. No information appears to be available that outlines the justification or the thought process that occurred in the making of the four models. Information that is lacking includes a complete list of the wreck sites contained in each of the models and the reasons they need to be protected under sanctuary manage-

ment. It is likely that the working group would have ranked each of the sites, but this was not made available. It would be important to know what their thinking was as to why they considered these to be particularly important sites, and not others. The reason for this might help answer the question as to the reasoning for drawing the particular boundary lines for each of the models.

Joyce Steinmetz hit the nail on the head with this insightful query: "When you look at the threats to shipwrecks you've got four: physical, biological, chemical, and anthropological, or man-made change. How will a sanctuary designation change any of these four threats?" NOAA had no answer.

As I have already remarked, NOAA has never done anything to address natural threats. NOAA does not even suggest a solution to these or any other threats. In fact, NOAA does not even acknowledge the existence of these threats. It simply states that, given totalitarian control, it will "protect" shipwrecks in the sanctuary.

In answer to the question, "Why expand?", NOAA wrote, "With preservation, these resources offer historians, maritime enthusiasts, recreational divers, fishermen, beachgoers and outdoor adventure seekers the ability to experience this unique region and celebrate our nation's maritime heritage."

My question is, how can all these people experience anything in the sanctuary when no fishing is allowed, and when diving access is restricted and requires a permit that is nearly impossible to obtain?

"How" remains a great unknown.

How does NOAA hope to "protect" shipwrecks from physical damage when a hurricane or fierce northeaster plows through the sanctuary, and deep ground swells thrash the wrecks with unchecked abandon?

How does NOAA intend to "protect" shipwrecks from the biological attacks of wood-boring teredos and the destructive glue of barnacles and other clinging organisms?

How is NOAA going to "protect" shipwrecks from rust and other types of destructive chemical corrosion on ferrous metals?

In the Monitor NMS, the greatest amount of physical damage was done by – guess who? – NOAA, when it tore the wreck apart in order to salvage the engine and turret.

In the latter case, the wreck would have been better protected without NOAA's infernal interference. Here is why . . .

Another Janus Face of NOAA

As long as I mentioned the subject of "protection," consider this. NOAA spent millions of dollars of taxpayers' money to fund a gross salvage operation on the *Monitor*. The job took six years to complete, from 1998 to 2002. The wreck was cut into little pieces in order to reach the major components that NOAA wanted to salvage: the propeller, engine, and turret.

The 9-inch-diameter solid-iron propeller shaft was sawed through by means of a hydraulically powered hacksaw. This was the least intrusive recovery operation because the components were unencumbered by other parts of the wreck.

The next step was to raise the engine. To do this, divers had to slice through the bottom hull plates that covered the upside down engine room. These riveted iron plates represented the largest intact segment of the hull and the highest point of relief. A huge gaping hole remained after the hull and engine were removed.

To remove the turret, divers had to cut through the armor belt that lay atop the iron cylinder. In this manner the entire stern of the wreck was effectively demolished. The remaining, dismembered components resembled nothing more than a junkyard of bent and twisted iron beams that looked like a drop of giant Pick-Up Sticks.

In other words, NOAA did on the *Monitor* the exact opposite of the kind of preservation that it firmly and resolutely advocated. "In situ" preservation means leaving the wreck to nature, not touching it, not removing anything. This is the kind of "preservation" that NOAA enforces in all its other sanctuaries. This is the kind of "preservation" that NOAA prescribed for the *Robert J. Walker*.

At this point let me repeat NOAA's emphatically stated conditions from the chapter "Nomination and Future" with regard to the *Robert J. Walker*: "As a matter of policy and practice, *in situ* preservation – leaving artifacts in place – is the preferred option for preserving the wreck."

Obviously, NOAA does not practice its own policy. NOAA does not practice what it preaches. What NOAA means is, "Do as I say, not as I do."

Understand that *I* do not accept the concept of "in situ preservation." The phrase is an oxymoron that only morons would follow. The word "preservation" is illogical in this context because in reality it means just the opposite. Anything that is left on the bottom of the sea is not only lost to public view, it is also left to the caprices of nature – as I have pointed out in previous chapters.

Would you hang your prize dresses on a tree during a tempest or snowstorm? Would you leave your valuable jewelry on rocks around your house? Would you store the family china on your lawn? Would you keep precious heirlooms on mountaintops in winter? The answer to these questions is obvious: no, you would not. No sane person would.

So why does NOAA believe that priceless antiquities can be "preserved" in the planet's most hostile and hazardous environment? You tell me and we will both know. Or is this – NOAA ignoring its own adopted policy – just a holier-than-thou attitude?

Furthermore, if artifacts are left on or under the seabed, the public at large will never be able to see or appreciate them, because the majority of people are not scuba divers.

The idea of "in situ preservation" is totally absurd. And in the real world NOAA believes that it does not apply to NOAA; it applies only to commoners, to the unwashed masses, and to recreational divers – who, by the way, are the very people who go out of their way, and spend their own time and money, to explore shipwrecks, discover artifacts, display rescued relics, and provide the clues that lead to a wreck's identity.

But the worst was yet to come. After saving the *Monitor's* most iconic components from the wild whims of nature, NOAA decided not to preserve – really *preserve* – those components after all, but abandoned them to limbo in The Mariners' Museum's conservation lab.

NOAA received numerous kudos in the press during the recovery operations. Newspapers and magazines were rife with photographs of the engine and the turret being pulled from the water and landed on the dock where cranes put them on flatbed trailers for the trip to The Mariners' Museum's newly constructed, multi-million-dollar

NOAA'S SNARK - TERRITORIAL DEMANDS

conservation lab. After the engine and turret were placed in tanks that were filled with preserving solutions, the fanfare was over and the relics were no longer visible. Nor did they garner any more press coverage. Thus they had no more value for promotional purposes. They were out of sight and out of the public's mind.

So NOAA – which claimed ownership of the items – quietly ceased funding the conservation efforts, and let The Mariners' Museum go into debt to the tune of nearly half a million dollars. As a result of NOAA's lack of interest, the lengthy and costly conservation process was abandoned. The laboratory was shut down, the lights were darkened, security cameras were switched off, and there the artifacts sit: untended, unconserved, with a future unknown.

Meanwhile, NOAA – having lost sight of its original goal – spent enormous amounts of money on taking its employees on recreational dives, so they could see other wrecks off the coast of North Carolina. NOAA employees got to dive on the German U-boat *U-701*, the torpedoed tanker *Dixie Arrow*, and other shallow-water wrecks that did not exceed the 130-foot limit that NOAA regulations imposed on its employees.

NOAA also used some of its ill-gotten money to work on its latest sanctuary expansion scheme. NOAA must have figured that it could justify expansion by locating other wrecks that participated in the so-called Battle of the Atlantic: discoveries that would again put NOAA in the limelight.

NOAA had grander goals than conserving the salvaged remains of the *Monitor*. To achieve those goals, NOAA was mandated by Congress to hold public meetings in order to hear – and ignore – the voices of the public.

I took this picture of a diver swimming past the armor belt (at the *Monitor's* stern) before a fishing boat caught it's anchor line in the propeller and dislodged it - all because NOAA refused to mark the site with a warning buoy, and also refused to publish the location of the wreck. In its wisdom, NOAA wanted anglers to stay away from a site whose position was unknown to them: a prime example of NOAA's lack of reasoning and logic. Ultimately, NOAA ignored its own protocol to preserve wrecks in situ; it severed the shaft and raised the damaged prop.

The Hunting of NOAA's Snark
Battle of the Atlantic National Marine Sanctuary?

Deep, Down, and Dirty

In 2008, NOAA embarked on a multi-year project to "survey" North Carolina shipwrecks from World War Two: largely those that were popular dive sites, and whose stories and locations were published in both volumes of *Shipwrecks of North Carolina: from the Diamond Shoals North* and *from Hatteras Inlet South*.

As noted in the previous chapter, NOAA started its "survey" of commonly visited wrecks by making recreational dives on the *Bedfordshire, Dixie Arrow*, and *U-701*. Other wrecks that NOAA divers were supposed to "survey" were the *Australia, Ciltvaira, City of Atlanta, Dixie Arrow, E.M. Clark, Empire Gem, Kassandra Louloudis, Keshena, Malchace, Manuela, U-85*, and *U-352*. Locations for all these wrecks were published in the shipwreck books that are noted in the previous paragraph, making it easy for NOAA to find them (without acknowledgment, of course).

Although NOAA claimed to have plans to "survey" these World War Two wrecks, it was not permissible for NOAA divers to descend to three of them because they exceeded NOAA's allowable depth on scuba for NOAA divers.

The three deep wrecks were the *E.M. Clark* (250 feet), *Malchace* (206 feet), and *Manuela* (155 feet).

If NOAA ever carried out its plans to "survey" these deep wrecks – and no public documentation is available to indicate that it actually did so – the surveys would have to have been conducted by qualified divers breathing mixed gas that was supplied from the surface vessel via hose, and with constant communication with surface personnel via cable; or by remote survey methods such as multi-beam sonar, side-scan sonar, drop cameras, or remotely operated vehicles.

The whole purpose of these so-called "surveys" was to lay the groundwork for NOAA's next territorial demand: the expansion of the Monitor National Marine Sanctuary, to be retitled the Battle of the Atlantic National Marine Sanctuary.

In addition to following in the footsteps – or finwash – of recreational divers, NOAA did one item of original research. It set its sights on locating the *YP-389*.

I first wrote about the dramatic events concerning the loss of the *YP-389* in 1989, in *Track of the Gray Wolf*. I then wrote an expanded version in *Shipwrecks of North Carolina: from the Diamond Shoals North*. Finally, I repeated the sad saga in *The Fuhrer's U-boats in American Waters* (2006). All three of these books included location

YP-389
(Courtesy of NOAA).

information from archival sources.

NOAA latched on to this story because, according to a NOAA news brief: "The story of the *YP-389* personifies the character of the Battle of the Atlantic along the East Coast of the United States, where small poorly armed fishing trawlers were called to defend American waters against one of Germany's most feared vessels. It is one of the most dramatic accounts of an engagement between Axis and Allied warships during the dark days of World War II."

In brief, the Navy dispatched the *YP-389* on anti-submarine patrol with a defective firing pin in its only deck gun. The converted fishing boat had the bad luck to encounter the *U-701*. The Nazi U-boat engaged the fishing boat with its deck gun. The *YP-389* was unable to return fire, so her skipper steered away from the U-boat and dropped depth charges in his wake. The patrol boat could not outrun the U-boat because the latter was much faster. The U-boat shot the wooden hull to pieces, setting it afire and killing six men in the process. A dozen survivors jumped overboard as the fishing boat sank. All of them were wounded from either shrapnel or burns. They drifted throughout the night until they were rescued by friendly forces in the morning.

In typical U.S. Navy fashion, the skipper was recommended for court-martial for failure to engage the enemy.

In 2011, I received a letter from one Rick Janhola. He was an ex-Navy sailor who had read about the *YP-389* in my book (he did not mention which one). Rick's father was one of the survivors of the patrol boat's final engagement. He informed me that – again, in typical U.S. Navy fashion – his father did not receive a Purple Heart for his wounds.

NOAA did not search randomly for the wreck, but as I noted in my newsletter for November of 2010:

> The wreck site was discovered in 1973 by a Duke University expedition that was searching off the Diamond Shoals for the Civil War ironclad *Monitor*. The side-scan sonar survey located more than a dozen targets during the course of a weeklong search. Examination of the side-scan images established that one of the sites was the *Monitor*. The other sites were relegated to the scrap heap because they were not relevant to the mission's only goal.
>
> The National Oceanic and Atmospheric Administration obtained the co-ordinates of the other sites from Duke University. In 2009, NOAA dedicated three weeks of expensive shipboard operating time on surveying these deep-water sites by means of a remotely operated vehicle (ROV). One of the wrecks was tentatively identified as the *YP-389*. The entire wreck was videotaped, and a photomosaic was created from frame captures. The photomosaic provides an overhead view from bow to stern, and clearly shows a deck gun that was mounted on the deck. Along with wreck-site dimensions that were scaled off a multi-beam sonar image, the gun lends credence to the supposition that the wreck is the *YP-389*.
>
> The location of the site is being kept from the public that paid for the survey. According to NOAA, the wreck lies at a depth of 300 feet.
>
> One might wonder why NOAA spent taxpayer's money to conduct shipwreck surveys that do not serve any useful function for American citizens.

The reason is NOAA's secret mission to expand its National Marine Sanctuary Program in order to increase its control over public property and resources. Congress created the NMSP for the express purpose of preserving areas of biological interest. On its own, NOAA has established a territorial imperative that goes far beyond the pale of its Congressional mandate.

NOAA wants to expand the boundaries of the Monitor National Marine Sanctuary and change its name to the Battle of the Atlantic National Marine Sanctuary. This newly designated Sanctuary will be thousands of times larger than the core Sanctuary on which it is formed, perhaps to encompass the entire Eastern Sea Frontier. During World War Two, the ESF was an operational area that extended from Maine to Florida to a distance of approximately 200 miles from shore.

If NOAA gets its way, it will eventually control every shipwreck off the American eastern seaboard.

In light of NOAA's current enforcement policies, and more restrictive policies that it is proposing, wreck-diving could then become a thing of the past.

I cannot say that I am happy about my prescience and accurate prediction. As I learned later, the weeklong search was actually a three-week expedition that lasted from August 4 to August 24, 2009.

Some NOAA sources now state that the depth of the wreck is 320 feet. I tried to obtain the GPS coordinates from NOAA, but NOAA refused to divulge them. Let me remind my readers that all information that NOAA gathers at the taxpayers' expense belongs to the taxpayers. NOAA does not have the right to withhold public information from the public. This is only another in a long list of NOAA's illegal practices.

The GPS numbers are 34-56.445 and 75-23.900. This information came willingly from commercial anglers who work out of Hatteras, North Carolina.

As always, NOAA immediately issued a press release as a way to pat itself on the back for identifying the wreck, and to draw attention to itself for its accomplishments. One mistake that I noticed in the press release was the number of survivors, which NOAA gave as eighteen. In fact, the total complement was eighteen. There were twelve survivors and six fatalities.

Itsa Not a My Boat, It Musta Be a You Boat

Five years passed before NOAA found and identified its next shipwreck; actually, a pair of shipwrecks whose losses were inextricably entangled.

By this time NOAA had lost interest in the *Monitor* artifacts that were being conserved at The Mariners' Museum's conservation lab. The engine and turret were no longer newsworthy now that they did nothing more than soak in a chemical bath. NOAA quit supporting the conservation effort for artifacts that it had recovered and for which it claimed ownership, and left The Mariners' Museum hanging with a debt of nearly half a million dollars.

These precious artifacts that NOAA recovered were supposed to be put on display.

The irony of this situation is that NOAA outspokenly claims that recreational divers do the same thing with artifacts that they recover from shipwrecks. NOAA continually

NOAA'S SNARK – BATTLE OF THE ATLANTIC

makes aspersions about divers rescuing artifacts for bragging rights, and having trophy rooms in which their artifacts were displayed. If this sounds a lot like NOAA's *Monitor* recoveries and The Mariners' Museum's display cases, so be it.

Recreational divers do not issue press releases to brag about their exploits the way NOAA does. NOAA does not believe that what is good for the goose is good for the gander – at least, not when such an attitude contradicts the light in which NOAA likes to portray recreational divers: especially those recreational divers who are more observant and competent than NOAA's divers.

Furthermore, when NOAA announced the wrecks that it wanted to "survey," it neglected to mention that most of those wrecks had been positively identified by relics that recreational divers had rescued from oblivion.

To keep the record straight, I once offered to donate my entire collection of artifacts to the Philadelphia Maritime Museum (now the Independence Seaport Museum). The board refused the offer. The one relic that was accepted was not displayed, but was stashed in the basement where visitors could not see it. Later I took it back.

In 2014, after five years of "surveying" shipwrecks, NOAA finally hit pay dirt with something that was newsworthy: the discovery of the merchant vessel *Bluefields* and the U-boat that sank her.

I covered this incident in my books. In short, the *Bluefields* was part of a convoy that consisted of nineteen merchant vessels, seven escorts, one blimp, and Navy aircraft. The *U-576* surfaced in the middle of the convoy, and fired a spread of torpedoes that struck three merchant vessels. The *Chilore* and the *J.A. Mowinckel* survived the attack, but the *Bluefields* sank in four minutes. The *Chilore* later sank under tow at the mouth of the Chesapeake Bay. (For full details, see *Shipwrecks of the Chesapeake Bay in Virginia Waters*.)

Counterattack was immediate. A shot from the deck gun of the SS *Unicoi* struck the U-boat aft. Two airplanes dive-bombed the U-boat and straddled it with depth charges. The Nazi U-boat went straight to the bottom. There were no survivors.

A NOAA press release was just as immediate upon discovery of the sites: "A team of researchers led by NOAA's Office of National Marine Sanctuaries have [sic] discovered two significant vessels from World War II's Battle of the Atlantic. The German U-boat 576 and the tanker *Bluefields* were found approximately 30 miles off the coast of North Carolina. Lost for more than 70 years, the discovery of the two vessels, in an area known as the Graveyard of the Atlantic, is a rare window into a historic military battle and the underwater battlefield landscape of WWII."

This press release was plastered everywhere, including Facebook and Twitter.

Again, NOAA neglected to release the precise locations of the wrecks, and refused to provide the GPS coordinates upon request. Again, commercial anglers from Hatteras made up for NOAA's deficiencies and intentional redaction.

The *U-576* rests in 690 feet of water at 34-45.733 and 75-30.449.

U-576. (Courtesy of NOAA.)

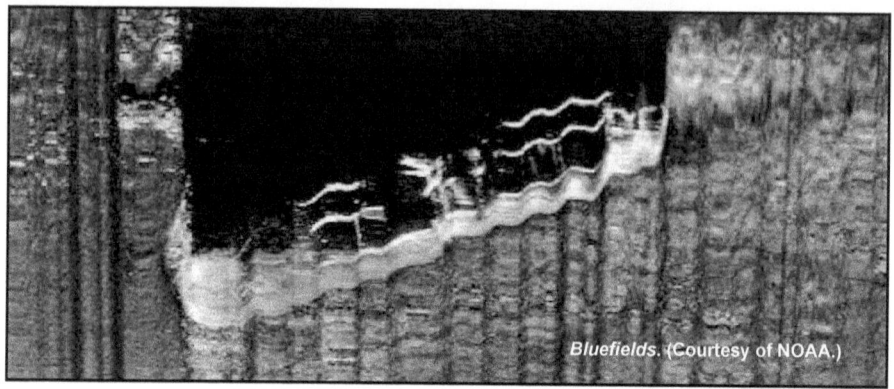
Bluefields. (Courtesy of NOAA.)

The *Bluefields* lies at a depth of 750 feet at 34-45.695 and 75-30.297. According to NOAA, the two wrecks lay only 230 yards apart: little more than a city block.

Ironically, at the bottom of the same release was this paragraph: "NOAA's mission is to understand and predict changes in the Earth's environment, from the depths of the ocean to the surface of the sun, and to conserve and manage our coastal and marine resources. Join us on Facebook, Twitter and our other social media channels."

The paragraph above caused many people to wonder why NOAA was spending the taxpayers' time and money on shipwreck research. What does that possibly have to do with NOAA's stated and Congressionally mandated mission, which NOAA openly acknowledged in its press release?

The answer is not quite "nothing." The answer is to obtain World War Two ammunition for NOAA's Battle of the Atlantic sanctuary designation; so NOAA could expand the boundaries of the Monitor National Marine Sanctuary; so NOAA could exercise totalitarian control over the vast coastal waters of the Atlantic Ocean: a designation that will severely limit the activities of commercial fishing, sport anglers, and recreational divers.

We can expect that NOAA's attitude toward expanding the Monitor NMS will eventually occur in the Sandy Hook Bay sanctuary. The proposed Sandy Hook Bay sanctuary is just another cog in NOAA's giant wheel, which is rolling toward overall control of the underwater world.

The Fictioneers

NOAA has a long and sordid history of disseminating falsehoods to the press as a way to alter the public perception of reality. NOAA's thesis is based on George Orwell's Ministry of Truth in his book *1984*: rewriting and revising history and spreading propaganda in order to misinform and mislead people about the need for marine sanctuaries.

NOAA constantly releases incorrect, untruthful, and misleading information to bolster its case for expansion. On April Fool's Day in 2016, NOAA spokesperson Tane Casserley was quoted as saying (about the proposed Battle of the Atlantic NMS), "We need to protect this as a battlefield and a monument for the fallen sailors of the war."

David Alberg, superintendent of the Monitor NMS, said that the expansion proposal "is about working together to honor this history, in so doing showcasing the heritage, and appreciation of the role North Carolina played in World War II. Not many Americans know about it and it needs to be honored."

Neither one explained why the only way to honor fallen sailors and to showcase their heritage is for NOAA to make a national marine sanctuary out of untold thousands of square miles of seabed, then restricting fishing and diving in the area.

To say that not many Americans know about the U-boat war off the eastern seaboard is to ignore the huge quantity of books, magazine articles, and newspaper columns that have been written – and continue to be written – about the U-boat war (including dozens of my own books and articles).

Nor did NOAA deny or try to correct the falsehoods that appeared in the same piece. It was claimed that "the bell of the *Dixie Arrow* was hanging as a trophy in a Cape Hatteras dive shop." This heart-wringing factoid was patently untrue. Yet this was the kind of rabid story that NOAA liked to perpetuate, because it reflected badly on recreational divers and helped to invigorate the need for sanctuary "protection." As I explained in *Shipwrecks of North Carolina: from Hatteras Inlet South*, U.S. Navy divers recovered the bell in 1944. It has not been seen since.

The last thing that NOAA wants is to work with stakeholders, as Alberg contended: "NOAA is aware of the concern from the fishermen and local citizens as their livelihoods are mainly from the Outer Banks. We are aware of it, we are being sensitive about it."

What political BS! NOAA has never been sensitive about local concerns in any of its other sanctuaries. As soon as it grabbed the reins it totally ignored local "concerns" and invoked strict regulations that put a stranglehold on locals and visitors alike. Even if NOAA was "aware" and "sensitive" of citizens' "concerns," NOAA never said what it was going to do about "it."

The real truth is that NOAA does not need to own or control torpedoed shipwrecks in order to honor the sailors and merchant mariners who perished on them. A memorial on land is far more effective in spreading the word about the U-boat war and its casualties, because more people will see such a memorial than will ever dive on the wrecks.

As a case in point, the British seamen who died in the torpedoing of the *Bedfordshire* have been honored in a cemetery that is maintained at Ocracoke, North Carolina. A memorial plaque explains the circumstances of their demise.

Furthermore, there are other areas off the coast of Florida and in the Gulf of Mexico that saw as much if not more U-boat action than NOAA's hypothetical Battle of the Atlantic. The North Carolina expansion proposal was shot down in 2012 because so many local citizens and out-of-state visitors showed up at the public meetings to voice their opposition; and because so many others submitted letters of opposition.

But wait! There's more. . . .

Instant Replay

As I noted in *NOAA's Ark*, when NOAA held a series of public meetings in 2012, it received overwhelming opposition to its scheme to expand the Monitor NMS and take over all the wrecks and bottomlands off the coast of North Carolina. NOAA hoisted its own petards by ignoring public opinion – both vocal and written – when it wrote a fictionalized account of the tenor of the meetings in which it stated that although some participants and stakeholders voiced "concerns" (NOAA's self-serving euphemism for "opposition"), the rabble were generally supportive of expansion. This clear-cut prevarication was submitted to Congress: a perfect case of fraudulent reporting. The report included the few letters that supported expansion, but excluded *hundreds* of letters that opposed expansion: facts that I duly pointed out in *NOAA's Ark*.

Now, as a stopgap solution to full expansion, which would include hundreds of square miles of seabed, in 2016 NOAA attempted a barely concealed step-at-a-time expansion in which it proposed a number of mini-expansions that would consume the most popular wrecks at first. Then, unspoken, NOAA would seek control of the rest of the offshore territory at a later date. No one was hoodwinked by this obvious ruse of piecemeal usurpation.

As far as the pubic was concerned, the question of expansion had been answered in 2012 by voluminous opposition. The people toed their Maginot Line and fired their canons during the latest set of public meetings, which NOAA called "scoping" meetings. They should be called "screwing" meetings.

I did not attend these meetings because they were held at locations that were geographically inconvenient from my home in Pennsylvania. However, commercial angler George Phifer contacted me about the meetings, the first of which he planned to attend. (There were five altogether; he attended the one that was held in Hatteras on February 1, 2016.) I asked him to record the session for me. He did, and he sent a copy of the voice recording to me so I could comment on the meeting in the present volume.

Public opinion had not changed or been swayed during the intervening years. Opposition to any and all expansion plans was unanimous.

The meeting was led by David Alberg, superintendent of the Monitor NMS. He announced that NOAA was authorized to expand the borders of national marine sanctuaries, but neglected to state where that authorization originated. In truth, NOAA authorized itself to expand its sanctuaries. Alberg forgot to mention that only Congress could authorize expansion – else why did NOAA have to write a report and submit it to Congress for approval and further action?

In *NOAA's Ark*, I quoted some of his dialogue for my readers. In answer to a question that was posed by Karen Flynn, here is an abbreviated sample of his answer for those of you who have not read the previous book:

> So, uh, in answer to your question, have, what have we been doing, have we been working on, where would it be, where would it not be, the truth is we haven't started it. That's why this is so important from our perspective, to begin that discussion. Nothing would make me happier than being able to hold, and, and, and the point was made last night, at, at uh, some of the other meetings, in terms of comments of the *Monitor*. It's fine. No one's really commenting about the *Monitor*. This is the, this is the issue. And nothing would make me happier than the ability to sit down with gentlemen like you, ladies like you, people that are, have a stake in this, and say, all is right, if we were ever to do this, provide me some feedback, because what's happened is that people, if you read the blogs, if you read the Internets, if you, in the postings that are out there, people unfortunately are responding to our lack of a position on the Internet: where it would be, what it would be. And the *Monitor* hasn't helped this. Because we've got forty year history on the *Monitor*, and it is the

most regulated site, argument the most regulated ship other than the *Arizona* in U.S. waters, um, although the *Portland* is, er, is regulated up in the Stellwagen Bank, it is natural for somebody to assume that if there was ever an expansion to the Monitor sanctuary, what has happened in this column of water would naturally go to these other sites. That is not true. Any revisions to the, to the management plan, any of the, the, uh, the, the, the, federal registers, er, uh, CFR bullets that you've identified, in, in your letter, any of those regulations would be, would be, happy to be looked at. So do you permit? Do you not permit? Is it every wreck? Does every wreck off the coast of North Carolina have historical significance? No, absolutely not. Does every wreck out there, um, important to the dive community? No. Is every wreck out there important to the fishing community? It's certainly a concern to them because of what might happen, but, what this action plan does, in this document, what we're proposing, is the ability to sit down, and start hearing from you, about what it would mean and what it wouldn't mean.

This diarrhea of verbiage went on and on and on without ever providing any useful information or coming to an intelligible conclusion. My reportage of Alberg's lack of communication skills must have impressed NOAA. For the new set of meetings, NOAA was smart enough not to let him speak. All he did was introduce a bevy of more articulate NOAA speakers. Although these speakers could talk grammatically, none of them ever explained how NOAA's shifty expansion maneuvers would "protect" or "preserve" the wrecks that NOAA wanted to place under its exclusive domination.

Mismeeting of Minds

In a meeting that lasted an hour and twenty-four minutes (84 minutes), NOAA speakers talked for 46 minutes: more than half the length of the meeting. Then, when the floor was turned over to the attendees, each attendee was limited to 3 minutes in which to voice his "concerns," (read "reasons for opposition") – although most of them overran their allotted time.

Furthermore, NOAA refused to answer any questions . . . about anything. Thus the audience that came for information was left in ignorance about the rules and regulations for the proposed Battle of the Atlantic NMS. NOAA simply said that they would be determined at a later date after consideration was given to the "concerns" of divers and anglers.

This caused one commercial angler from Florida to stand up and inform attendees about how NOAA screwed Floridians who fished – excuse me, who *used* to fish – in the Florida Keys NMS. He cautioned local anglers, "Be careful what you give up, because you're not getting it back." He had two horror stories to relate.

In the first fish tale, when the Florida Keys NMS was first proposed, NOAA promised not to restrict fishing or diving in the sanctuary. After the sanctuary was designated, NOAA changed the rules and prohibited both fishing and diving in certain areas, then later expanded the prohibited zones. It has been proven in this and other sanctuaries that once NOAA took control, it did whatever the hell it wanted to do, bad-faith promises notwithstanding.

In the second fish tale, because fishing for grouper and file fish was prohibited within sanctuary boundaries, any fishing vessel that had prohibited fish in her holds was not allowed to pass through the sanctuary; if they did, NOAA had no way of knowing whether those fish were caught within or without the sanctuary. This meant that fishing boats were forced to go all the way around the sanctuary on their return to port: a measure that was costly in terms and time and fuel.

He cautioned attendees to make NOAA put all its promises in writing. Yet even that measure was pointless when dealing with NOAA, because it has never adhered to its promises when it suited itself to rewrite rules and regulations.

NOAA reps talked about the so-called "need to protect additional maritime heritage territory," but never stated why such protection was needed . . . nor how NOAA was going to afford such protection from the elements of nature. This was merely NOAA doubletalk that was effective when declared to ignorant media types, but not to people who knew the truth of the situation. "Protect" was NOAA's euphemism for "control."

NOAA reps gloated about how it had partially funded the Graveyard of the Atlantic Museum (in which the first meeting was held), but neglected to mention that because of its funding it assumed control over how the museum was operated. It neglected to mention that it did not allow artifacts to be displayed if those artifacts had been recovered by recreational divers. It also neglected to mention that it broke its own stance by allowing two such artifacts to be displayed. As a result of NOAA's ban and hatred of recreational divers, the museum had only those two artifacts on public display. Visitors must feel cheated when they see nothing but two artifacts in a building that could exhibit hundreds or thousands of artifacts.

On one of my expeditions I photographed, videotaped, and rescued dozens of bottles from the *Monitor*. Many were mustard bottles that are shown below: first in situ where they were falling out of storage bins and in danger of being smashed as the iron hull collapsed around them. The on-board NOAA observer asked me to recover them, so I did. They all ended up at The Mariners' Museum in Newport News, Virginia.

This begs the question: What was the point of having a multimillion dollar building to display only two artifacts? Worse, although the museum was located only 16 miles from the wreck of the *Monitor*, no *Monitor* artifacts were on display there. All the *Monitor* artifacts were shipped to The Mariners' Museum in Hampton Roads, Virginia.

As long as NOAA seized the majority of the meeting time, its reps took time to suggest that the entire eastern seaboard was in fact a battle zone in two world wars, but that it was interested (for now) only in the area off North Carolina. But to worldly-wise folks, the handwriting was on the wall: North Carolina was not NOAA's only area of interest; it was just a starting point for later additional expansion.

Keep in mind that in accordance with current sanctuary rules, there was no fishing, no diving, and no drifting allowed.

NOAA reps wanted the *Bluefields* and the *U-576* to be recognized by being included in a national marine sanctuary that was under NOAA control. Such recognition put the cart before the horse. NOAA's media blitz promoted the fact that NOAA's survey vessels discovered both wrecks, but failed to mention that the purpose of the survey and ultimate discovery was a devious way of gathering ammunition to create a sanctuary that the public did not want. (I covered both wrecks in *The Fuhrer's U-boats in American Waters*.)

NOAA's overused phrase "interpretative outreach" could be achieved by numerous alternative methods.

NOAA reps then blamed sanctuary expansion on "working groups." I reiterate this scheme: the members of so-called working groups were hand-picked by NOAA. The only way to be part of a working group was to be in agreement with NOAA nefarious goals. In other words, a working group was nothing more than a NOAA sockpuppet. The working group advised the Sanctuary Advisory Council (another NOAA sockpuppet), which then advised NOAA the way it wanted to be advised: a devious and circumlocutory means of getting what it wanted without giving the appearance of wanting it; that in fact it was forced upon NOAA by the working group and SAC.

When NOAA finally got tired of beating its breast and patting itself on the back, the public was allowed to comment . . . but not to ask questions.

First up was the commissioner of Dare County. His position was that to the effect that "We can govern ourselves; we don't need NOAA to govern us." And, "We can protect our own resources without NOAA's intervention."

As an example of government takeover, he noted that when the National Park Service moved into the county and made the Outer Banks a Park, the public was denied continuous access. The NPS imposed restrictions around every corner and atop every dune. Restricted public access meant reduced tourism. Reduced tourism meant less income for local services and businesses. There were other places for people to go where restrictions were not imposed and where people were free to roam.

The corollary could be extended seaward. If fishing and diving were restricted or forbidden, anglers and divers would go elsewhere, and Dare County would dry up and become a tomb that was buried in sand and federal regulations.

The commissioner made it clear that Dare County wanted no part of NOAA's creeping encroachment: no way, no how.

George Phifer noted that NOAA refused to put guaranteed shipwreck access in writing. He also noted that once offshore North Carolina became federal property, there was no way to prevent other government agencies – such as the Environmental Protection Agency – from imposing additional restrictions on bottomlands that were now freely accessible. Why would anyone agree to have his hands tied behind his back so he could be kicked whenever NOAA felt like it?

NOAA reps promised to "look at" the restrictions for the expanded sanctuary but would not address the issues and offered no guarantees until after it gained control: a blank check which everyone knows never to sign or endorse.

Phifer wanted answers about restrictions against fishing – his livelihood – but NOAA refused to furnish them.

Other anglers and divers made statements that emphasized their suspicions of NOAA and stressed their dissatisfaction with the manner in which NOAA was handling the situation by not providing information that the people desperately wanted to have. NOAA kept everyone in ignorance.

All in all, the meeting went just about the way I expected it would. Nothing was accomplished as far as the public was concerned. NOAA expressed its desire to "protect" shipwrecks by placing them in a sanctuary, but never stated how sanctuary designation would prevent hurricanes from destroying them. No one can outlaw the weather.

NOAA cannot even *forecast* the weather, much less outlaw it.

A Rotating Revolution

The only thing that pleased me about the meeting was to hear one of the NOAA speakers talk about the *Monitor's* rotating turret. This statement directly if unknowingly addressed a pet peeve of mine.

In *Ironclad Legacy: Battles of the USS Monitor* (1993), I wrote:

> In naval parlance turrets that turn around their centers are called revolving turrets. Strictly speaking, this usage is imprecise. "Revolving" generally implies orbiting around a central point, whereas an object that spins on its axis is said to be "rotating." Thus the Earth rotates on its axis and revolves around the Sun. In order to be grammatically correct I will ignore naval custom and describe the turret on the Ericsson battery as a rotating turret: appropriate because that is the time when the phrase came into misuse.

Once embedded in the collective human consciousness, a fallacy is usually impossible to correct. Nonetheless, I continued to employ the phrase "rotating turret" in all my books about naval actions and shipping catastrophes. My books are read by Navy and NOAA personnel. Apparently, some of them accepted my emphasized fact that the traditional usage of revolving turrets was indeed incorrect, and made a conscious effort to remedy an age-old tradition.

Before the publication of *Ironclad Legacy*, everything I read about warships with turrets referred to them as revolving. In recent years I have read books and articles about naval history in which the author now referred to warship turrets as rotating. Some of these authors were navy personnel; others were civilian historians. This growing awareness and change in word usage has brought great personal satisfaction to me. Out of the mouths of babes . . .

The Hunting of NOAA's Snark
The U-boat Conundrum

The Sleazy Dog Syndrome

Although NOAA is faster than lightning when it comes to issuing press releases, it does so only when it wants to call attention to its actions. In other situations, when NOAA acts illegally or unethically, when it wants to impose a cover-up or divert attention from inappropriate actions, and when it does not want the public to know what it has done, it forgoes the press release and remains silent on the subject.

In NOAA's press release about the three-year search for the *U-576* and the *Bluefields*, it was noted, "Until this discovery, only four U-boats were known to have been lost off the coast of North Carolina, and all had been discovered."

This statement was patently false. As long ago as 1989 I published a list of five U-boats that were lost off North Carolina: *U-85*, *U-352*, *U-548*, *U-576*, and *U-701*. One can only presume that *NOAA* did not know of the existence of one of them, while tens of thousands of my readers certainly knew, after reading *Track of the Gray Wolf.* NOAA confers its own ignorance on the rest of the world.

So far, NOAA has been unsuccessful in expanding the Minotaur NMS – er, that is, the Monitor NMS. Remember that NOAA claims that it wants to promote fishing and diving in its sanctuaries, but its actions speak louder than its printed words. Much of the Florida Keys sanctuary is off limits to fishing and diving. Severe restrictions apply to the California mega-sanctuary. Other sanctuaries are also bound by various restrictions – most of which I covered in *NOAA's Ark*, so I will not repeat those perfidies here.

In addition, NOAA has gone out of its way to secretly impose restrictions on wreck sites that lie outside of national marine sanctuaries: shipwrecks on which NOAA has no legal authority. I already mentioned how NOAA nominated the *Robert J. Walker* for inclusion on the National Register of Historic Places, in which the location was restricted. But did you know that NOAA has conferred the same status on many other wrecks over which it exercises no control?

Case in point. After locating the *U-576* and the *Bluefields*, NOAA quietly nominated both of them for inclusion on the National Register of Historic Places. Both nomination forms are address restricted. That is, the locations on the forms have been redacted so that the public is excluded from having access to public information.

Where were the press releases for these nominations?

It gets worse.

In retaliation for not getting its way with the proposed 2012 expansion of the Monitor NMS, NOAA nominated the *U-701*.

And the *U-85*.

And the *U-352*.

Thanks to NOAA, these wrecks are now subject to diving and fishing restrictions. Here is NOAA's hollow justification for nomination: "Archaeological work by

NOAA on the U-boats off North Carolina, *U-85*, *U-352*, U-576, and U-*701*, has developed information about U-boat design, construction, and use as well as more complete interpreting the Battle of the Atlantic and its role in American history."

This statement is pure BS. Everything about the design and construction of U-boats is well documented on the original construction plans, which are readily available. Nothing more can be learned by looking at the rusting remains of the hulls.

Everything about the way in which U-boats were used in war is also well documented: by massive amounts of German records and by direct observation of contemporary Allied participants. And anyway, how can NOAA possibly expect a dead submarine that is lying on the bottom of the sea to divulge information about U-boat tactics and strategy? This is absurd. And if such a determination could be made from U-boat hulls, it could better be made from existing U-boats that serve as tourist attractions.

Plus, everyone who wants to know about the U-boat's role in American history and the Battle of the Atlantic either already knows it, or can read any one of hundreds of books on the subject. Again, nothing can be learned or interpreted about a U-boat's so-called "role" by examining the hull of a sunken Nazi U-boat.

This kind of "archaeological assessment" may look good on paper to an ignorant Nerp rubberstamper, but it is meaningless in reality. This is an example of NOAA snowballing Nerp reviewers as a means to take control of shipwrecks that have been in the public domain since World War Two.

The nomination form includes a table of U-boat losses that was taken right out of my books (either uncredited, or credited to someone who copied the information from my books). The same is true for most of the historical information.

NOAA tries to make people believe that each and every U-boat is somehow unique, and that this uniqueness must be "preserved" – by NOAA of course. We have already seen how NOAA "preserves" shipwrecks: by leaving them in situ in a destructive environment. In the nomination form, NOAA made no promises about how it was going to prevent these U-boat from further deterioration. So what was the point of putting them on the list of preserved places if NOAA was not going to preserve them?

Besides, as I have already detailed, being listed on the register of historic places is no more important than being listed in the phone book. No one who submits a completed nomination form or phone number ever gets turned down.

But, there is a method to NOAA's apparent madness and senseless nominations. NOAA can then point to these registered places and claim that because they are classified as historic, they are in need of protection that NOAA can provide by means of including them in a national marine sanctuary.

In other words, these nominations are part of NOAA's master plan to expand the Monitor NMS. If you do not believe me, understand that this scam has already been used to create a NOAA sanctuary. In 1974, the *Monitor* was nominated for inclusion on the National Register of Historic Places. The following year, the *Monitor* became the first National Marine Sanctuary – despite the fact that the marine sanctuary program was created to preserve *natural* resources. The word "shipwreck" does not appear anywhere in the Marine Protection, Research, and Sanctuaries Act.

Thus the claim for creating the Monitor MNS was baseless and illegal.

And while I am on the subject, NOAA has also nominated the *Dixie Arrow, E.M.*

NOAA'S SNARK – U-BOAT CONUNDRUM 191

Clark, Empire Gem, Lancing, and *Light Vessel 71* (the *Diamond Shoals* lightship).

Following the *Monitor* precedent, NOAA has set out to gobble up all these popular diving and fishing sites by fair means or foul, mostly foul. That way it can point to them and say, "See, they are all on the Register because they are historically significant. That's why we need to include them in a national marine sanctuary." Undoubtedly NOAA will nominate other merchant vessels unless it gets its way.

The Snake Oil Sellers

Under the category of the "significance" of the discovery of the *U-576* and the *Bluefields,* NOAA claims, "There are many unanswered questions about the battle and the order of events, but now with these two sites identified, archeological examination of the sunken vessels might offer explanations."

Again, this sounds good on paper if you are trying to impress someone who does not know any better. But NOAA neglected to identify any "unanswered questions," or how examining the wrecks "might offer explanations." NOAA's sentence is mere fluff that lacks any semblance of substance.

In the chapter "Nomination and Future" I disavowed the meaning of what the U.S. Navy and NOAA refer to as the "property" clause in the Constitution. The Navy's and NOAA's intentionally fictitious interpretation is blatantly unconstitutional.

NOAA also stated its intentional misinterpretation of the "legal status of U-boat 576: "The U.S. recognized Germany's ownership and that as a sovereign vessel, it is immune from arrest under the law of salvage and otherwise."

Unless the upper case "U.S." was a typo that was meant to spell lower case "us" that included NOAA and the Navy, this statement is definitely *false*. The United States most ardently does *not* recognize Germany's ownership of U-boats. Nor does the United States agree with the quote that NOAA published and attributed to the German Foreign Office, which read:

> In legal succession to the former German Reich, the Federal Republic of Germany, as a rule, sees itself as the owner of formally Reich-owned military assets, such as ship or aircraft wreckages. The Federal Republic of Germany is not interested in a recovery of the remnants of the *U-576* and will not participate in any such project."

The Potsdam Agreement

What NOAA and the Navy intentionally ignore are the terms of Nazi Germany's unconditional surrender.

In accordance with the terms of the Potsdam Agreement, Germany was completely stripped of its army and navy. It was not allowed to produce either arms or ammunition; indeed, Krupp (Germany's primary arms and armor manufacturer) was largely dismantled, and what remained of the company was converted to the manufacture of kitchen appliances. Germany's entire navy – its few remaining capital ships as well as hundreds of U-boats and even part of its merchant fleet – was seized by the Allies for reparations or disposal.

Each of the three major Allied powers (U.S., U.K. and U.S.S.R.) kept a number of U-boats "for technical assessment and experimental purposes." The remainder were scuttled at sea: hundreds of them, most in the North Sea.

It was stipulated in the Potsdam Agreement that Germany was not allowed to possess instruments of war of any kind: tanks, cannons, artillery, rockets, surface warships, and particularly U-boats. Winston Churchill went as far as to *specify* that Germany must be stripped of all U-boats, that they must be either dismantled or destroyed, and that Germany was never again allowed to build or own another U-boat.

What the Potsdam Agreement means in relation to the subject at hand is that the present-day German government does not and never has owned the Nazi U-boats that were sunk off the American eastern seaboard – or anywhere else in the world, for that matter. All existing U-boats have officially been disowned.

Because the provisions of the Potsdam Agreement specifically forbid Germany from ever again possessing U-boats, the German government has no claim to sunken U-boats.

I will mention only two instances that relate to this particular issue. In 1993, Danish millionaire Karsten Lee funded the salvage of Nazi U-boat *U-534*. The hull was raised intact, and is now on public display in Birkenhead, England.

The German government neither protested the salvage nor had any say in how or where the U-boat should be exhibited.

Instance number two occurred over a two-year period in 1990 and 1991. The U.S. Navy conducted a massive salvage operation in which Navy divers used airlifts to exhume some 10,000 cubic feet of sand, mud, silt, and human remains from the interior of the *U-352*, and spewed the waste material through an exhaust pipe into the water column, after which the current spread it across the ocean floor. The Navy did not ask Germany for permission to disturb a grave site, and there was no word of protest from the German government. The Navy just went and did it. (For exhaustive details about this major salvage operation, see *The Great Navy Wreck Scam*.)

To reiterate, the legal rationale of the Potsdam Agreement applies to all U-boats everywhere in the world, including those that were sunk off the eastern seaboard of the United States. This means that Germany has no claim to the *U-576*. To repeat, Germany has been dispossessed of all existing U-boats.

Both NOAA and the Navy continue to lie about the true legal status of Nazi U-boats. A lie remains a lie no matter how often it is repeated.

The fact that NOAA either lies about and/or refuses to recognize the Potsdam Agreement poses an interesting problem. If NOAA truly believes its own guff – that present-day Germany owns the *U-576* – how can NOAA nominate another country's vessel for inclusion on the National Register of Historic Places, which is a United States government organization? Such an action constitutes theft.

"Curiouser and curiouser," cried Alice, in *Alice's Adventures in Wonderland*.

Perhaps NOAA's adage is a quote from the Queen in the same book, "Sometimes I've believed as many as six impossible things before breakfast."

Or has NOAA adopted Humpty Dumpty's philosophy that is found in the same book: "When I use a word, it means just what I choose it to mean."

You will have to go *Through the Looking Glass* to understand NOAA.

The Hunting of NOAA's Snark
Freedom of Information – Not!

Data Corruption

In this chapter you will learn how hard NOAA fights to keep from disseminating public information to the public. Keep in mind that everything that NOAA does is paid by the taxpayers. Therefore, taxpayers have a constitutional right to access information that NOAA has collected.

Nonetheless, NOAA decides what information it will release to the public, and what information it wishes to keep *from* the public. In writing about the *Robert J. Walker*, the only information that I could obtain from NOAA was what it published on its website.

When I asked NOAA for a high resolution scan of a low resolution side-scan image that was posted on NOAA's website, NOAA replied that it no longer possessed the original high-resolution image because it had been transferred to the National Archives. It is absurd to think that NOAA would not keep a copy of its own image, especially as that image was created only the year before. Information is not transferred to the National Archives until it is no longer needed by the agency that obtained it – that is, until that information assumes historical quality.

When I contacted the National Archives about the image in question, and submitted NOAA's response to my query, the Archives told me that it did not have the image, and informed me that it is not NOAA's repository for recently acquired information. Thus NOAA gave me a runaround because it did not want me to have public information to which I was entitled.

This is not a new issue. NOAA has blocked the dissemination of information to me ever since I started dealing with it, in 1984, when I submitted my first request to dive on the Civil War ironclad *Monitor*. Some important information for the second of my four lawsuits against NOAA was not released to me until six years later, and then a court order was required to obtain it. (See *Ironclad Legacy* for more in this regard.)

By now, I have been actively fighting NOAA for more than three decades. In all that time it has employed a whole gamut of obstructionist tactics to prevent the release of public information. I wrote about a number of my information requests in *NOAA's Ark* (2013). The lengths to which NOAA will go to prevent the dissemination of public information to the public is nothing less than phenomenal.

The most oft used tactic is simply not replying to a query. Leaving a FOIA request in limbo is not a denial. After several repeat queries, I generally forwarded my information request to my Congressional representative, who then used the authority of his position in the government to force NOAA to release the information that I requested. This approach did not always work, as you will see in the following recent example (which is not annotated in *NOAA's Ark*).

The Billy Mitchell Wrecks

In 2011, NOAA made the fictitious claim that it had "discovered" the wrecks that were known collectively as the Billy Mitchell Wrecks. In reality, NOAA did not "discover" these wrecks because I had already discovered them, between 1990 and 1995. I published a Special Report in *Shipwrecks of Virginia* (1992) in which I recounted the history of the wrecks, and provided coordinates for those that I had dived and identified up to that time: three out of eight.

In 1999, I published a step-by-step account of all the expeditions that I led during that six-year period: scores of pages that were part of *The Lusitania Controversies*. By that time in my publication history, I had discovered and dived on seven of the eight wrecks.

These wrecks were World War One German warships that were brought to the U.S. after the signing of the Armistice. They consisted of the battleship *Ostfriesland*; the light cruiser *Frankfurt*; the destroyers *G-102*, *S-132*, and *V-43*; and the U-boats *U-117*, *U-140*; and *UB-148*. The only one that eluded me was the *S-132*.

I named them the Billy Mitchell Wrecks because General Billy Mitchell was responsible for the aerial bombing tests that sank some of them, in 1921. Some were sunk by means of naval gunfire.

The first one that I dived – with Ken Clayton and Pete Manchee – was the *Ostfriesland*. It lay at a depth of 380 feet. The *Frankfurt* was the deepest, at 420 feet. The U-boats were the shallowest: between 230 feet and 275 feet. The destroyers lay at 350 feet. These deep dive discoveries received a large amount of media attention, not only in technical diving magazines but in a six-part television series. I wrote magazine articles about some of my exploits, and included them in *Shipwreck Sagas* (2008).

Thus NOAA was well aware of my discoveries when, inspired by them, it set out to look at the wrecks through the lenses of underwater cameras. Despite my wealth of published material, NOAA claimed that "exact locations of the wrecks are unclear as is the condition of the wrecks." This is another big lie. The locations were known. Just as in the case of the *Robert J. Walker*, NOAA did not have to search for the Billy Mitchell Wrecks. All it had to do was go to the precise coordinates that I had published two decades earlier.

Similarly, on another survey trip a NOAA vessel "found" the battleship *Washington*. I discovered and dived on the *Washington* in 1989. In *Shipwrecks of Virginia*, I wrote a chapter about the history of the battleship, described my dive to 290 feet, and published the coordinates.

In 2012, the headline of one NOAA article announced in large boldface letters: "Billy Mitchell Shipwrecks 'Found.'"

Another claimed, "The German light cruiser we dove on today was oriented upright," giving the impression to an unknowledgeable public that NOAA employees dived to the wreck on scuba, the way I explored these wrecks, whereas in fact they deployed a remotely operated vehicle (ROV) that did their "diving" for them while they sat in the comfort of a dry cabin in front of a television monitor.

In order to distance itself from my discoveries, NOAA changed the name that I gave to the Billy Mitchell Wrecks to the Billy Mitchell Fleet. A rose by any other name . . .

NOAA claimed that it was going to "generate high-resolution photomosaics" of the Billy Mitchell Wrecks from multi-beam surveys. It was the multi-beam scan of the *Ostfriesland* that I tried to obtain when I was told that NOAA no longer possessed it –

NOAA'S SNARK – FREEDOM OF INFORMATION   195

which begs the question, how was NOAA going to generate a photomosaic if it did not have the multi-beam survey in its possession?

To date, no photomosaic of any kind has been made available to the public which paid for NOAA's costly expeditions.

To add insult to injury, in addition to not giving me credit for priority in discovering the Billy Mitchell Wrecks, NOAA then claimed, "We have evidence that divers have damaged some of them."

If divers *had* damaged some of the wrecks, that admission on the part of NOAA proved that divers had already discovered the wrecks, and not NOAA.

Due to the extreme depths at which the Billy Mitchell Wrecks lay, only a few dozen divers have ever visited these wrecks in person. Most of them were on my expeditions; others were on J. T. Barker's expeditions. Now these intrepid explorers were being accused of damaging "some" (more than one) of the wrecks. I did not believe it.

First NOAA lied about my priority of discovery, then it made unsupported allegations that denigrated the integrity of highly skilled recreational divers. These unscrupulous gambits constituted standard operating procedure for NOAA, to which malfeasance was an everyday practice.

To understand the absurdity of NOAA's aspersion, consider how much damage the wrecks incurred before they were scuttled. The centerpiece of the Billy Mitchell Wrecks was the *Ostfriesland*. Mitchell started the bomb test by having a flight of eight Martin biplanes drop 25-pound bombs on the deck. A group of Naval inspectors then examined the battleship in order to ascertain how much damage had been done.

The next flight of biplanes dropped thirty-two 230-pound bombs on the warship. Again a group of Naval inspectors examined the damage.

The third flight dropped twelve 550-pound bombs. Naval inspectors examined the damage.

The fourth flight dropped twelve 600-pound bombs. Naval inspectors boarded the battleship and took notes of the damage.

The fifth flight dropped fourteen armor-piercing 1,100-pound bombs. Naval in-

Bomb fragments and chunks of metal from the deck and superstructure are blown hundreds of feet into the air and splatter the ocean an equal distance from the hull of the *Ostfriesland*.

Courtesy of the National Archives.

spectors examined the damage.

The sixth flight dropped fourteen 1,000-pound bombs. Naval inspectors did their duty. By this time the upperworks were riddled with holes, and the hull had been hammered so hard that it was settling in the water.

The seventh flight dropped eleven 2,000-pounds bombs, which finally caused the ship to roll over and sink.

Altogether, more than one hundred bombs were dropped on or next to the *Ostfriesland*; that is more than 80,000 pounds (40 tons) of bombs. The overall damage was devastating. When last seen, the *Ostfriesland* resembled a junkyard of bent and twisted metal more than a sleek battleship.

Then, after 91 years of collapse and gross deterioration, NOAA observers claimed that they could distinguish between the massive damage that was wrought by more than a hundred high-explosive bombs, nearly a century of corrosion, natural decay and degeneration, and through a thick covering of marine fouling organisms – and alleged "damage" that was done on a few dozen dives, each of which lasted little more than ten minutes in length. This was preposterous.

NOAA operates under the theory that you can fool some of the people all the time, and all of the people some of the time, and who cares about the ones you don't fool. Quantity counts. In character assassinations, the bullets that hit count more than those that miss.

Now the question that is begged is, Why is NOAA in the shipwreck location business?

According to NOAA, its objective "is to assess that damage and to try to find a way to preserve these iconic shipwrecks . . . and management work has only just begun."

I have stated it before but I will state it again: You cannot "manage" shipwreck deterioration; you can only watch it occur.

NOAA also stated, "The shipwrecks are being assessed for the possibility of their being listed on the National Register of Historic Places, a designation that would help protect an important chapter in nautical and aviation history."

There is that empty-headed word again, "protect." NOAA neglected to explain how a political designation would protect the Billy Mitchell Wrecks from chemical disintegration and the brutal and unchecked forces of nature. Next thing you know, NOAA will ask Congress to repeal the law of gravity.

Now it all becomes clear. For the same reason that NOAA nominated U-boats and merchant vessels off the coast of North Carolina, for the same reason that NOAA nominated the *Robert J. Walker*, for the same reason that NOAA wants to create the Sandy Hook Bay NMS, NOAA wants to use the Billy Mitchell Wrecks to create a new sanctuary which it can later expand to join the other East Coast sanctuaries. These are all parts of a grandiose scheme to create an East Coast mega-sanctuary that will eventually encompass the entire eastern seaboard.

East Coasters heed this dire warning. Californians did not; now they are saddled with a mega-sanctuary that covers nearly all the waters off the State's Pacific coast.

Pâté de FOIA Gras, or Goose Poop on Rye

There are two things that American citizens need to know about the Freedom of

NOAA'S SNARK – FREEDOM OF INFORMATION   197

Information Act: the way it is supposed to work, and the way it actually works – or does not work, as is more often the case.

The way FOIA is supposed to work is that everyone has the freedom to obtain government information freely and in a timely manner. The way it works in actuality is quite different. Consider this:

When I was writing *NOAA's Ark*, I tried to obtain information about a remark that the manager of the Monitor NMS made at a scoping meeting. Here is my FOIA letter:

> National Oceanic and Atmospheric Administration   May 18, 2012
> 1401 Constitution Avenue, NW
> Room 5128
> Washington, DC 20230
>
> At a recent scoping meeting, NOAA spokesperson David Alberg stated that NOAA had received complaints from officials in Germany with regard to diving on Nazi U-boats in American waters. In addition to U-boats in general, he mentioned specifically the *U-85*, *U-352*, *U-576*, and *U-701*. In accordance with the Freedom of Information Act, 5 U.S.C. Sec. 522 et seq., I hereby request copies of all correspondence, documents, emails, notes, telephone transcripts, inter-office memos, and any other form of documentation to which Alberg referred: not only correspondence addressed *to* NOAA and other government agencies, but all replies, correspondence, documents, emails, notes, telephone transcripts, inter-office memos, and any other form of documentation *from* NOAA with regard to Nazi U-boats in American waters. Digitized documentation is acceptable, and may be sent to me via email.

NOAA's response? None. I never even received acknowledgment of receipt of my request. Nor did I receive an acknowledgment to my follow-up request; or to the next follow-up; or the next; or the next . . . I am still waiting.

You get the picture. This is not the way a responsible government agency is supposed to operate.

Here is a copy of my next FOIA request, two years later:

> National Oceanic and Atmospheric Administration   July 16, 2014
> 1401 Constitution Avenue, NW
> Room 5128
> Washington, DC 20230
>
> Re: Freedom of Information Act Request
>
> In 2012, NOAA published an article about shipwrecks of the so-called Billy Mitchell fleet, in which it was claimed "we have evidence that divers have damaged some of them."
>
> In accordance with the Freedom of Information Act, 5 U.S.C. Sec. 522 et seq., I hereby request copies of all reports, correspondence, emails, notes, telephone transcripts, inter-office memos, photographs, and any other form of documentation, relating to this "evidence" or supporting the aforementioned claim.
>
> Digitized documentation is acceptable and may be sent to me as email

attachments or on compact disks.

Note that I called the Billy Mitchell Wrecks the Billy Mitchell fleet. I did that because that was how NOAA called it in its online post. I did not want any confusion to intrude in my request.

This time NOAA took a different tack. As always, I sent my request via U.S. Postal Service. NOAA waited two weeks, then sent the following letter via email:

> Mr. Gentile,   July 30, 2014
> The NOAA FOIA Office uses FOIAonline* which is located at:
>   https://foiaonline.regulations.gov
> Please choose one of these options:
> 1) Enter your request into FOIAonline as a Guest or establish an account
> 2) Reply to this email that you agree to have the NOAA FOIA Office staff copy and paste your request into FOIAonline for you. This means that you will not be able to take advantage of the benefits of FOIAonline*.
> If you do not reply by August 7, 2014, the NOAA FOIA staff will enter the request for you.
> Please let us know if you have any questions.
> *FOIAonline is a multi-agency FOIA tracking and processing system which provides a single interface through which you may submit requests to NOAA and other participating agencies. FOIAonline will automatically provide tracking numbers for requests. Registered users may view the status of all your requests online, eliminating the wait time for replies from agency staff. It will provide NOAA a convenient place to post FOIA documents in electronic format after they have been released to the requester. Many users will choose to search these records before filing requests in the future.

This all sounds very official, but in fact it was just an obstructionist tactic that was intended to sound as if I was receiving just treatment when in fact NOAA had no intention of fulfilling my request. I followed instructions nonetheless.

The following day I received this protracted tome:

> Dear Mr. Gentile
> This letter is in regards to your Freedom of Information Act (FOIA) request entered into FOIAonline on July 31, 2014, regarding "shipwrecks of the so-called Billy Mitchell fleet."
> You asked for a waiver of fees. Pursuant to procedures established in 15 CFR, Part 4.11(k), I will rely on the following factors in determining whether the statutory standard for granting a fee waiver has been met:
>   1) The subject of the requested records must concern identifiable operations or activities of the Federal Government.
>   2) The disclosable portions of the requested records must be meaningfully informative about Government operations or activities in order to be "likely to contribute" to and increase public understanding of those operations or activities.

3) The disclosure of the requested information must contribute to the understanding of a reasonably broad audience of persons interested in the subject, as opposed to the individual understanding of the requester. For example, tell us about publications or websites where the information will be posted.

4) The disclosure of the requested information is likely to contribute "significantly" to the public's understanding of Government operations or activities.

5) Whether the requester has a commercial interest that would be furthered by the requester.

6) Whether any identifiable commercial interest of the requester is sufficiently great, in comparison with the public interest in disclosure, such that the disclosure is not primarily in the commercial interest of the requester.

After reviewing your request, I determined that your fee waiver justification did not provide us with all the necessary information to make an informed decision as to whether or not to appropriately grant you a fee waiver for these specific records. If you would like further consideration of your fee waiver request, please explain in detail how disclosure of the records requested would satisfy all the requirements for a fee waiver. A detailed fee waiver justification should cover all information described in your request.

Please reply to this letter by August 21, 2014. The clock is stopped until you reply or the due date in this letter whichever comes first.

If the fee waiver is not granted your request will be processed under the "All Other" fee category.

This lengthy letter undoubtedly took more time to write that it would have taken to make a phone call to the NOAA scribe who wrote the article that instigated my FOIA request, and to ask him how he obtained the so-called "evidence" that I was requesting – which, I was certain, did not exist.

NOAA was playing games with me. Keep in mind that NOAA knew exactly who I was, because they had been dealing with me for more than thirty years. The NOAA file on me – which included four federal lawsuits – was colossal.

Noticeably missing from the list of "musts" was a promise to provide me with unredacted documents. In other words, should I be able to jump through all of NOAA's hoops, NOAA reserved the right to send the pages on which the requested information appeared, but to redact the very text that I was requesting. Thus the situation was more of a roulette gamble than an assurance to properly respond to my FOIA request.

Furthermore, most of NOAA's conditions were purely subjective. For example, how does one determine whether the information that I requested is "likely to contribute," or "significantly?"

Keep in mind that my request was not broad. I asked for a specific and quantifiable item of information which a NOAA employee had already identified.

Worse yet, after submitting my appeal, NOAA claimed that it had never been received. This trick enabled NOAA to deny my fee waiver out of hand, with the excuse that I had not replied by the due date.

On August 22, 2014, NOAA sent me a letter of fee waiver denial. To wit:

After reviewing your request I sent you email correspondence via FOIAonline on July 31, 2014, asking for additional information. You did not provide any additional information. Since you have not addressed the factors above, I made the determination that your incoming fee waiver justification was insufficient in detail for the records listed above. Specifically, you did not identify a government operation or activity and show how you would share the records to increase the public understanding.

This constitutes a denial of your fee waiver request. You have the right to appeal. Your appeal must be received within 30 calendar days of the date of this initial denial letter by the Assistant General Counsel for Administration.

Even though I knew that NOAA was playing a game of cat and mouse with me, I decided to play this out and see how far NOAA would go to prevent me from obtaining the requested information. I submitted my appeal to the email address that was provided in the letter. The daemon mailer bounced my email because the address was invalid.

I lodged a complaint on FOIAonline. NOAA provided a different address. I resubmitted my appeal thus:

I received a denial of fee waiver for the FOIA request that is attached. The fee waiver was denied on the grounds that I did not respond to NOAA's letter of July 31, 2014. I did respond, but perhaps my response was misplaced or was not received.

As noted in my original FOIA request, NOAA claimed to possess evidence that divers damaged some of the shipwrecks which NOAA calls "the Billy Mitchell fleet." This claim was not substantiated by any documentary evidence. Making unsubstantiated allegations to be interpreted as fact demonstrates a bias in government activities of which the general public should be made aware. Releasing the putative evidence will contribute to an understanding of the manner in which the government in general (and NOAA in particular) operates with regard to maligning sectors of the American public by publicizing allegations without furnishing evidence to support those allegations. The American people need to be made aware of the government's (and NOAA's) rationale for making claims while withholding documentary evidence to support those claims.

I plan to publish this information in my free online newsletter, which reaches thousands of American subscribers who are concerned about government activities. Additionally, some of my subscribers forward my newsletters to other concerned citizens. Furthermore, some of my subscribers republish my newsletters on blogs, website, and chat groups that have their own vast subscriptions. Anyone can subscribe to my newsletter for free by visiting my website, clicking the link named Contacts, and entering an email address to which the subscription should be sent.

By making unsubstantiated allegations, the government (and NOAA) gives the appearance of a purposeful intention to malign scuba divers unfairly. Disclosure and distribution of this information will help to enable Americans in general (and scuba divers in particular) to understand why NOAA would make a deleterious claim without providing documentation to support that claim.

I have no commercial interest in making this information public. My goal is to set the record straight. If NOAA possesses such evidence, I plan to publish (for free in my newsletter) the evidence that NOAA relied upon when it published its allegations.

Understand that preceding the time of this FOIA request, David Alberg – superintendent of the Monitor NMS – had deprecated recreational divers by telling reporters, "Two of the U-boats, *U-352* and *U-85*, have been severely impacted by salvage operators and souvenir hunters." He neglected to mention that the worst salvage operators and souvenir hunters were U.S. Navy divers, who scooped 10,000 cubic feet of sand, silt, mud, and body parts out of the interior of the *U-352*, and who pulled apart sections of the *U-85* in order to take a spare torpedo as a souvenir.

Alberg also said that recreational divers "are going to a grave and looting a grave."

NOAA archaeologist Joseph Hoyt said that a lot of recreational divers, "if they find a skull, or remains, will decide that others want to see it, so will move it out and bring it up on deck." Again, Hoyt neglected to mention that it was the U.S. Navy that sucked all the body parts out of the *U-352*: a monumental case of grave desecration.

The readers of this book – that is, those who have not read *NOAA's Ark* – need to understand how much bad press NOAA was feeding to the media. The offensive declaration about recreational divers on the Billy Mitchell Wrecks was not an isolated item. It was one instance among many in which NOAA went out of its way to give recreational divers a foul reputation in a public forum.

Appended to my appeal was a fact that NOAA already knew: "I would like to add that NOAA staff members number among the subscribers to my free online newsletter. NOAA keeps informed of diving activities by reading my newsletter."

NOAA did not lower the boom on me until October 2, 2014.

> We estimate that the cost to search for responsive records will be approximately $296. This estimate is based on approximately 4 hours of Search and Review time at the actual salary rate of the employee conducting the search and review, ($64/per hour), plus 16 percent of the employee's salary rate. This estimate does not include the cost of reproducing documents because until the initial search is complete, we have no way to estimate how many documents, if any, would need to be copied.

Understand that the only information that FOIA will provide is that which is printed on paper (or nowadays, that which is typed digitally in a computer file). Because I knew – or suspected with conviction – that the malodorous statement in question was only an allegation, and that there was no paperwork to support it, I would expect to receive (for hundreds of dollars of my money) nothing more than a bland declaration that would be worded something like this:

"After an exhaustive search through our records, we found no documents that were responsive to your request."

NOAA also added the qualifier, "Please be aware that not all responsive documents are necessarily releasable under the FOIA."

This meant that NOAA could exercise its option not to disclose the requested information if it might prove to be injurious to NOAA's public image. This attitude presents a problem for all investigative reporters who try to find damaging information about a government agency *from* that government agency, because the agency can always claim that the requested information was not releasable. Asking for censorious information is like asking an agency to confess its sins to the world at large.

According to the Department of Justice, "The Freedom of Information Act (FOIA) is a law that *gives* you the right to access information from the federal government. It is often described as the law that keeps citizens in the know about their government." According to *The American Heritage Dictionary*, "give" is defined as "to make a present of; bestow."

There are exemptions to FOIA that deal with issues such as classified information and invasion of privacy. Plus there are hundreds if not thousands of loopholes that an embarrassed or impeachable agency can slink through in order to justify its refusal to release clearly responsive documents. Then there are denials that are purely arbitrary and capricious. And finally there is willful intent to cover-up mistakes, aberrant behavior, criminal activity, and the like. An agency can suppress information under any pretext that it can imagine, and the requester will never know.

There is no way to ascertain what an agency did *not* send you. A requester's only recourse is to file a suit against the agency. That route costs thousands or tens of thousands of dollars to the individual, while the agency being sued has unlimited legal resources that are funded by the taxpayers.

Although FOIA has been mandated by Congress, in a very real sense any compliance is purely voluntary.

On October 7, 2014, I wrote this appeal to NOAA:

> To justify a fee waiver for my FOIA request, I was asked to disclose how widespread I was planning to distribute the information received pursuant to my request. I did so. (See attachment.) As my fee waiver was denied on these grounds, I would like to know the circulation threshold that NOAA has established for a fee waiver. As noted in my letter, circulation of my newsletter ultimately reaches thousands of concerned citizens. What is the minimum number of people that NOAA has established must receive this information before NOAA will waive the fee? The number cannot be arbitrary, so NOAA must make a determination that is based on a precise number that is quantified in Federal regulations.

Whereas a government agency is obligated to respond to a FOIA request and furnish responsive documents, an agency is not required to *create* a document. In other words, an agency is not obligated to answer letters or questions. In this case, NOAA ignored my letter and never answered my question – I suspect because there is no such threshold number. NOAA just used that as an excuse to charge me for information that is supposed to be free.

FOIA is not an end-all mechanism. In doing shipwreck research, I have submitted

FOIA requests to the Navy and the Army Corps of Engineers that were never even answered. Never. They simply ignored my request and dozens of follow-up letters. There is no way to win against an agency that is entrenched in obstruction of justice.

On October 27, NOAA replied to my appeal with a three-page letter that is a masterpiece of fabulous rationalizations that is worth repeating in full, in order to show the extreme lengths to which NOAA went in order to extract $296 from me, in return for which I would probably receive nothing but a note that no responsive documents had been found:

> Dear Mr. Gentile:
> This is in response to your August 22, 2014, filing of a Freedom of Information Act (5 U.S.C. § [paragraph] 552) (FOIA) appeal via FOIAonline of the National Oceanic and Atmospheric Administration's (NOAA) denial of your fee waiver request for FOIA request # DOC-NOAA-2014-001400.
>
> The FOIA provides for the waiver or reduction of fees if disclosure of the information "is in the public interest because it is likely to contribute significantly to public understanding of the operations or activities of the government and is not primarily in the commercial interest of the requester." 5 U.S.C. § 552 (a)(4)(A)(iii). Both prongs of this two-part test (the public interest prong and the commercial interest prong) must be satisfied by the requester before properly assessable fees are waived or reduced. Department regulations establish how these two prongs may be satisfied pursuant to the statutory standard. 15 C.F.R. § 4.11(k). We have reviewed the information you provided in support of your request for a fee waiver, and have determined that NOAA's decision to deny your fee waiver request is in accordance with the standards set forth in the FOIA and the Department of Commerce's regulations, 15 C.F.R. § 4.9(c). Therefore, your appeal is denied.
>
> In order to determine whether the first prong has been met, there are four criteria which should be considered by the agency: (1) whether the subject of the requested records concerns the operations or activities of the government; (2) whether the disclosure is likely to contribute to an understanding of government operations or activities; (3) whether disclosure is likely to contribute significantly to public understanding; and (4) whether the disclosure is likely to contribute significantly to public understanding of government operations or activities. 15 C.F.R. § 4.11(k)(2). It is the influence of all four factors considered together, rather than the failure or success of meeting any particular factor that is determinative. Overall, these four factors can be broken down into two broader considerations: (1) whether the information requested will contribute to a significant public understanding of a specified operation or activity of the government and (2) whether the requester has established that he or she has the means to and will actually disseminate the information.
>
> In your appeal, you state that the requested information will contribute to an understanding of the manner in which government, particularly NOAA, operate with regard to maligning sectors of the American public by publicizing allegations without furnishing evidence to support them. However, you fail to provide any information as to how the requested information will allow

you to extract meaningful information about NOAA's decision making process and actually shed light on any identified government operation. See Jarvik v. CIA, 495 F. Supp. 2d 63, 67 (D.D.C. 2007). In fact, you have not even clearly identified a government operation or activity. Thus, you have failed to show that release of the requested information will contribute to a significant public understanding of a specified operation or activity of the government.

Further, unless a member of the news media, a requester must substantiate his ability to disseminate information in order to show that he can contribute to the understanding of the public at large. See Judicial Watch, 122 F. Supp. 2d at 9-11; see also, Carney v. U.S. Dep't of Justice, 19 F. 3d 807, 814 (2d Cir. 1994). You are identified as an "All Other Requester;" therefore you have the burden of proving your ability to disseminate the requested information. You state in your appeal that you will disseminate the information you receive by publishing it in your free online newsletter for the benefit of other concerned citizens. Other than these statements, you offer no further explanation as to how the requested information will be disseminated.

While posting requested information on social media sites or in newsletters can be part of a plan to disseminate information, these must be a part of a broader campaign to convey the information to the public. See Judicial Watch v. Rossotti, 326 F.3d 1309, 1314 (D.C. Cir. 2003) (Judicial Watch was granted a fee waiver when it stated its mission, and provided nine ways in which it could communicate the collected information, including: via press releases; a newsletter with a monthly circulation of "over 300,000 copies nationwide"; a website on which people can view copies of documents and that has "logged up to 1,000,000 visitors in a single day"; an "Infonet" listserve with "over 60,000 subscriber[s]" congressional testimony; a nationally syndicated news and information television show Judicial Watch helps to produce; a Judicial Watch-produced weekly radio program which "airs nationwide on thirty-six radio stations and the Internet"; appearances by Judicial Watch employees on television and radio programs; and conferences organized by Judicial Watch). In fact, courts have upheld agency fee waiver denials where the requestor had done no more than cite his or her publication of prior articles, and note that the requested information would be published on its website while failing to provide an actual estimate of the number of people likely to view the cite [sic] or to demonstrate any other ways in which the information would be disseminated. Cause of Action v. Federal Trade Comm'n, 961 F. Supp. 2d 142, 157 (D.D.C. 2013). Because you have only indicated that you will publish the requested information in your newsletter that reaches and undefined number of people, and have not indicated how these individuals would have a particular interest in the requested information you have failed to establish an ability to disseminate the requested information in a way that will contribute to the understanding of the public at large.

We have considered your appeal by applying the four factors 15 C.F.R. § 4.11(k)(2) and determine that you fail to show that the requested information is in the public interest because it is likely to contribute significantly to public understanding of the operations or activities of the Government. Because this request failed to meet the requirements of 15 C.F.R. § 4.11(k)(2), the public interest prong, there is no need for the Department to determine whether or not it meets the commercial interest prong at 15 C.F.R. § 4.11(k)(3).

We note that NOAA did not provide a fee estimate to you when it denied your request for a waiver. NOAA has informed this office that a fee estimate has been sent to you. Upon the payment of the fee estimate provided by NOAA, NOAA will begin a search and process your FOIA request. Note that even with payment of anticipated fees, all or part of responsive information may be withheld under applicable FOIA exemptions. . . .

Based on the foregoing reasons, your appeal is denied. This is the final department of the Department of Commerce. You have the right to obtain judicial review of this denial of your FOIA fee waiver appeal as provided for in 5 U.S.C. § 552(a)(4)(B).

The final sentence meant "Sue and be damned."

Other threats and insinuations implied that even if I succeeded in meeting the as-yet undetermined threshold of the first prong, NOAA was holding a second prong joker up its illegitimate sleeve. This joker would not be played until I satisfied all the criteria in the first prong.

Note that NOAA made an unfair comparison between me and a multi-million dollar nationwide media organization, without establishing any middle ground that would constitute a threshold.

NOAA now made an unveiled threat that even if it located documents that were responsive to my request, it might at its own (in)discretion withhold the information on those responsive documents by making excessive redactions.

NOAA also admitted that the cost could be much more than the original amount that was quoted to me. In other words, it wanted me to sign a blank check before it would commence the search for responsive documents. Then, if I did not pay an additional trumped-up amount, it would refuse to release the documents to me. Now it was holding wild cards in addition to jokers.

This whole situation was a pyrrhic victory for NOAA. The cost for paralegals to look up so much case law, and for so many lawyers to compose so many protracted letters, must have exceeded by tenfold the amount of money that NOAA wanted me to pay. It would have been far less expensive to simply call the NOAA publicist who wrote the article on NOAA's website, and get the answer to my question – if indeed there was one.

Meanwhile, anticipating a denial, on October 22, 2014, I sent the following letter to my Congressional representative, Senator Pat Toomey:

> On July 29, 2014, I submitted a FOIA request for documentation to substantiate NOAA's published claim that recreational divers damaged some of the German warships that were scuttled by Billy Mitchell's bombers in 1921. (See enclosure).
>
> Instead of complying with my request, NOAA submitted a lengthy questionnaire in which it demanded that I justify my reasons for requesting the information. My reply is enclosed.

Subsequently, NOAA refused to release the information unless I made a down payment of $296 in advance, to which it reserved the right to make additional charges as it might see fit, without guaranteeing that it would release (and/or not redact) all the documents that were responsive to my request.

As information, FOIA stands for Freedom of Information Act. It does not stand for Make Money for NOAA Act.

As an American citizen who is concerned about the operations of his government, I have the right to make bona fide requests for information which NOAA alleged but neglected to document with evidence . . . especially when NOAA itself was responsible for maligning recreational divers while withholding the information that may (or may not) substantiate its accusation against them.

I am asking for your help in forcing the free release of this public information.

NOAA dallied for six months before stooping to answer the senator from Pennsylvania, on April 27, 2015:

Dear Mr. Gentile,
Thanks you for contacting my office to share the difficulties that you are experiencing with the National Oceanic and Atmospheric Administration (NOAA). I submitted an inquiry on your behalf to NOAA, and have received a response from their office. I received the following via email:

"Thank you for the Senator's letter to the National Oceanic and Atmospheric Administration (NOAA regarding constituent Gary Gentile's FOIA request. NOAA received Mr. Gentile's original FOIA request on July 31, 2014, and following some communications with Mr. Gentile, NOAA notified him that it was denying his fee waiver request because he had provided insufficient support for his request. Mr. Gentile appealed that decision to the Department of Commerce (of which NOAA is a part). The Department denied Mr. Gentile's appeal in writing on October 27, 2014. The Department's letter to Mr. Gentile described the requirements that a requester must meet to be granted a fee waiver and explained why Mr. Gentile did not meet those requirements."

While this response is not what we hoped, I trust this information is helpful to you.

By then I had long since obtained the information from another source.

The Truth Will Out

I was discussing the issue of NOAA's base accusation with regard to the Billy Mitchell Wrecks with J.T. Barker when he said that he knew where NOAA had obtained its so-called "evidence": from his website.

On a 1999 trip to the *Ostfriesland*, Barker's dive buddy spotted a porthole lying in the sand off the wreck. He swam it to the grapnel and secured it to the tie-in line. The porthole was retrieved after the dive when the anchor line was pulled up. Barker then posted the story of the dive, accompanied by a photograph of the porthole.

NOAA and the Navy constantly surf the Internet for instances of recreational divers intruding on what NOAA and the Navy believe is their private domain. As I suggested in the previous section, NOAA used shills with fake names to subscribe to my online newsletter as a way to keep in touch with recreational diving activities. As a result of NOAA's and the Navy's threatening posture, many recreational divers have gone "underground" in addition to underwater by not announcing new shipwreck discoveries on the Internet.

Now I knew why NOAA went to such great lengths to prevent me from having free access to its files. Now I knew – or suspected with conviction – that NOAA would never release – *could* never release – responsive information to me, even if I did agree to pay for it. Because NOAA did not possess any such information.

For one thing, NOAA had not actually documented any evidence of diver damage to the Billy Mitchell Wrecks. All it had to make its malicious allegation was unsubstantiated hearsay from Barker's website. Hearsay was not admissible in a court of law.

The absence of a porthole could not be observed unless NOAA had prior knowledge of the porthole's existence and placement. As the write-up concerned NOAA's first exploratory trip, NOAA had no prior knowledge other than what its employees had read in my books and on Barker's website. At this point, everything that NOAA knew about the Billy Mitchell Wrecks came from the few recreational divers who had discovered and explored the wrecks. NOAA had no firsthand knowledge.

For another thing, the only documentation that NOAA might have on paper would have to have been written in the "correspondence, emails, notes, telephone transcripts, inter-office memos" which I requested. It could not have any original "reports" because its sole source of information was Barker's website, which NOAA would not want to admit, and which likely would have been redacted had I paid for the search, in order for NOAA to keep its source confidential.

Now let us take a closer look at NOAA's denunciation: "We have evidence that divers have damaged some of them."

This sentence claims that NOAA *has* or possesses evidence (present tense). Because this sentence was embedded in a report on NOAA's first underwater robotic exploration of the Billy Mitchell Wrecks, it *implies* that NOAA observers actually spotted such evidence. In fact, NOAA did not obtain the so-called evidence from any one of the wrecks. NOAA *inferred* the evidence from hearsay on Barker's website. NOAA then used this slender thread of hearsay to denigrate recreational divers in a public forum.

Note, too, that NOAA claimed that it had evidence of damage to "some of them" (plural). This part of the sentence goes beyond inference to vile prevarication. NOAA did not specify which wrecks were damaged, perhaps because to do so it would appear awkward if it did not specify what *kind* of damage it *had*.

Rescuing a porthole from the sand off the wreck does not constitute damage to the nearby *Ostfriesland* – even if the so-called "damage" held any meaning in context with the enormous amount of real damage that the wreck suffered as a result of the bombing raids and subsequent deterioration and collapse. The porthole had not been removed from the actual wreck; it had been blown off the warship by raining bombs, or it had been removed under water by natural collapse.

On the other hand, NOAA used the robotic arm of an ROV to take a souvenir that it called a "ballast brick from one of the destroyers from the 'Billy Mitchell Fleet.'" This admission constitutes "damage" by NOAA's definition of the word, because such a brick would have been located inside the hull, where the ballast bricks were stacked.

When all is said and done, the actual perpetrator cast blame where it did not belong. Such an action is standard operating procedure for NOAA in its ongoing persecution of recreational scuba divers.

Semantics is an important tool that NOAA uses to the fullest. When a recreational divers rescues an artifact, NOAA calls it "looting." When NOAA takes an artifact, NOAA calls it "recovering." This name calling convention is a tactic that NOAA employs as a way to denigrate recreational divers in the media. According to NOAA's definition, a looter is anyone who took something from a wreck that NOAA would have taken if NOAA had found it first. NOAA claimed that this ballast brick was an "archaeological sample" that contained "significant archaeological information." This description is a stretch of imagination that rivals the tall tales of Baron Munchhausen and Paul Bunyan. The photo is courtesy of NOAA, which proudly displayed the trophy on the Internet as a means to demonstrate its prowess in recovering relics which, in accordance with NOAA's protocol of in situ preservation, violates its own proclamation.

The Hunting of NOAA's Snark
Copyright Infringement

A Warped Program

WORP is the acronym for NOAA's Wreck Oil Removal Program: an ambitious effort to identify American coastal shipwrecks that may contain petroleum products which NOAA believes could spill suddenly and catastrophically and then drift onto beaches where the viscous substance might cause contamination that would adversely affect the environment. The program is not only ambitious; it is largely fictitious.

According to the Project Background, "The past century of commerce and warfare has left a legacy of thousands of sunken vessels along the U.S. coast. The public has long been fascinated by shipwrecks because of their significance to history and culture. However, there is a growing concern about their potential environmental impacts from eventual release of their cargo and fuel."

In 2013, WORP identified 87 sunken tankers that "might" pose a threat to the environment if their submerged cargoes were released all at once due to instantaneous failure of the bulkheads that comprised the cargo tanks.

The Sunken Tanker Project

According to the program's statistics, of the 87 vessels that were on the list, 53 (or 61%) were lost during World War Two, nearly all in 1942 when the German U-boat blitz was the most active and successful.

In 1967, the U.S. Coast Guard conducted the Sunken Tanker Project. This project had the same goal as NOAA's current project: to ascertain if the threat of extreme oil release was real. The Coast Guard put divers on the *Gulftrade, R.P. Resor, Varanger*, and *Coimbra* (all of which were sunk in 1942). As a result of this in-water survey, "no oil was found in sufficient quantity for analysis." That means not even a test tube full.

To explain the loss of oil from compartments that appeared to be intact – that is, the bulkheads were standing and seemed to be in good condition – the Coast Guard speculated, "Best estimates are that the oil has escaped by rising through the tank ventilation systems. This would most likely have occurred gradually over an extended period of time, allowing the oil to be assimilated by the surrounding sea through bio-degradation of the persistent oils and evaporation of the volatiles to the atmosphere from the non-persistent oil cargoes."

The Coast Guard also stated, "There is indication that a cargo will probably be lost from tanks thru [sic] ventilation or other fittings before plating and other structure corrodes away." Finally, the Coast Guard determined that long before a tank bulkhead would collapse abruptly, the ongoing process of corrosion would thin the plating and create microscopic holes that would permit the escape of oil on a drop-by-drop basis. These droplets would be assimilated unnoticeably by the environment one at a time.

In its final report, the Coast Guard announced, "Evidence gathered from this project indicates that tankers sunk during World War II do not present a potential pollution threat to the American coastline."

Thus the current "catastrophic failure" concept for World War Two wrecks is a myth. In fact, there has never been a case of catastrophic failure from World War Two wrecks. Such a scenario was found wanting nearly half a century ago.

Why WORP?

If World War Two tankers contained no perceptible amounts of oil after 25 years on the bottom, why would NOAA contend that they might contain oil 46 years later, by which time the wrecks had lain on the bottom for 71 years? And what would make NOAA believe that the *Northern Pacific*, for example – an ocean liner that sank in 1922, and on the WORP list – would contain *any* oil after lying on the seabed for 91 years?

My guess is that NOAA wanted to scam the American people out of the millions of dollars that NOAA convinced Congress to authorize for a new investigation of sunken tankers – and purely a paper investigation at that.

NOAA did no field work.

For each of the 87 targeted tankers on the WORP list, NOAA produced a packet that averaged 40 to 45 pages in length. After creating a template, each packet consisted of boilerplate language followed by a brief synopsis of the circumstances of loss, which did not come from primary archival documentation but was quoted from Internet sites, or from paper-published material that was already part of NOAA's library. All of the vessel statistics and background information came from secondary sources that NOAA "investigators" – and I use the term loosely – found on the Internet.

Some of this information was lifted straight out of my books (uncredited). I have written historical narratives on 36 of the wrecks on the list, and have personally surveyed 13 of them. I have made a number of dives on the *Northern Pacific*, whose hull is separated in two places, and whose outer plates are either fractured or have fallen off; no oil slicks have ever been detected near this wreck, nor is there any possibility that large quantities of fuel oil remain in its bunkers.

Despite the documented facts in my books, NOAA wrote, "The vessel is not broken and remains as one contiguous piece." Bad enough that NOAA has never surveyed the wreckage, its "investigators" could not even copy my survey report correctly.

Here are some other facts that NOAA "investigators" got wrong. According to the report, "The *Northern Pacific* was taken over by the military for World War I, armed, and used as a fast troopship. During her military service, the *Northern Pacific* made 13 round-trips to Europe, and was severely damaged in a grounding off Long Island. She was repaired, but later lost while under tow to be sold. The vessel never saw a day of civilian use, and is properly thought of as a Navy ship."

In fact, the *Northern Pacific* commenced her career in 1915 in the service of the Great North Pacific Steamship Company. She and her sister ship, the *Great Northern*, transported people and freight along the West Coast in summer, and to Hawaii in winter. After the United States declared war against the Central Powers, she was commissioned into the Navy, on November 3, 1917. She was decommissioned on August 20, 1919, at which time she was transferred to the U.S. Army Transport Service.

On February 22, 1922, the *Northern Pacific* was sold to the Pacific Steamship Company. She was under tow *after* she was sold, with a skeleton crew aboard, when she caught fire and sank off the coast of Delaware. She became a popular dive site in the 1960's, and has been one ever since.

NOAA's gross misinformation runs through the gamut of vessels on WORP's list. This is what happens when you do all your research from the vacuum of an office, where false information is gathered from unproven Internet sources, and realism is based on what is seen on a computer monitor.

If NOAA cannot even get a few historical facts straight, how much credence can be given to the rest of the report? The result is a waste of taxpayers' money, times 87.

Nonetheless, NOAA contended that its "research has revealed that 87 wrecks pose a potential pollution threat."

Once a template was formulated, all NOAA had to do was to fill in the blanks and add color to make the "report" look official and attractive so that Congress would think that it got its money's worth.

According to the program's statistics, of the 87 vessels that were on the WORP list, 47 (or 54%) "have unknown or unconfirmed locations." What was the point of listing vessels that NOAA could not possibly examine under water? Was this just padding to make Congress think that NOAA had done a thorough investigation?

Even granting that there is some overlap between the 53 wrecks that were lost during World War Two, and therefore do not constitute a threat to the environment, and the 47 wrecks whose locations were unknown, and therefore nothing can be done about them, some three-quarters of the wrecks on the WORP list either do not constitute a threat or cannot be found for confirmation purposes. WORP lists the *Coimbra* as a potential threat even though Coast Guard divers examined the wreck 46 years earlier, and could not find enough oil to sample.

According to SLRAP *Coimbra*: "The *Coimbra* is classified as High Risk for both oiling probability and for degree of oiling for water column socio-economic resources." The report goes on and on with pompous academic lingo that makes NOAA's evaluations sound factual and important. But if you read between the lines you realize that NOAA is using a lot of pretentious language to misdirect the reader, and to prevent him or her from apprehending that the report has nothing to say.

This snow job reminds me of the saying, "If you can't dazzle them with brilliance, baffle them with bullshit."

Assembling speculative risk factor tables and adding fancy colored graphs that show probable current directions add nothing useful to reports of wrecks that the Coast Guard found long ago did not represent a hazard. The same goes for wrecks who positions were unknown, in most cases because they lie in water that is too deep for clean-up operations.

Appended to each report (including the *Coimbra*) are pages and pages of risk factors, release scenarios, environmental impact models, potential shoreline impacts, long lists of bird species and other animals that could be affected by a catastrophic oil release – and this on wrecks that have already been proven to contain no oil.

Each of the 87 WORP reports is called a Screening Level Risk Assessment Package (SLRAP), even if the wreck in question was disqualified as an environmental hazard because it dated from World War Two, and even if its location was unknown, making the report superfluous. I think that the words "screening level" should be replaced with Canard, or Charade, or Concocted, or Chimerical (for those wrecks that have never been found). Either of these words would result in a more accurate acronym.

The *Cayru* Caper

Throughout this book I have quoted liberally from NOAA documents and website posts. Using such quotes is legally allowable because everything that the government publishes, photographs, or otherwise creates is automatically part of the public domain. This is because those creations were funded by the taxpayers, and therefore they belong to them.

On the other hand, everything an individual publishes, photographs, or otherwise creates is protected by copyright. Under current copyright laws, the copyright belongs to the creator for the rest of his or her life plus fifty years. No one is allowed to publish your writings, copy your photographs, record your songs, recite your poetry in a public venue, copy movie dvd's, or otherwise reprint your copyrighted works without specific written permission from the creator.

Which brings us to the point of this section. One of the useless WORP reports is about the *Cayru*. The wreck has never been found. After many years, I came to the conclusion that – well, no sense rewriting the story. Here is how I originally phrased it:

> In the 1970's, when I began conducting historical research for my Popular Dive Guide Series, I noticed certain aberrations with respect to the location and identification of World War Two shipwrecks. One prime example is the *Cayru*. This large passenger-freighter was torpedoed by a German U-boat off the coast of New Jersey. Wartime Naval documents provided coordinates of the site. In 1950, the U.S. Coast and Geodetic Survey conducted a wire-drag survey of the wreck, and subsequently plotted its position on the charts. Despite this apparent authentication, no one has ever been able to locate the wreck. I organized several search trips that came to naught. I also continued my archival research. Eventually I unearthed the original Descriptive Report of the 1950 survey. I was shocked to learn that the surveyors stated specifically that they had not located the wreck, and in fact recommended that the wreck symbol be deleted from the chart. For some reason, the symbol was never deleted, and still appears today on modern charts. The *Cayru* has yet to be found. Probably it lies far offshore. Corroboration for this likelihood can be found in the deck log of the *U-94*, in which Oberleutnant zur See Otto Ites recorded coordinates that are farther off the coast than Allied documents indicated.

While perusing the various WORP reports, I was shocked to discover that NOAA had infringed on my copyright by quoting me in its WORP report on the *Cayru*. NOAA had never asked me for permission to reprint my assessment; it just took what it needed to justify why it did not know the location of the wreck.

Understand that I am a professional author and photographer. My words and my photographs are my business; they are my livelihood. I lose money when someone or some entity steals my work, my intellectual property rights, because the value of my work is diminished every time it is republished. A photograph loses its uniqueness and appeal when it is published more than once. My written words possess more value when they appear in only one book, which a person must purchase in order to obtain the information.

NOAA'S NARK – COPYRIGHT INFRINGEMENT

And worse, NOAA published my work in an online public document where it was subject to repeated infringement. People generally believe that everything in a public document is in the public domain.

As an ordinary part of my business, I have a form letter for dealing with situations such as this. Consequently, I wrote to NOAA and enclosed a copy of my standard waiver:

> National Oceanic and Atmospheric Administration   March 16, 2014
> 1401 Constitution Avenue, NW
> Room 5128
> Washington, DC 20230
> Re: Copyright infringement
>
> It has come to my attention that NOAA has infringed upon my copyright. In "Screening Level Risk Assessment Package *Cayru*," NOAA quoted 214 words which are copyrighted in my name.
>
> In accordance with my standard "GGP Waiver for Quotes, Interviews, Research, Appraisals, and Consultations" (a copy of which is included with this notification) my standard charge for quotes is:
>
> **$1 per word** for material quoted or restructured from written works (books, reports, articles, electronic media, Internet, memos, correspondence, and all published and unpublished forms of expression). Credit must be given. Word fee is doubled when credit is not given. Word fee is tripled when permission is not sought or is denied, as this constitutes copyright infringement. **Misquoting and quoting out of context are expressly forbidden.**
>
> Because NOAA did not seek permission to quote my material, the triple fee applies. Promptly remit payment in the amount of $642 for infringing on my copyright.

NOAA lawyers should have known that NOAA's conduct clearly violated federal copyright law. Yet NOAA did not reply to my demand for payment. A month later, I submitted another demand along with a late payment fee of $10, plus an interest charge of 1.5% per month. I had adopted the standard practice that credit card companies applied for delinquent payments. Again NOAA chose not to reply – not even to acknowledge receipt of my demand. Not even to apologize for infringing on my copyright.

In addition to submitting monthly bills, I later offered an alternative to payment in full for the money that NOAA owed me.

If you contemplate the timeframe of concurrent events between this chapter and the previous one, you will see by the dates on the letterheads that my submissions for payment for copyright infringement soon overlapped my FOIA request for information about damage to the Billy Mitchell Wrecks.

The irony of these ongoing situations must be appreciated: on one hand NOAA infringed on my copyright and owed me money, while on the other hand NOAA wanted me to pay for public information that should have been provided for free.

Eventually I thought that I would be generous by offering a compromise. I allowed NOAA to deduct the FOIA charges from my copyright infringement fee. NOAA balked at my settlement proposal.

214   NOAA'S SNARK – COPYRIGHT INFRINGEMENT

After submitting ten monthly bills for copyright infringement, I received this letter from NOAA:

> We are in receipt of your letter, dated March 16, 2014 but sent in December 2014, in which you demand that the National Oceanic and Atmospheric Administration (NOAA) remit payment of $830.82 to you for quoting a 214-word passage written by you in its publication, *Screening Level Risk Assessment Package: Cayru*.
>
> In NOAA's scholarly publication, it quoted an excerpt from a larger work created by you for the purpose of illustration in an educational context. Additionally, NOAA attributed the quoted excerpt to you and provided a website immediately after the excerpt to direct readers to your publication where the excerpt may be found. Accordingly, NOAA considers its use of the 214-word excerpt by you to be one of fair use pursuant to 17 U.S.C. § 107, and therefore, payment will not be provided.

NOAA may consider anything it wants, but with *my* material it is my consideration that counts, not NOAA's. Furthermore, considering how many mistakes and how much misinformation the CRAP package contained, it hardly qualified as scholarly.

To add injury to insult, NOAA refused to delete the infringed paragraph from its report. It is still there.

Go Away Kid, You Bother Me
(With deference to W.C. Fields)

I posted my copyright infringement travails in a newsletter. Undoubtedly half the people in the world did not read it, as NOAA used as an excuse to deny my FOIA fee waiver, but Kim Dixon read it and told me that she had had the same problem with NOAA. In July of 2013, she attended a meeting with NOAA about the possible identification of the *Robert J. Walker*. She was very curious about this issue because she had dived on the $25 Wreck many times, and often wondered about its identity. After the meeting she read NOAA's report and found that NOAA had taken descriptions of the site from her blog, and used them to help in identifying the wreck.

NOAA had never asked permission to publish her blog report in a public document. She later got in touch with James Delgado and asked him to delete her name and blog description from the *Robert J. Walker* report. He said he would but he never did. She removed her post in order to protect her copyright, and decided never again to publish that kind of material on her blog.

Then there are the other 86 WORP reports. Nearly every one of them is gorged with copyright infringements. I would venture to guess that most of the people whose words NOAA purloined are unaware that NOAA has infringed upon their copyrights.

NOAA does not care what people feel or think about its infringement policies. NOAA takes what it wants, and fails to deliver that which it is mandated to give.

In *The Great Navy Wreck Scam* (2015), I parodied a sentence from the *Bible*, "The sea giveth, and the sea taketh away. But the Navy only taketh." That same sentiment applies to NOAA.

The Hunting of NOAA's Snark
Global Warming – Another Not!

Rotten to the Core, or The Spy Who Came in from the Heat

While most of this book has dealt with the National Marine Sanctuary Program, that program is only part of a much larger picture of deceit and fabrication. In *NOAA's Ark*, I covered numerous other agencies within NOAA in which fraudulent activities ran rampant enough to force the head of NOAA to resign. I will not repeat that illegitimate behavior here.

The latest in NOAA's long list of fraudulent activities has come to light only recently. It deals with falsifying data about global warming in order to fit preconceived political notions that was being thrust down the public's throat.

Anyone who believes in manmade global warming should have spent last winter at my house in Pennsylvania. It was the coldest winter in memory. After snow fell near the end of December, we never saw the ground again until April. For three months straight the temperature never rose above freezing. The lowest temperature that I recorded at my house was 7° below zero; neighboring communities recorded temperatures as low as 16° below zero. Ice anglers loved it because all the local reservoirs were frozen solid, with ice that measured 16 inches in thickness. Even streams and the Lehigh River froze all the way across.

Geologists will tell you that the Earth is still coming out of an Ice Age that started to thaw some 10,000 years ago. This is a *natural* event, not manmade. It has nothing to do with chimney smoke, carbon dioxide, or aerosol propellants in the atmosphere.

I keep my household thermometer away from the house and in the shade. If I had wanted to cheat on recording temperatures, I could have placed the thermometer next to the dryer vent in the sun. Only a moron would do that. A moron, and NOAA.

That's right, folks. In order to register temperatures that were politically correct, NOAA placed its thermometers next to the engine intakes of its survey vessels, where the air was warmed by friction and an increase in density. No one could be that stupid, so it must have been intentional. Other temperature sensing instruments have been equally badly placed: low and close to asphalt which absorbs and holds heat. When thermometers did not display anticipated results, the recorded temperatures were "adjusted" to correct for instrument errors; this was called "bias correction," but the phrase neglected to indicate whose bias was being corrected. These and other forms of tampering with the evidence produced exactly the results that NOAA wanted to achieve.

On the other hand, although satellite sensors were the most accurate instruments available to obtain global temperature readings, they were ignored when they conflicted with predetermined conclusions.

Another method that NOAA employed to achieve its desired assumptions was to retrofit historical records by claiming that old-fashioned instruments gave readings that were higher than actual. By reducing past data a couple of degrees, the adjusted colder temperature made today's temperatures appear warmer.

Proposed environmental regulations were seen as a good thing because they would create jobs and help to alleviate a flagging economy. Whether the regulations were necessary or not was politically irrelevant. This was a case of a short-term political agenda ignoring long-term natural reality as a means to fool the public into believing that the government had its finger on the pulse of a potential problem. Much like WORP.

According to the *Washington Times*, "NOAA appears to pick and choose only data that confirms their bias. NOAA then disseminates this incomplete data to the media who manufacture alarming headlines but ignore the uncertainty of the conclusions."

Efforts to force NOAA to release all its temperature information has been blocked by, you guessed it, NOAA. I am not glad to be the only one whose FOIA requests have been denied. Ours are important issues that need to be addressed. NOAA constantly circumvents the system of checks and balances on which this nation was founded.

Hundreds of scientists worldwide have proclaimed that NOAA's global warming predictions were faked, that human intervention had nothing to do with temperature fluctuations, and that the blame on irregular temperature changes should be placed on the fickleness of the sun.

To make matters more absurd, after leaving office, ex-Vice President Al Gore was awarded the Nobel Peace Prize . . . for promoting a non-existent environmental threat.

Nero may have fiddled while Rome burned, but NOAA fiddles with data in order to make the planet hot.

Global warming is neither a problem nor a fact; it is an invention.

Parting Shot

I could have gone much farther in the preceding section, but what is the sense of beating a dead horse?

I would like to leave my readers with food for thought. NOAA belongs to the Department of Commerce. The purpose of the Department of Commerce is, as you might guess, to facilitate commerce.

As I amply noted in *NOAA's Ark*, instead of facilitating commerce NOAA uses its position to impose fines that amount to hundreds of thousands of dollars on commercial anglers, for violations as trivial as catching one fish more than NOAA's allowable limit, or for drifting a few feet into a no-fishing zone, or for accidentally overlooking a single out-of-season fish in a trawl of several thousand look-alikes.

The Marine Sanctuary Program disallows fishing in much of its underwater holdings, and severely restricts diving in all of them. These overregulated sanctuaries spell economic disaster for local citizens, who depend of the tourist trade to charter boats, purchase tackle, buy bait, eat in restaurants, purchase groceries, obtain lodging, and hundreds of other activities in which vacationers engage.

Thus NOAA in general and the Marine Sanctuary Program in particular engage in numerous activities that are diametrically opposed to their reason for existence: to promote commerce. NOAA now serves only itself instead of the public for which it was organized.

To truly serve the people, the Marine Sanctuary Program must be abolished, and NOAA should be reorganized and started anew with all fresh administrators and employees. Only then can freedom ring in the vast underwater land that used to be free.

INDEX

Absecon lighthouse historical site: 95-97
Adams, John Quincy: 8
Advance: 59
Alamo: 10
Alaska Purchase: 14-15
Alberg, David: 69, 173, 182-185, 197, 201
Alden, James: 33
Alice's Adventures in Wonderland: 192
American Oil Institute: 174
American Civil War: 13-14, 53, 56, 71
American Heritage Dictionary, The: 202
American Oil Institute: 174
Arizona (State): 11
Arizona (warship): 185
Arkansas: 11
Armstrong, James: 36
Army (U.S.): 85
Army Corps of Engineers: 203
Atlantic Divers: 65-66, 68, 83, 120, 161
Australia: 178
Automated Wreck and Obstruction Information System (AWOIS): 63-64
B. & J. Baker: 60
Bache, Alexander: 43-44, 53-54
Bache, Mary: 7
Barker, J. T.: 195, 206-207
Basta, Dan: 69
Battle of Hampton Roads: 138
Battle of the Atlantic: 177, 183, 190
Battle of the Atlantic NMS: 178-188
Bedfordshire: 178, 183
Beecher, Henry Ward: 7
Bibb: 26, 27-28
Biddle, Nicholas: 10
Billy Mitchell Wrecks: 193-208, 213
Black, George: 66, 68
Black Laser Learning: 77, 79
Bluefields: 181, 187, 189, 191
Bonaparte, Napoleon: 26
Boston Navy Yard: 36
Boyle, Eddie: 66, 68, 80, 83
Brandywine: 36
Brazil: 36
Brown, John: 12
Buchanan, James: 11, 13

Buffalo, New York: 7
Burnite, Emily: 79
California: 11
Cape May (New Jersey): 37, 48
Capone, Vince: 77, 79
Capt. Harry's Fishing Supply: 166
Carr, Lieutenant: 12
Casserley, Tane: 182
Cat and Ship Islands (Mississippi): 28
Cayru: 212-214
Cedar Keys (Florida): 31
Chaparra: 64
Chattahoochee: 57-58
Chilore: 181
China: 35-36, 55-56
Choctaw: 9
Ciltvaira: 178
City of Atlanta: 178
Civil War, American: 13-14, 53, 56, 71
Clark, William: 26
Clay, Henry: 10
Clayton, Ken: 194
Clemens, Samuel (Mark Twain): 29
Clifford, Charles: 40-42, 49
Clinton, Bill: 90-91
Coast and Geodetic Survey: 63, 212
Coast Guard: 71
Coast Survey: 11, 26, 45, 53, 71, 80, 92, 96
Cochrane, Essex: 48
Coimbra: 209, 211
Confederate States of America: 13-14
Congress of the United States: 89-92, 170, 171, 182, 202
Constitution of the United States: 87-89, 93, 191
Cora F. Cressy: 85, 87
Daily Union History of Atlantic County: 50
Dallas, George M.: 7
Dare County Commissioners: 172-174, 187
Davis, Charles: 27
Davis, Jefferson: 13, 14
Deebold, Frank: 68
Delaware: 48

Delgado, James: 53, 65, 68-69, 72, 76, 78, 80, 81, 83-84, 96, 98, 109, 121, 214
Department of Commerce: 91, 92, 96, 157, 203, 205, 206, 216
Department of Justice: 202
Department of the Treasury: 11
Department of Transportation: 92, 96, 157
Diamond Shoals lightship: 191
Dixie Arrow: 177, 178, 183, 190
Dixon, Kim: 214
Donofrio, Jim: 168
Dry Tortugas (Florida): 168
Dudas' Diving Duds: 73
Duke University: 179
East Carolina University: 65, 72
Eastern Sea Frontier: 180
Ellis, John W.: 55
E. M. Clark: 178, 190-191
Empire: 26
Empire Gem: 178, 191
Entler, Joel: 80
Environmental Protection Agency: 188
Ericsson, John: 104
Evert, Steve: 79
Fanny: 41, 43, 49, 50, 53-54
Federal Republic of Germany: 191
Fields, W. C.: 214
Fiorentino, Joe: 79
Flirt: 35-36
Florida: 66, 71
Florida Keys NMS: 185, 189
Flynn, Karen: 184
Foote, A.H.: 36
Forney, John W.: 15
Fort Pickens (Florida): 34
fractional currency: 13-14
Frankfurt: 194
Fraser, Alexander: 17
Freedom of Information Act (FOIA): 74, 86, 193-208, 213-214, 216
Frolic: 59
G-102: 194
Gallatin: 28
Gentian: 61-63

Germany (Federal Republic): 191
Germany (Nazi): 191
Glang, Gerd: 71
global warming: 215-216
Goliath: 104
Gore, Al: 216
Graveyard of the Atlantic: 181
Graveyard of the Atlantic Museum: 172, 173, 186
Great Mobile Hurricane: 32
Great Navy Wreck Scam, The: 87, 214
Guadagno, Kim: 168
Gulf of Mexico: 28, 31, 71, 96, 183
Gulftrade: 209
Guthrie, John Julius: 34-60
Gypsy: 66, 83
Haas, Mike: 79
Hatteras Island (North Carolina): 172, 173
Hepler, Paul: 77
Hepler, Ruth: 79-80
Hesper: 85-86
Hitler: 167, 168, 169
Holland Land Company: 7
Holmes, Silas: 31
Hong Kong: 36
Hoyt, Joseph: 201
Hudson, Shepherd S.: 38, 40, 44, 46, 48, 50-52, 54
Hudson River: 26
Huger, Thomas B.: 34
Huidekoper, Harm Jan: 7
Humpty Dumpty: 192
Huron: 59-60
Independence Seaport Museum: 73, 181
Indian Removal Act: 8-9
Indians: 8
in situ preservation: 93-94, 116, 176, 177, 186, 190, 208
Ironclad Legacy: Battle of the USS Monitor: 188
Ice Age: 215
Isherwood, Benjamin: 26
Ites, Otto: 212
Jackson, Andrew: 8, 10
J. A. Mowinckel: 181

INDEX

Jefferson, Thomas: 26, 71
John Adams: 35
Johnson, Andrew: 59
Jones, Catesby ap Roger: 57
Judge Advocate General: 54
Kansas: 7, 11-13
Kassandra Louloudis: 178
Keller, Dave: 67
Kennebeck: 37, 41, 48
Keshena: 178
Key Biscayne (Florida): 168
Lake Huron: 104
Lancing: 191
Lavitt, Mike: 79
lead: 29-31
Lead Wreck: 73
Lecompton Constitution: 12
Legare: 26
Levant: 36, 55-56
Lewis, Meriwether: 26
Liberia: 56
Liberty ship: 16
Lieb, Dan: 76, 79, 81
Liederman, Carl: 166
Life-Saving Service: 59
Lighthall, William: 18-26, 70
Light Vessel 71: 191
Lincoln, Abraham: 13
Lloyd's War Losses: 16
London, England: 14
Luther Little: 85-86
magnetism: 31
Mahew, Captain: 49
Malchace: 178
Manchee, Pete: 194
Manuela: 178
Marine Protection, Research, and Sanctuaries Act: 73, 190
Mariners' Museum, The: 171, 174, 176-177, 180-181, 186-187
Marine Sanctuary Program: 215-216
Martin, W.E.: 4, 80
Mason's Paddle Wheeler: 66
Massachusetts: 15
Matagorda Bay, Texas: 33-34
McPheeters, William: 35

Mexican-American War: 11
Mexico: 10
Ministry of Truth: 182
Mississippi (State): 8-10, 14
Mississippi River: 8, 17, 26
Missouri (State): 11, 13
Missouri River: 7
Mobile (Alabama): 26, 31
Mobile and Ohio Railroad: 29
Mobile Bay (Alabama): 28-29, 71
Monitor: 68, 73-75, 75, 77, 79, 117, 138, 169-177, 179-187, 190, 193
Monitor Center and Foundation: 174
Monitor NMS: 69, 74-75, 168-177, 178, 180, 182, 189-190, 197, 201
Monitor National Marine Sanctuary Management Plan and Environmental Assessment: 170
Nagiewicz, Steve: 76-77, 79, 96
National Archives: 73, 193
National Civil War Naval Museum: 58
National Geospatial Intelligence Agency: 96
National Historic Preservation Act: 91
National Marine Sanctuary Association: 79
National Oceanic and Atmospheric Administration (NOAA): 18, 65, 68-99, 165-216
National Park Service: 85, 87, 187
National Register of Historic Places: 78, 84-87, 92, 98-164, 189-190, 192, 196
Naval Historical Center: 89, 91
Naval History and Heritage Command: 89-90, 93
Navesink Maritime Heritage Association: 167
Navesink River: 165
Navy (U.S.): 54, 87-90, 93, 179, 183, 188, 191, 192, 201, 203, 207, 214
Navy (U.S.) Board of Commissioners: 22-23
Navy Wreck List: 63
Nevada: 11
New Jersey Historical Divers Associa-

tion: 76, 78, 81
New Jersey Maritime Museum: 80, 92
New Mexico: 11
New Orleans (Louisiana): 26
New York City: 26
New York Herald: 39-42, 72
New York Times: 37-39, 42
Nightingale: 56
Nigro, Matt: 79
1984: 182
NOAA's Ark: the Rise of the Fourth Reich: 74
Nobel Peace Prize: 216
Non-Submarine Contacts: 63-64
North Carolina: 38, 55-56
Northern Pacific: 210
Northumberland, Pennsylvania: 7
Nute, Reverend Mr.: 8
Oak Hill Cemetery: 15
Ocracoke Civic & Business Association: 174
Ohio River: 26
Oklahoma: 9
On-Ka-Hy-e: 35
Oregon Ship Building Corporation: 16
Orwell, George: 182
Ostfriesland: 194-195, 206-208
Outer Banks (North Carolina): 172, 183
Outer Banks Association of Realtors: 174
Papp, Robert J.: 71
Patterson, Carlile: 33
Penn, William: 84
Pennsylvania Supreme Court: 7
Pensacola (Florida): 32
Pentagoet: 78
Persephone: 63
Peterson, Gene: 65-66, 68, 83, 120, 161
Phifer, George: 184, 187-188
Philadelphia Maritime Museum: 181
Pittsburgh, Pennsylvania: 7, 18
Pizzio, Mike: 79
Poff, Walter: 79
Poindexter, Senator: 10
Polk, James: 11
Popular Dive Guide Series: 212
Portland: 85, 185

Portland Gale of 1898: 78
Portsmouth: 36, 56
Potsdam Agreement: 191-192
Pradith, Vitad: 68, 72
Presidential Statements: 90-91
Purple Heart: 179
Quickmatch: 16
Radford, Andy: 174
Raiders of the Lost Ark: 54
Recreational Fishing Alliance: 168
Revel Resorts: 79
Revenue Marine Service: 11, 17, 26, 71
R. G. Johnson: 38
R. G. Porter: 40, 44, 46, 48, 50-52, 54
Richard Stockton College Marine Science Field Station: 79
Robert J. Walker (man): 7-16,
Robert J. Walker (vessel): 16-165, 176, 189, 193, 194, 196, 214
Roecker, Harry: 79
Ronald W. Reagan National Defense Authorization Act for Fiscal Year 2005: 89
Rosin Wreck: 76-77
R. P. Resor: 209
Russia: 15
S-132: 194
Sanctuary Advisory Council: 166, 169, 170, 174, 187
San Diego: 64, 94
Sands, Benjamin Franklin: 34
Sandy Hook Bay NMS: 165-168, 182, 196
San Jacinto: 36, 56
San Saba: 64
Santiago de Cuba: 59
Saramac: 36
Saratoga: 56-57
Screening Level Risk Assessment Package: 211, 213
Sea Horse Key (Florida), 31
Second Opium War: 36
Segars, Herb: 77
Segars, Ronnie: 81
Seward, William H.: 15
Seward's Folly: 15

INDEX

Sewell, Joseph: 40, 42, 46
Shanghai: 36
Shaw, Johnny: 66
Shields, Chelsea: 79
Shipwrecks of New Jersey – North: 94-95
Shrewsbury River: 165
slavery: 7-8, 11-12, 56
Spratley, Louisa Sarah: 60
SRVx: 69
Statute of Limitations: 92
steering conventions: 43
Steinmetz, Joyce: 65-66, 68, 72, 73, 74, 77, 175
Stellwagen Bank NMS: 78, 85, 168, 185
Stellwagen Bank Robbery: 74-75
St. Georges Sound (Florida): 32
Stimers, Alban: 138
Stoeckl, Eduard Andreevich: 15
Straub, Peter: 79
Sumner, Charles: 15
Sunken Military Craft rider: 89-90
Sunken Tanker Project: 206-210
Superstorm Sandy: 69, 94
survey slate: 76-77
Susquehanna River: 7
Sweeney, Shawn: 79
Taylor, James: 79
Taylor, Zachary: 11
Texas: 10, 11
Theberge, Albert: 72
Thomas Jefferson: 69, 72
Through the Looking Glass: 192
Timm, Heinrich: 16
Tomlinson, Joseph: 18
Toomey, Pat: 205-206
Toy Wreck: 78
Trail of Tears: 9
Treaty of Dancing Rabbit Creek: 9
Troy: 26
$25 Dollar Wreck: 65-66, 72, 80, 214
U-85: 178, 189-190, 197, 201
U-94: 212
U-117: 194
U-140: 194
U-352: 178, 189-190, 192, 197, 201
U-534: 192

U-576: 181-182, 187, 189-192, 197
U-701: 177, 178-179, 189-190, 197
U-862: 16
UB-148: 194
Unicoi: 181
Union: 35
University of Pennsylvania: 7
U.S.S. San Diego: the Last Armored Cruiser: 94
Utah: 11
V-43: 194
Van Buren, Martin: 11
Varanger: 209
Varina: 34
Venture III: 77
Vincent's Semi-Annual United States Register: 45-46, 47
Virginia: 138
Vogel, Al: 79
Vraim, Tony: 64, 66
Walker, Duncan: 8
Walker, Robert J. (the man): 7-16, 105
Walker Tariff: 11
Warren: 35
War Shipping Administration: 16
Washington (North Carolina): 35
Washington (warship): 194
Washington *Chronicle*: 15
Washington Times: 216
Webster, Daniel: 10
West Point: 35
William H. Young: 58
Wilson, Senator: 7
Wiscasset (Maine): 85
working groups: 166, 174, 175, 187
World Hydrography Day: 95-96
Wreck Information List: 63
Wreck Oil Removal Program: 209-214
yellow fever: 32
YP-389: 178-180
Yucatan: 10

Books by the Author

The Popular Dive Guide Series

Shipwrecks of Maine and New Hampshire
Shipwrecks of Massachusetts: North
Shipwrecks of Massachusetts: South
Shipwrecks of Rhode Island and Connecticut
Shipwrecks of New York
Shipwrecks of New Jersey (1988)
Shipwrecks of New Jersey: North
Shipwrecks of New Jersey: Central
Shipwrecks of New Jersey: South
Shipwrecks of Delaware and Maryland (1990 Edition)
Shipwrecks of Delaware and Maryland (2002 Edition)
Shipwrecks of the Chesapeake Bay in Maryland Waters
Shipwrecks of the Chesapeake Bay in Virginia Waters
Shipwrecks of Virginia
Shipwrecks of North Carolina: from the Diamond Shoals North
Shipwrecks of North Carolina: from Hatteras Inlet South
Shipwrecks of South Carolina and Georgia

Shipwreck and Nautical History

Andrea Doria: Dive to an Era
Deep, Dark, and Dangerous: Adventures and Reflections on the Andrea Doria
Great Lakes Shipwrecks: a Photographic Odyssey
The Great Navy Wreck Scam
The Fuhrer's U-boats in American Waters
Ironclad Legacy: Battles of the USS Monitor
The Kaiser's U-boats in American Waters
The Lusitania Controversies: Atrocity of War and a Wreck-Diving History (Book 1)
The Lusitania Controversies: Dangerous Descents into Shipwrecks and Law (Book 2)
The Nautical Cyclopedia
NOAA's Ark: the Rise of the Fourth Reich
Shadow Divers Exposed: the Real Saga of the U-869
Shipwreck Heresies
The Shipwreck Research Handbook
Shipwreck Sagas
Stolen Heritage: the Grand Theft of the Hamilton and Scourge
Track of the Gray Wolf
The $25 Dollar Wreck of the Robert J. Walker
Underwater Reflections
USS San Diego: the Last Armored Cruiser
Wreck Diving Adventures

BOOKS BY THE AUTHOR

Dive Training
Primary Wreck Diving Guide
Advanced Wreck Diving Guide
The Advanced Wreck Diving Handbook
Ultimate Wreck Diving Guide
The Technical Diving Handbook

Nonfiction
The Absurdity Principle
Lehigh Gorge Trail Guide
Lehigh River Paddling Guide
Wilderness Canoeing

Science Fiction
A Different Universe
A Different Dimension
A Different Continuum
Entropy (a novel of conceptual breakthrough)
A Journey to the Center of the Earth
The Mold
Return to Mars
Second Coming
Silent Autumn
Subaqueous
Tesla and the Lemurian Gate
The Time Dragons Trilogy: *A Time for Dragons*
Dragons Past
No Future for Dragons

Sci-Fi Action/Adventure Novels
Memory Lane
Mind Set
The Peking Papers

Supernatural Horror Novel: *The Lurking: Curse of the Jersey Devil*

Vietnam Novel: *Lonely Conflict*

Videotape or DVD
The Battle for the USS Monitor

Visit the GGP website for availability of titles:
http://www.ggentile.com

www.ingramcontent.com/pod-product-compliance
Lightning Source LLC
Chambersburg PA
CBHW051049160426
43193CB00010B/1126